D0463580

DATE			

The Limits
of Social Policy

Also by Nathan Glazer

The Lonely Crowd
(with David Riesman and Reuel Denney)

Faces in the Crowd
(with David Riesman and Reuel Denney)

American Judaism

Studies in Housing and Minority Groups
(Editor, with Davis McEntire)

The Social Basis of American Communism

Beyond the Melting Pot
(with Daniel P. Moynihan)

Remembering the Answers: Essays on the American Student Revolt

Ethnicity: Theory and Experience
(Editor, with Daniel P. Moynihan)

Affirmative Discrimination: Ethnic Inequality and Public Policy

The Urban Predicament
(Editor, with William Gorham)

Ethnic Pluralism and Public Policy
(Editor, with Ken Young)

Ethnic Dilemmas, 1964–1982

Clamor at the Gates: The New American Immigration
(Editor)

The Public Face of Architecture
(Editor, with Mark Lilla)

The Limits
of Social Policy

Nathan Glazer

Harvard University Press
Cambridge, Massachusetts
London, England

Library of Congress Cataloging-in-Publication Data

Glazer, Nathan.
  The limits of social policy / Nathan Glazer.
    p. cm.
  Includes index.
  ISBN 0-674-53443-3 (alk. paper)
  1. United States—Social policy. 2. Public welfare—
United States. 3. Welfare state. I. Title.
HN59.G57 1988
361.6'1'0973—dc19   88-4029
                          CIP

Preface

This book appears at a time when the media regularly assail us
with reports of devastating social problems—homelessness, drug
addiction, teenage pregnancy, educational failure, crime—but
when, paradoxically, political discourse has almost nothing to
propose for dealing with them. Even the inevitable "Spend more"
is not often heard; it would sound hollow at a time when federal
budget deficits are enormous and when no candidate for office
will advocate tax increases. The heady days of high hopes and
grand proposals are now far in the past, even though the problems
that afflict the poor are more salient than ever. At the root of
this paradox, clearly, is a deep distrust of large-scale national
schemes. Some of those that have been initiated have not done
much good, and a good deal of harm has been mixed in with the
good.

The chapters in this book describe the evolution of this national
mood of caution and skepticism. But they also suggest what
course social policy should take in the future. I explore the steady
pressure to break up the large programs and to introduce important roles for states and cities, for nongovernmental communities
and institutions, and for beneficiaries and clients. This is the
course now being taken in welfare reform, in the expansion of
medical insurance to those not covered, and in the provision of
housing for the poor and shelter for the homeless. Finally, I consider why the pursuit of a uniform and fully developed welfare
state, which has been carried so far in other economically advanced societies, has found so much less favor in American eyes.
America is different, I argue, and in this difference Americans
find value.

Contents

The Limits
of Social Policy

Toward the end of the 1960s, during a period of vigorous expansion of social programs, an insight came to me that was to dominate my response to social policy from that time onward. I had participated in the Kennedy administration as an urban sociologist in the Housing and Home Finance Agency in 1962–63, had taught about social policy in the years following at the University of California at Berkeley, and had written about social policy. I thought of myself as liberal, as we in America understand that term; I participated as a writer, and occasionally as an official or consultant, in the remarkable burst of social reform that accompanied the Kennedy and Johnson administrations and that was to continue, scarcely abated, through the Nixon administration.

We believed in those years, despite the Vietnam War, that our rich country had both the material resources and the intelligence to eliminate poverty, eradicate slums, overcome the differences between the educational achievement and health of the rich and of the poor. Social scientists—economists, sociologists, political scientists, anthropologists—were pulled into the design and administration of new government programs aiming at these results.

A new discipline of policy sciences or policy studies expanded, and new schools were founded to teach it. *The Public Interest,* for which I wrote and which I was later to edit, was founded in 1964 by Daniel Bell and Irving Kristol and reflected this new mood: it heralded a new age in which we would rationally and pragmatically attack our domestic social problems. We could relegate the ideological conflicts between conservatives and liberals and radicals to the past because we now knew more and because we had the tools, or were developing them, to do better.

By the end of the 1960s I was not alone in thinking that something had gone wrong, that we had been somewhat too optimistic. My insight, probably not original, derived entirely from my experiences with social policy and not at all from reading any theorist or social philosopher, was that we seemed to be creating as many problems as we were solving and that the reasons were inherent in the way we—liberals, but also the moderate conservatives of the day (recall that they were such people as Richard Nixon and Nelson Rockefeller)—thought about social problems and social policy.

Let me characterize the dominant view of the day (still the dominant view, I would say, among liberals): we believed the advanced industrial world in which we lived had undergone progressive, if jerky, improvement since the days of early industrialism. In the unimproved world of early and high capitalism, market forces prevailed unobstructed, or nearly so. The enormous inequalities they created in wealth, power, and status were added to the still largely unreduced inequalities of the preindustrial world. In this situation most people lived in squalor, while a few, profiting from the labor of many, could live in great luxury and acquire huge fortunes. Our developing social conscience saw this as evil and dangerous: evil because of the huge inequalities and the failure to ensure a decent minimum for all, dangerous because it encouraged the destitute to rebel against industry and order. And so in Bismarck's Germany and Disraeli's England conservative statesmen became worried about rebellion and revolution and joined with liberals to protect workingmen against complete destitution brought about by industrial accident or age. We moved on to develop programs for help with unemployment and medical care and housing. The countries of northwestern Europe were in the lead and competed with each other for more effective and complete provision of social services. We in the United States were far behind, but we had made a good start in the first two terms of Franklin D. Roosevelt, were completing the job under John F. Kennedy and Lyndon Johnson, had converted Richard Nixon, and indeed were beginning to show Europe a thing or two by plunging ahead with daring experiments in community participation and social planning to complete the attack on poverty.

In this prevailing view, then, we have a sea of misery, scarcely diminished by voluntary charitable efforts. Government then starts moving in, setting up dikes, pushing back the sea, and reclaiming the land, so to speak. In this view, although new issues may emerge, they are never really new—rather, they are only newly recognized as issues demanding public attention. This point of view is paradoxically calculated to make us feel both guilty and complacent: guilty for not having recognized and acted on injustices and inequalities and deprivations earlier, because they were after all always there, but also complacently superior to our forebears, who didn't recognize or act on them at all.

This may be something of a caricature, but it gets, I think, to the essence of the liberal view of social problems. The typical stance in this view of social policy is blame—not of course of the unfortunates suffering from the social problem the social policy is designed to remove, but blame rather of our society and our political system. The liberal stance is: for every problem there is a policy, and even if the problem is new, the social system and polity must be indicted for failing to tackle it earlier.

The liberal view further sees vested interests as the chief obstacle to the institution of new social policies. One such interest is simply those who are better off—those who are not in need of the social policy in question and who would have to pay for it in increased taxes. But there are other, more specific vested interests in each area of social policy: landlords and real-estate interests in the field of housing, doctors in the field of health, employers subject to payroll taxes in the field of social security, and so on.

But as I worked on our policies in housing, health, social welfare, quite a different point of view impressed itself upon me, and I can summarize it in two propositions:

1. In our social policies we are trying to deal with the breakdown of traditional ways of handling distress. These traditional ways are located in the family primarily, but also in the ethnic group, the neighborhood, the church.

2. In our efforts to deal with the breakdown of these traditional structures, our social policies are weakening them further and making matters in some important respects worse. We are making no steady headway against a sea of misery. Our efforts to deal with distress are themselves increasing distress.

Despite the pleasing symmetry of this view, I did not believe in any automatic law. The basic problem was the breakdown of traditional structures. But other problems continually frustrated our efforts to complete the structure of social policy so that we could be satisfied improvement was occurring and that we were not making things worse than before.

Whatever our actual success by some measure in dealing with a social problem, it seemed that discontent steadily increased among the beneficiaries of these programs, those who carried them out, and those who paid for them, particularly in the 1960s when we were doing so many things to improve matters. We were enmeshed in a revolution of rising expectations, a revolution itself fed by the proposals for new social policies. Their promise, inadequately realized, left behind a higher level of expectation, which a new round of social policy had to attempt to meet, and with the same consequences. In any case, by the nature of democratic (and perhaps not only democratic) politics, again and again more must be promised than can be delivered. These promises are the chief mechanisms in educating people to higher expectations. But they are, of course, reinforced by the enormous impact of mass literacy, the mass media, and expanding levels of education. Rising expectations continually enlarge the sea of felt and perceived misery, whatever happens to it in actuality.

Alongside rising expectations, and adding similarly to the increasing difficulties of social policy, was the revolution of equality. This is the most powerful social force in the modern world. Perhaps only Tocqueville saw its full awesome potency. It first expresses itself in a demand for equality in political rights and in political power; it moves on to demand equality in economic power, in social status, in authority in every sphere. And just as there is no point at which the sea of misery is finally drained, so, too, there is no point at which the equality revolution comes to an end, if only because as it proceeds we become ever more sensitive to smaller and smaller degrees of inequality. More important, different types and forms of equality inevitably emerge to contradict each other as we move away from a society of fixed social orders. "From each according to his abilities, to each according to his need": so goes one of the greatest of the slogans invoked as a test of equality. But the slogan itself already incorporates two terms—"abilities" and "needs"—that open the way for conflict between conceptions of equality and a justification of some inequality. We live daily with the consequences of the fact that "equal" treatment of individuals does not necessarily lead to "equality" for groups. And we can point to a host of other contradictions which virtually guarantee that the slogan of "equality" in any society will continue to arouse passions, lead to discontent, and never be realized. Possibly claims for equality do not dominate, to the exclusion of other values, the American people, or even American workers and low-income groups (see Chapter 9). But some claim of unequal treatment was the easiest basis on which advocates for any group could claim more: such claims steadily drove the expansion of social policy, only to create new inequalities that other advocates could seize on to demonstrate mistreatment (welfare clients versus the working poor? social security recipients versus social security tax payers? government employees versus private sector employees? and on and on).

Social policy thus, in almost every field, created new and unmanageable demands. It was illusory to see our social policies as only reducing a problem; any policy has dynamic aspects such that it also expands the problem, changes the problem, generates further problems. And social policy is then challenged to deal adequately with these new demands that follow the implementation of the original measures.

Demands that required enormous expenditure for their fulfillment were often presented, not only by advocates but by experts, as if they were absolute minima for a decent society. We in this country in the late 1960s and early 1970s suffered from the illusion that the money tied up in the arms budget and the war in Vietnam was enough to satisfy all our social needs. Yet if we looked at a country like Sweden, which spent relatively less for arms—and which, owing to its small size, its low rate of population growth, and its ethnic homogeneity, presented a much more moderate range of social problems than did the United States—we could see how even the most enlightened and least conflict-ridden effort to deal with social problems led to a public budget that took half of the Gross National Product in taxes. And new demands steadily joined even Sweden's ample compendium of social programs, which could potentially raise that percentage even higher. For example, one could still raise the number of Swedes who go on to higher education. The Swedes still lived for the most part in apartments and would prefer houses. And so on.

In this country, of course, we still have a long way to go. By comparison with Sweden and with other developed nations of northwestern Europe our taxes are still relatively low, and there is that huge 7 or 8 percent of the GNP devoted to defense and arms that might be diverted, at least in part, to the claims of social policy. But social demands can easily keep up with the new resources made available by arms cuts. We now spend about 11 percent of the GNP on health, about 6 percent on education. It would be no trick at all to increase our expenditures on education or on health by 50 percent, simply by adopting sensible proposals made by leading experts in these fields. We could with no difficulty find similar enormous expenditures to make in housing.

My point is not that we either cannot or should not raise taxes and use the arms budget for better things. Those matters should be argued independently. It is that when we look at projected needs and at the experience of other countries, we know that even with a much smaller arms budget and much higher taxes, social demands will continue to press on public resources. And we may suspect that needs will be felt then as urgently as they are now.

Another source of discontent flowed from the professionalization of services. Professionalization means that a certain point of view is developed about the nature of needs and how they are to be met. It tends to handle a problem by increasing the number of people trained to deal with that problem. When we expand a program, we first run out of people who are defined as "qualified" (social workers, counselors, teachers, and so on). This naturally creates dissatisfaction over the fact that many services are being handled by the "unqualified." Further, questions arise from outside the profession about the ability of the "qualified" themselves to perform a particular service properly. We no longer—and often with some good reason—trust social workers to handle welfare, teachers and principals to handle education, doctors and hospital administrators to handle health care, managers to handle housing projects, and so on. And yet there is no one else in whose hands we can entrust these services. Experience tells us that if we set up new programs and agencies it will be only a very few years before a new professionalism emerges which will be found limited and untrustworthy in its own turn. So, in the poverty program we encouraged the rise of community-action agencies as a way of overcoming the bad effects of professionalism, and we soon found that the community organizers had become another professional group, another interest group, with claims of their own which had no necessary relation to the needs of the clients they served.

But perhaps the most significant limitation on the effectiveness of social policy is simply lack of knowledge. We are in the surprising position of knowing much more than we did at earlier stages in the development of social policy—more about income distribution, employment patterns, family structure, health and medical care, housing and its impact—and simultaneously becoming more uncertain about what measures will be most effective, if effective at all, in ameliorating pressing problems in each of these areas. In the past there was a clear field for action. The situation demanded that something be done, whatever was done was clear gain, and little as yet was expected. Little was known, and administrators approached their tasks with anticipation and self-confidence. Good administrators could be chosen because the task was new and exciting. At later stages, however, we began dealing with problems which were in some absolute sense less serious, but which were nevertheless irksome and productive of conflict. We had already become committed to old lines of policy; agencies with their special interests had been created; and new courses of action had to be taken in a situation in which there was already more conflict at the start, less assurance of success, and less attention from the leaders and the best minds of the country.

Thus, if we look at the history of housing policy, for example, we will see that in the earlier stages—the 1920s and 1930s—there was a good deal of enthusiasm for this subject, with the housing issue attracting some of the best and most vigorous minds in the country. Since little or nothing had been done, there was a wide choice of alternatives and a supply of good men and women to act as administrators. In time, as housing programs expanded, the issue tended to fade from the agenda of top government officials. Earlier programs limited the possibilities for new departures, and as we learned more about housing and its effects on people, we grew more uncertain as to what policies, even theoretically, would be best. Housing, like so many other areas of social policy, became, after an initial surge of interest, a field for experts, with the incursions of general public opinion becoming less and less informed and less and less useful. This process is almost inevitable: there is always so much to know.

Perhaps my explanation of the paradox of knowledge leading to less confident action is defective. More knowledge should permit us to take more confident and effective action. Certainly we do need more knowledge about social policy. But it also appears that whatever great actions we undertake today involve such an increase in complexity that we act generally with less knowledge than we would like to have, even if with more than we once had. This is true, for example, of the reforms in welfare policy, which I shall discuss below, that have dominated discussions of social policy for two decades.

But aside from all these problems of expectations, cost, competency, limitations of knowledge, there is the simple reality that every piece of social policy substitutes for some traditional arrangement, whether good or bad, a new arrangement in which public authorities take over, at least in part, the role of the family, of the ethnic and neighborhood group, of voluntary associations. In doing so, social policy weakens the position of these traditional agents and further encourages needy people to depend on the government for help rather than on the traditional structures. This is the basic force behind the ever growing demand for more social programs and their frequent failure to satisfy our hopes.

To sum up: against the view that to every problem there is a solution, I came to believe that we can have only partial and less than wholly satisfying answers to the social problems in question. Whereas the prevailing wisdom was that social policies would make steady progress in nibbling away at the agenda of problems set by the forces of industrialization and urbanization, I came to believe that although social policy had ameliorated some of the problems we had inherited, it had also given rise to other problems no less grave in their effect on human happiness than those we had addressed with modest success.

Did I have a solution? I began by saying that the breakdown of traditional modes of behavior is the chief cause of our social problems. I am increasingly convinced that some important part of the solution to our social problems lies in traditional practices and traditional restraints. Since the past is not recoverable, what guidance can this possibly give? It gives two forms of guidance: first, it counsels hesitation in the development of social policies that sanction the abandonment of traditional practices, and second, and perhaps more helpful, it suggests that the creation and building of new traditions, or new versions of old traditions, must be taken more seriously as a requirement of social policy itself.

These views are sharpened by the debate over welfare reform that began in the late 1960s and dominated the 1970s. A nation's welfare system provides perhaps the clearest and severest test of the adequacy of its social policy system in general. Welfare, which exists in all advanced nations, is the attempt to deal with the distress that is left over after all the more specific forms of social policy have done their work. After we have instituted what in America is called social security (and what may generally be called old-age pensions); after we have expanded it to cover widows, dependent children, and the disabled; after we have set up a system of unemployment insurance; after we have enabled people to manage the exceptional costs of housing; after we have instituted a system to handle the costs of medical care and to maintain income in times of illness—after all this (and we have not yet done all this) there will remain, in any modern society, people who still require special supports, either temporarily or for longer periods of time.

But as we expanded our system of social security, in theory the number of those needing to resort to welfare should have declined; instead, welfare grew, to the confusion of policy analysts and to the unhappiness of taxpayers. Some welfare experts and policy analysts assured us that there was nothing much to worry about, except that our welfare benefit levels were too low, and our policies in determining eligibility too intrusive and stigmatizing. Nevertheless, the view prevailed that extensive reform was necessary: welfare became the central issue on which our emerging discipline of social policy cut its teeth, it became the issue on which we employed our most sophisticated models to develop and test policies. Welfare was a burning domestic policy issue of the late 1960s and early 1970s, continued to be a significant issue through the 1970s, was for a while pushed off the public agenda in the 1980s, but is returning with vigor to the agenda of public discussion as the Reagan administration comes to an end.

Despite the fact that welfare was far from the biggest of our social programs, it was seen, and with good reason, I would argue, as being closer to the heart of our social problems than larger programs such as social security, or aid to the disabled, or Medicare, or Medicaid. It was forcefully imposed on our attention during the 1960s, when it grew mightily—at a time when unemployment was low. In 1955, 30 out of every 1,000 American families received welfare. By 1969 this had doubled to 60. In 1960 there were, for example, 250,000 persons in the family categories (parents and their children) on welfare in New York City; in 1969, about 800,000. Yet during the same period there had been a substantial drop in unemployment in New York City.

Why welfare grew was a subject of intense argument. It had been designed primarily for families headed by women with children, living without the support of a working husband and father, because of death or divorce or desertion. In the 1950s and 1960s the number of widows on welfare was declining to a small fraction. Welfare families were increasingly composed of mothers who were not receiving support from the fathers of their children; the men had left them, whether or not they had been married to them. That with expanding systems of social security and unemployment insurance there should be a rising number of such families meant something was amiss with our social arrangements.

Welfare, we were assured by some experts, was working. More of the poor were taking advantage of it because the stigma of taking welfare was being reduced, because they were being organized to do so, because low-income jobs were disappearing or could not provide enough to support a family, and it was right that welfare should grow. Indeed, the chief problem, some authorities assured us, was that welfare did not pay enough—even while others demonstrated that in some places, such as New York, it provided more than a low-wage job could, and the program might encourage men to leave their wives and children so they could be supported by a more ample welfare check.[1]

These reassuring efforts to explain welfare did not reduce public dissatisfaction with its expansion. Although one could argue that welfare was no great drain on our financial resources—which was true, compared with other large social programs—it did have an unsettling way of increasing when it should be declining, and, further, it was connected with a nexus of other, rising problems. Was it not likely that it was the children raised on welfare without resident fathers who did worse at school, were most subject to dropping out, most susceptible to juvenile delinquency, to drugs, and to crime? These connections could only rarely be demonstrated (in time some were) but the feeling was widespread that the dependence on welfare of increasing numbers of mothers and their children was a problem of more than simply providing the public funds to support them. The connection of welfare with other social problems was plausible. Welfare reform became an urgent issue, and the economists and sociologists who were working on social programs obliged with a program that represented the best thinking on social policy of the time.

The program was the Family Assistance Plan (FAP) of the Nixon administration, which drew on much social research and analysis. Its chief mover was Daniel P. Moynihan, who played a unique role in linking the researchers on these issues with the political actors who could implement their findings and expectations. The FAP had four major features, and all its variants for the next few years were to contain these features in one or another mix.

First, it created a national welfare benefit floor. The setting of welfare benefit levels was in the hands of the states (with federal participation in funding and a substantial and important federal role in setting the rules). Welfare varied enormously in what it provided from state to state: the northern and western states were more generous, the southern states much less so, and the differences from the most generous state to the least were on the order of magnitude of four or five to one. The national welfare floor expressed the belief among policy analysts that these state differences were irrational, based on prejudice and suspicion—more apparent in some parts of the country than others—and encouraged migration to high-welfare states by people who were most likely to become welfare beneficiaries. (Whether this kind of migration was actually occurring was unclear, but it seemed reasonable that it was if people responded, as we assumed they did, to economic incentives.)

But the second and third features were the heart of the program. The second was an *incentive* for adults on welfare to enter the labor market and become self-supporting workers. Many on welfare did work, with welfare supplementing their earnings. But if the welfare grant was cut dollar for dollar on the basis of earnings, there was no economic incentive to work. The FAP would reduce payments in accordance with earned income, but not to the full extent of earnings: a dollar earned would mean a reduction of less than a dollar in the grant. Those on welfare would thus be encouraged to become productive workers.

But this required a third crucial feature: the program could no longer be just for mothers and children, that is, primarily broken families, but would also have to include unbroken families with children. Otherwise the income of the welfare family, with its combination of welfare and earned income, would exceed that of families of low-income workers. The fact that welfare would not be reduced dollar for dollar for earned income meant that families could continue to receive welfare while their total income moved considerably higher than the definition of need on the basis of which they had first become eligible for welfare, and higher than that of many families dependent on low-wage jobs, and not on welfare. This would encourage working heads of families with low-wage jobs to redefine themselves as incapable of work, or at least full-time work, in order to get the higher income of welfare plus work, which was not desirable. It was also politically impossible to have a system in which many of those on welfare had more income than those in unbroken families dependent on low-wage jobs. Thus working and nonworking family heads, complete families and broken families, would be included in the same system. This was *family* assistance, regardless of the composition of the family or the number of hours the adult mother or father worked.

An additional reason for including all families, those headed by man and wife as well as those headed only by a woman, in the new Family Assistance Plan, was that if welfare was available only to female-headed families (as it was in many states), it encouraged families to break up to get the benefits of welfare. This incentive might operate on the father, who by departing could ensure welfare for the mother and children, or on the mother, who by separating from the father could also ensure her children's support from welfare.

With these new economic incentives, welfare would become a "machine that would go of itself" and thus could be divorced from remedial social services and intrusive investigation. The stigma of welfare would be reduced. Many of those who had proposed and supported the FAP called it, after one of its theoretical fathers, Milton Friedman, "a negative income tax." Those who received the negative tax should be as little marked by stigma as those who paid the "positive" income tax or received refunds for overpayments. There was the hope that in its administration FAP would become an impersonal income-maintenance program, divorced both from the suspicious investigation of families applying (after all, the government takes our calculation of our positive income tax—for most of us—on faith), and from the assumption that social services were necessary and should be provided.

A final feature of the proposed reform was that in addition to the incentive to work, there would be a requirement that every adult capable of work register for job training and employment. If there was a father, he had to register; if there was no father presesnt, the mother had to register if she had no children below school age.

This was the plan that dominated our thinking about welfare for years to come, however we modified its name or its specific features. But just about the time that this plan, the triumph of our research and thinking about social problems and how they might be addressed through social policy, reached fruition, doubts as to whether it would work—I leave aside the political problems which actually defeated it—grew in my mind. These doubts were initially hardly theoretical: they were based on the fact that most of the new features the FAP was to introduce for most of the country were already in effect in the liberal state of New York, and even more so in the liberal city of New York. Yet one could see there none of the positive consequences that we hoped would follow from the national reform. There was an incentive to work: in New York City part of earned income could be retained. The unbroken family was eligible: a father and husband could apply for supplemental welfare aid for himself and his family if his earnings did not reach the minimal need level for a family of that size. Income from welfare was increasingly divorced from services. It was becoming true income maintenance, or as true as one could imagine under any real political system.

And yet income maintenance in New York City did not seem to encourage work participation by the heads of welfare families, and, what was worse, the rate of family breakup was rapidly growing.[2] I could see some positive consequences of the FAP. It would have raised the abysmally low welfare payments in the South. It might, by setting a national floor (New York would still be well above that, because the floor would have to be between southern levels and the New York level), have reduced migration to the big cities of the North. It would have provided some fiscal relief to the states and local jurisdictions with high welfare benefits. All this was to the good. But what the new program could not have done was to strengthen the family or substantially increase the number of those on welfare willing to enter the labor market. If it had had these desirable results, just how it accomplished them would have been a mystery, because similar arrangements had not done so in New York and other states in which some features of the new plan, such as the eligibility of complete families with unemployed fathers for welfare, were in effect. The forces leading to the breakdown of male responsibility for the family among a good part of the poor were greater than those the new program brought into play to counteract them.

The number of abandoned families had grown enormously in the 1960s. More liberal welfare eligibility and benefits were one factor that had encouraged this increase. More generally, the constraints that traditionally kept families together had weakened. In some groups they may not have been strong to begin with. Our efforts to soften the harsh consequences of family breakup spoke well of our compassion and concern, but these efforts also made it easier for fathers to abandon their families or mothers to disengage from their husbands.

And yet, what alternatives did we have? The Family Assistance Plan was, after all, the most enlightened and thoughtful legislation to be introduced in the field of welfare in some decades.

My own tendency, following from the basic considerations I have suggested, would have been to ask how we might prevent further erosion of the traditional constraints that still played the largest role in maintaining a civil society. What kept society going, after all, was that most people still felt they should work—however well they might do without working—and most felt that they should take care of their families—however attractive it might appear on occasion to desert them. Consequently we should have tried to strengthen the incentive to work. The work-incentive provision was the best thing about FAP, but we needed to make it even stronger. Our dilemma was that we could never make this incentive as strong as it was when the alternative to work was starvation or the uncertain charity of private organizations. Nor was it politically feasible to increase the incentive by reducing the levels at which we maintained the poor. The only alternative, then, was to further increase the incentive to work by increasing the attractiveness of work. For example, we could have begun, and we still can and should, to attach to low-income jobs the same kind of fringe benefits—health insurance, social security, vacations with pay—

that now make higher-paying jobs attractive, and that paradoxically are also available in some form to those on welfare.[3]

The dilemma of income maintenance was that, on the one hand, it permitted the poor to live better, but on the other, it reduced their incentive to set up and maintain those close units of self-support—family, in the first case, but also larger units—that have always, both in the past and still in large measure today, formed the fabric of society. Our reform efforts sought to improve the condition of the poor without further damage to those social motivations and structures which are the essential basis for individual security everywhere. But the Family Assistance Plan and its successors did not still the fears that we had not found a way to do this.

In 1984 the developing critique of the social policies of the 1960s and 1970s burst on the public with the publication of Charles Murray's *Losing Ground*. Murray argued that one could discern patterns of improvement among the poor until the middle or late 1960s, but that then matters worsened as social policies expanded, when we considered such measures as the number of people in poverty, participation of blacks in the labor force, illegitimacy, and family breakup. He made his argument with a host of statistics, but the most vivid presentation of his case came in a provocative fictional account of Phyllis and Harold, a young unmarried couple, the girl pregnant, the young man unemployed. Murray contrasted their situation in 1970 as against 1960; he attempted to show that in view of the paucity of welfare benefits in 1960, it paid Phyllis and Harold to get married, and Harold to go to work; in 1970 it paid to stay unmarried, and Phyllis to go on welfare.

Murray then carried the story further, proposing as a thought experiment the elimination of all benefits. How would all the Phyllises and Harolds react? He thought it might be all for the best in the end: they would get out of poverty the way tens of millions of immigrants from abroad and migrants from the farms have regularly gotten out of poverty, by working in an expanding economy.

Murray was sharply disputed on the relationships he discerned. In particular, it was hard to demonstrate a direct relationship between economic benefits and the behavior that maximized economic return on the basis of these benefits. Thus, despite the great variation from state to state in welfare benefits, the rate of increase in family breakup shows no direct relationship: the incentives have varied, the behavior that is presumably the result of the incentives has not. Similarly with illegitimacy.

All this may be true. But Murray stood his ground: more was happening than simply changes in welfare levels and eligibility, and what was happening was teaching young poor people that it didn't pay to maintain a stable family and work at a stable job. In addition to the changes in the welfare package and the eligibility rules, "reforms in law enforcement and criminal justice increased income from the underground economy . . . The breakdown in inner-city education reduced job readiness . . . the reforms diminished the stigma associated with welfare and simultaneously devalued the status associated with working at a menial, low-paying job."[4]

I think all this was indeed happening in the 1970s, and other things were happening too: for example, the change in the culture, which glorified a variety of ways of "dropping out" of organized society. This cultural change, through novels, magazines, radio, and popular music, was able to penetrate to young people who might have been expected to be immune to such influences, owing to the failure of their education. But one could hear from young delinquents the very explanations and excuses that social psychologists and sociologists were making for behavior that damaged society—and themselves.

By the time of the publication of Charles Murray's book, much had changed. The period of welfare reform based on economic incentives to work and maintain family stability ended when the research that tested this approach came up with surprising results (see Chapter 2). The Reagan administration which took office in 1981 approached welfare in a very different way: traditional behavior was now expected rather than rewarded (Chapter 3). A new consensus emerged on welfare, linking conservatives and liberals, and the newest welfare reforms take as their starting point the requirement that fathers support their children and that adults on welfare undertake work training and seek work, with no reward beyond that provided from the marketplace. This is the thrust of the reforms proposed in 1987 by Senator Daniel P. Moynihan, who was so closely identified with the rather different approach of the Family Assistance Plan.

The traditional virtues were now assumed and required. Other changes have been afoot for the past few years: school reforms are reining in the great increase in freedom of choice and behavior that characterized the 1970s. We talk more now of punishing than of explaining crime. The messages from the culture too are changing, as conservatism enjoys a renaissance, with the fortuitous assistance of the AIDS epidemic.

The next debate on social policy will be whether this hardening in the

1980s, the changing of the incentives, has had the effects Murray somewhat optimistically hoped for in his thought experiment. Whether, in other words, the clock can be run backward.

It was not only in welfare that one could see the impact of the breakdown of traditional measures, traditional restraints, traditional organization. Even in an area apparently so far removed from tradition as health and medical care, the weakening of traditional forms of organization can, upon examination, be found to be playing a substantial role. This was clear even twenty years ago, when drug addiction was the chief cause of death—and of who knew what other frightful consequences—among young men in New York. We now know that one of these frightful consequences was AIDS.

Ultimately, we are not kept healthy primarily by new scientific knowledge or more effective cures or even better organized medical care services, although they are all important. But we are also kept healthy by certain patterns of life. These, it is true, are modified for the better by increased scientific knowledge, but this knowledge is itself communicated through such functioning traditional organizations as the school, voluntary organizations, the family. We are kept healthy by having access to traditional means of support in distress and illness, through the family, the neighborhood, informal social organization. We are kept healthy by decent care in institutions where people in certain traditional occupations (like nursing and cleaning) still manage to perform their functions. Who now needs to argue the case for the significance of traditional patterns in maintaining health?

One major objection, among many, that can be raised to the emphasis I have placed on traditional behavior has to do with the greater success of social policy in a country like Sweden, which shows a greater departure from traditionalism than America does. And it is indeed true that social services in Sweden, and England as well, can be organized without as much interference from tradition-minded interest groups of various kinds (including the churches) as we have to contend with in this country. Certainly this is an important consideration. But I would insist that behind the modern organization of social services in the advanced European countries are at least two elements that can legitimately and without distortion be called traditional.

One is authority. Authority exists when social workers can direct clients, when doctors can direct nurses, when headmasters can direct teachers, when teachers can discipline students and can expect acquiescence from parents. Admittedly this feature of traditionalism itself serves the movement *away* from tradition in other respects. The authority may be used, as in Sweden, to institute sex education in the schools, to ensure that unmarried girls have access to contraceptives, to secure a position of equality for illegitimate children.

But another feature that can legitimately be called traditional sets limits in these countries on how far the movement away from the traditional—toward indeed a new tradition—may be carried, and that is a greater degree of ethnic and religious and racial homogeneity. In America, by contrast, it is the very diversity of traditions—ethnic, religious, and social—that makes it hard to establish new forms of behavior that are universally accepted and approved, and that also makes it impossible to give the social worker, the teacher, the policeman, the judge, the nurse, the doctor, the same authority they possess in more homogeneous countries.

In the chapters that follow, I develop and explore the approach to social policy I have laid out, and try to see how far we can go in developing alternative approaches. In Chapter 2, I go into further detail on our attempts to reform welfare. In Chapter 3, I describe how the early Reagan administration instituted a new approach to welfare and to social policy generally. In Chapter 4, I consider the great explosion of programs in education and work training for the poor of the late 1960s and 1970s, and what we have learned from them. In Chapter 5, I discuss one element of the vision that dominated liberal social reform in those decades, the hope of universal social programs that would eliminate any differential treatment of people on the basis of income. Chapters 5 and 6 explore some new approaches to social policy that developed in the 1970s and 1980s. Chapter 8 ponders the disappointing experience of social scientists in trying to introduce a more scientific approach to social policy. Chapter 9 explores the reasons why the thrust to equality, which to so many social philosophers and analysts is self-evidently the central goal of public policy, does not make more headway. And in Chapter 10, I consider why the American welfare state, which, many believe, scarcely deserves that description, has been left, in comparison with European models, so incomplete, and why it is likely to continue so.

2 | Reforming the American Welfare Family, 1969–1981

Between 1969 and 1981 the United States was engaged in a major effort to solve in what was considered a rational and systematic way the problem of the poor and dependent family. In 1969, under the Nixon administration, a Family Assistance Plan (FAP) to replace welfare—need-based, noncontributory maintenance income for the poor—was proposed. It had a checkered career over the next few years; the character of the proposed program varied with each year of congressional action in response to political criticism and emergent findings from major social experiments. The welfare system was not reformed under Presidents Nixon and Ford. But President Carter vowed to take up this reform again in his campaign, and proposed a variant of the Family Assistance Program shortly after he came into office. This too represented what we may call the best thinking of the time—thinking I will summarize shortly—on how to reconcile the need to support families incapable of earning sufficient income in the labor market with the concomitant danger that some would become permanently dependent on government aid and would avoid the actions—work in the labor market, or marriage to those who could, through work, support dependents—that would lead to economic independence. This program, the Program for Better Jobs and Income (PBJI), also failed. When Reagan assumed the presidency, the effort to reform welfare, through analysis of the conditions that made it necessary and of the incentives and disincentives that together maintained a substantial welfare program, ceased. The age of welfare reform was over: the primary interest of the Reagan administration was to cut federal costs, to make it harder for people to get on welfare and easier to get people removed, and to reduce benefits to those who did get on welfare (see Chapter 3).[1]

This failed reform had been driven by a specific theory of family behavior, and in particular by the notion that economic incentives and dis-incentives played a key role in family instability and illegitimacy, and could be manipulated to reduce instability and illegitimacy. Leslie Len-kowsky has dubbed this the "incentive" theory. In one respect, it is not new. Feminists and critics of the bourgeois family have long argued that women are forced into marriage against their will in order to receive main-tenance for themselves and their children; failing marriage, they were once forced into domestic service or prostitution, and whether married or unmarried were forced into low-paying jobs. One could say the security hoped for from marriage served as an incentive to become married.

But the incentive theory went much further than this. It was created in response to an anomaly: that a program meant to reduce the distress of widows and unmarried mothers and their children, and designed to main-tain them at a minimal but decent level, seemed to be accompanied by a rising number of such women. While it could never be proved—perhaps because social scientists were so reluctant to give any support to a thesis which turned poor women into calculating economic agents—it was widely believed, among ordinary people (including the poor) and their representatives in Congress, that welfare assistance to destitute mothers and children might be serving as an incentive for fathers to leave their families, or, in a more sophisticated version, for mothers to push fathers out of the home, and for young girls and older women to have illegitimate children because of the assurance that support would rise with need, mea-sured by the number of children.

If welfare had created incentives that most Americans saw as per-verse—for whatever their tolerance and wide experience of divorce, mar-ital stability was still the norm to which most Americans aspired—could the system not be redesigned so that economic incentives served to *strengthen* the family? This was the remarkable basis of the welfare re-form efforts of the Nixon and Carter administrations: whereas in the past (and now again) social policy for the poor was seen by the left as some-thing demanded by charity, decency, or the basic human rights of all mem-bers of a single community, and by the right as something that was just too expensive, for ten years Republican and Democratic administrations operated, not from motives of liberal social impulse or conservative bud-get-cutting, but under the influence of a sophisticated economic analysis which explained how current social policy had put in place perverse incen-tives and how new social policies could replace them with benign incen-tives. The aims of family stability and legitimacy were no longer to be argued for on religious grounds or moral grounds, no longer to be promoted by threats of hellfire or exhortations to do good: they were to be realized through well-designed economic incentives.

The new approach offered a hope that constraint and command imposed by bureaucrats and social workers, as when they required welfare recipients to work by regulations or urged family responsibility, would be replaced by new incentives reaching the same result, incentives unaccompanied by requirements and propaganda. Just as Keynesian economics fine-tuned the economy, social policy tested by econometric models would fine-tune the family and control the distressing increase in female-headed families and illegitimate children. A noble objective, and it bears much in common with Adam Smith's invisible hand, in which each man pursuing his own interest produces good for the community. At a higher level, of course, this hand was all too visible: the new system had to work its way through all the processes of legislation. But once in place, it would operate like clockwork: fewer families would break up, more new ones would be created by remarriage, fewer illegitimate children would be born, and these most intimate of all behaviors would be regulated by well-designed social and family policy, as economic behavior was regulated by the market.

This entire enterprise was shaped by changing ideas of what was going on in the American family, ideas held by people in general—taxpayers and their representatives—and by academic researchers—economists and sociologists. There were some contradictions between the ideas of taxpayers and those of academic scholars as to the proper normative character of the family and how it was being affected by welfare. But by 1969 both were in substantial agreement as to what should be done: certain actions in public policy, the scholars asserted, and the public cautiously agreed, would prevent normal families (families headed by men, working to support their wives and children) from becoming abnormal (female-headed, supported through welfare).

As Congress worked on the policies aimed at by FAP and PBJI, problems emerged, the main one being that the research set afoot by the scholars, with the support of many millions in federal money, began to show disconcerting results. It turned out that the econometric analysis of the scholars, an analysis that seemed supported by common sense, did not work in reality: that a program designed to institute incentives to maintain stable families and to encourage work behavior would do neither. The research designed to support the program that had emerged from economic-sociological analysis, to the dismay of those who conducted the research, did not do so. A decade in which economists and sociologists dominated welfare reform came to an end, and so did welfare reform.

The story is best begun with the program of Aid to Families with Dependent Children, the program that is preeminently known as "welfare" in the United States, which has given this perfectly decent word a rather disreputable connotation. This federal program, conducted together with the states, and initially designed as part of the Social Security Act of 1935, is one of the enduring monuments of the Roosevelt administration. The social security system of the United States included a major program for retirement and disability, which is *the* social security system in the popular mind, which is entirely conducted by the federal government, and which is contributory; an unemployment insurance program, also contributory, which is a combined federal-state program, and a residual noncontributory program for children in families with no economic resources to maintain them. Eligibility for this program was defined by the presence of children, by poverty in the family in which they lived, and by the absence of a male (expected in those distant days to be the father) capable of working to support them. The entire social security program had a certain symmetry, and it was expected that all contingencies had been accounted for: social security retirement and disability benefits would take care of the aged and their families, as well as those families in which the head did not reach retirement age because of death or disability; unemployment insurance would take care of families in spells of unemployment; and those women and children in situations where there was no working male connected to the labor market would get welfare assistance.

As Gilbert Steiner has pointed out, it was expected that the numbers of these would not be large and would decline as the social security system came to maturity.[2] Mothers and children were expected to have husbands and fathers, the husbands and fathers were expected to be in the labor force, and by being in the labor force they would acquire rights to retirement and disability income and unemployment insurance. (It is well known that there was one great hole in the Rooseveltian scheme of social insurance, medical insurance, and this was in part plugged under President Johnson in 1965 with Medicare—medical insurance for the aged— and Medicaid—payment for health costs of the poor.)

The reality of the family situation in which this program was launched was one in which relatively few women with young children worked, or were expected to work. If their husbands died or deserted, it was inevitable that some form of aid would be provided. Before the depression, much of this was private, though many advanced states had state programs of mothers' aid or widow's aid. With the huge increase in need for aid in the depression, the private agencies were overwhelmed; soon the states were overwhelmed too, and so the federal-state program of AFDC (then known as Aid to Dependent Children) was launched to provide for those in this type of need. If the system worked, the number of those in this status would decline as the maturing insurance programs took care of their needs.

It didn't work. In the early 1960s, during the Kennedy administration, there was concern over the growing population on welfare, and an emergent body of researchers and analysts pondered what to do about it. The welfare reforms of the Kennedy administration (1962) were dominated by social workers. We never stopped to find out whether they were of any use or not, because, with the poverty program of 1964, a radical change came over American thinking about the poor and their problems. Social workers gave way to community organizers, and these, after a hectic few years, gave way to economists. After all, the 1960s were the age of economic preeminence: the Kennedy tax cut, designed on Keynesian principles, worked and brought prosperity; it was believed that the economy could be "fine-tuned"; Nixon himself said, "We are all Keynesians now." And there seemed to be no reason why economists, operating from their major citadel at the Institute for Research on Poverty at the University of Wisconsin, Madison, created with funds from the Office of Economic Opportunity, should not tackle the persistent and pesky problem of the welfare family.

Why was AFDC seen as a problem in the early 1960s, one that required major reform? One reason was that the expectations of the framers of the social security package of 1935 were not fulfilled. This expectation was that with the maturation of the social security system for retirement and death and disability insurance, and the development of the unemployment insurance system, the need for Aid to Dependent Children—welfare— would decline. This expectation may have been naive, but it was widespread. If mother's aid, the predecessor of welfare, was considered the program that took care, prototypically, of the widow of a West Virginia coal miner killed in an accident, social insurance would now take over the job (not to mention the increasingly strong pension or insurance plans that covered workers in many industries, among them mining).

By the early 1960s something that was increasingly being called a "crisis in welfare" was being analyzed. The number of mothers and children on welfare was increasing, not declining, as the social insurance system matured. And there was a second reason for crisis: the composition of those on welfare was changing. The miner's widow was less and less in evidence, and indeed widows in general were less and less in evidence. The women on welfare were those who had been divorced or deserted by living spouses, or, increasingly, had never been married at all and were the mothers of one or more illegitimate children. "Whereas public assistance once compensated for irreversible, involuntary tragic dependency (widowhood), that situation ceased to fit most of the customers by the early 1950's, when only one in five cases involved death of the father. By the 1960's the figure had dropped to one in fourteen, by 1973 to one in twenty, by 1975 to one in 27."[3] AFDC by 1970 was no longer a widows' program: it was not even a program primarily for divorced women, or women whose husbands had deserted them. It was increasingly a program for the mothers of illegitimate children.

That the program grew when it was expected to decline was a problem. That it no longer responded to emergencies created independently of the will or action of those who had recourse to it was another problem, one which could not easily be discussed openly. It had become a program for blacks, who made up about half of the recipients of welfare aid. That there should be more family breakup and more illegitimacy among blacks than whites was understandable in view of the hard economic circumstances under which blacks lived as compared to whites, the particularly great difficulty black men encountered in finding stable jobs, the inferior education blacks received.

In describing welfare as a problem arousing increasing concern in the early 1960s, we must of course specify to *whom* it was a problem and what kind of problem. To liberal social workers and the left in general, the problem of welfare was that its benefits were niggardly, its administration was harsh and showed no respect for the feelings of those who had to resort to it, and as a result far too many poor people refused to subject themselves to it even for its palpable money benefits. To the liberals and the left, then, its benefits should be raised, its administration made more neutral, and its coverage widened. The first proponent of a "negative income tax" (NIT) to replace welfare may have been the conservative economist Milton Friedman, but the idea that welfare could be dispensed the way the income tax was collected—perhaps by the same agency, and with the same level of trust and suspicion with which ordinary taxpayers were viewed by government—became very attractive to liberals thinking about suitable reforms in those expansive days when budget receipts rose automatically and when people could even worry (as they did in the late 1960s!) about what to do with the automatic budget surplus brought in by taxes. The left was not insensitive to the attractions of the NIT, but devoted its energies to enrolling more people on welfare, putting pressure on administrators to ease the rules, going into court to have practices they found disrespectful to the poor declared unconstitutional (such as the "midnight search" in which welfare workers went into the house to see if, as against the mother's declaration, a male capable of supporting her was living there).

To the right, of course, the problem was quite different: it was the rising numbers of welfare, the rising costs of welfare, the rising number of broken families and illegitimate children. To neutral social policy analysts, the problem was that welfare was not working the way it was expected to. To states and local communities, which bore about half the costs of welfare (the federal government bearing the other half) it was that welfare was becoming a strain on their budgets.

One response to the changing character (and increasing size) of the welfare population was to stiffen the rules. This stiffening generally was a matter of action by states or local communities, and was generally resisted by the federal partner in welfare funding and administration in Washington, which was always more enlightened, even under the Republican Eisenhower administrations. Thus, one southern state tried to exclude illegitimate children from welfare: Washington would not allow it. A northern community tried to put the welfare recipients to work on public projects to recoup some part of the cost: Washington's reaction to this was hostile.

Under the Kennedy administration, the reforms put in place were modest (basically, additional federal funds for the advice and counseling of social workers). Under the poverty program, quite another strategy toward the poor was adopted: psychologically oriented social workers were out, community organizers were in, and it was hoped that organizing the poor into protest blocs would in some way improve their circumstances, primarily by a greater responsiveness of local government in providing aid and jobs.

Protest of course, was set afoot not only by the community action program of the Office of Economic Opportunity; it was also the favored tool of black civil rights groups in the early 1960s, and eventually reached massive national success in the passage of the Civil Rights act of 1964. But by the middle 1960s a growing body of opinion held that neither social-work counseling, nor government-sponsored community action, nor civil rights protest, would solve the problem of the growing welfare population. Something responsive to neither counseling nor protest, it seems, was happening. And it took Daniel P. Moynihan, a scholar-politician, to put it on the national agenda.

In 1965 he prepared a report for the Labor Department, of which he was assistant secretary, titled "The Negro Family: The Case for National Action."[4] Moynihan pointed out that the Negro family was in trouble. There was a high proportion of families headed by women, a high proportion of illegitimate births, and female-headed families with illegitimate children were almost inevitably going to be poor and dependent families. He also pointed out that while the number of families on welfare had seemed to increase and decrease together with the rise and fall of unemployment until the early 1960s—suggesting that there was a common-sense relationship between hardship for working males and the need for families to go on welfare—this relationship no longer obtained in the early 1960s: the number of families on welfare kept going up, despite the fact that unemployment was going down.

The report, when it was leaked, created a sensation, not because it pointed to a serious social problem, but because it identified the problem as being black family instability. This was also the era of black pride, and a storm of protest, mostly entirely uninformed, enveloped the report: any serious discussion of the black family was placed under a ban for the next fifteen years because no white investigator dared face such an attack again, and blacks found less embarrassing topics to write about—or, if they wrote about the black family, insisted that it was strong and hardy and no problem at all. Black social scientists argued that what appeared to white middle-class social scientists as instability was simply rational adaptation to the black situation, and that illegitimacy created no special hardship for black children, who were cared for by a kinship network of female relations.

Undoubtedly the reaction to the report was only one nail in the coffin of the social work approach, which assumed a middle-class professional had something useful to impart to a black mother. But the celebration of black power did not seem any adequate answer either, unless one took the position that there was no problem except getting sufficient economic resources for these families, and that this could be managed by increasing the numbers on welfare and the benefits of welfare. This was indeed a popular approach: its chief propagandists were Richard Cloward and Frances Piven. It is hardly likely that many potential welfare clients read their books and articles. But community action had created organizers and organizations galore, and their chief success in the later 1960s was in expanding greatly the numbers on welfare, by organizing potential clients, and increasing their benefits, through the pressure of such groups as the Welfare Rights Organization and its liberal allies. Undoubtedly also assisting the rapid expansion of the numbers on welfare and the costs of supporting them were the summer riots that plagued the ghettos of American cities in the years from 1964 on. It is clear that one response to these riots was an expansion of social programs, not very difficult in a time of prosperity and rising revenues, and among these programs was welfare.

As the Johnson administration came to an end and the Nixon administration came into office, the welfare population was rising explosively, the nation was shaken by recurrent summer riots in the ghettos, the costs of welfare were becoming a serious problem for local communities and states in which liberal policies prevailed (New York, California, Massachusetts, Illinois), the instability and illegitimacy that Moynihan had pointed to was on the rise (though no one referred to it), and it was clear that welfare reform would be on the agenda of the new administration. What was surprising, however, in a Nixon administration was that Moynihan, a Democratic policy analyst who had devoted much effort to thinking about the relationship between social policy and the poor, became the chief domestic policy analyst, and that a liberal Republican, Robert Finch, became the secretary of Health, Education and Welfare, the agency responsible for welfare. It was clear in this concatenation of events that the response of the Republican administration would not be harsh budget cutting and harsh regulations. It was, instead, the Family Assistance Plan, first incarnation of the incentive theory of family formation and breakup.

Before proceeding to the program the incentive theory proposed, I must be more specific in explaining the negative incentives analysts and congressmen saw in the existing welfare system and how they hoped to overcome them. First, in half the states only mothers without husbands capable of supporting them (a husband could be present only if disabled) were eligible for welfare. The disincentive here was to a stable marriage: a husband making very little money or unemployed might desert to make his wife and children eligible for welfare; and a low-income woman would have no economic incentive to keep a marriage together, since she would be supported by welfare (possibly more handsomely) if her husband or the father of her children disappeared. Young girls or older women would have no economic incentive to limit the number of their children: income rose with each additional child.

The Family Assistance Plan would come into effect on the basis of income alone, regardless of whether a husband-father was present or not: low income would be supplemented as long as there was one child. This would eliminate the family breakup incentive, but it could reduce another important positive incentive: the incentive to seek paying work. If the husband-father saw as an alternative to a low-paying job the new FAP, for which he was now eligible, what would maintain work incentives? Here the social policy engineers had another solution, the one proposed by Milton Friedman in the negative income tax: FAP would be reduced as earned income went up, but not to the full extent of earned income. A family in which neither mother nor father earned would get the full FAP benefit. Earned income would reduce the benefit, not dollar for dollar, because that would reduce work incentive (why work if additional money earned led to an exact reduction in the FAP grant?), but at some rate that preserved the work incentive. The favored rate was a 50 percent reduction: for each dollar earned, FAP was to be reduced fifty cents.

This was the overall structure of both FAP and PBJI: coverage of intact families to eliminate the incentive for family breakup, retention of some percentage of the FAP grant with rising earned income to maintain the work incentive.

I leave out innumerable difficulties in the details, difficulties which prevented the passage of either FAP or PBJI despite presidential support, for I wish to concentrate on the incentive theory as a unique development in family policy. Note that families were to be held together because the economic incentive that encouraged instability was to be removed. Note that work was to be encouraged because one would make more money working than not working. Note too what was not involved: no difficulty was put in the way of family breakup—policy was to be neutral as between families headed by women and families headed by a husband-wife, mother-father pair—and work was to be not so much required as encouraged by incentives. Note that alternatives are possible: it was not so long ago that divorce was very difficult in many countries, and in the Soviet Union one is *required* to work, regardless of the array of incentives and

disincentives inherent in wage rates and social policy. Admittedly the programs did not depend on pure economic incentive: in one way or another,
Congress kept on trying to strengthen the requirement that fathers of children be sought out and made to pay for them and that FAP or PBJI recipients seek work. But in the large, for those who proposed these programs
and argued for them, the economic incentives were expected to work,
regardless of the other compulsions independent of incentive (not very
onerous) put into the program.

Would it work? Here we come to the most remarkable part of the story,
the introduction of research findings that said it wouldn't. No one doubted
that the changes in incentives for marital breakup would work: it stood to
reason. Moynihan had pointed to the disastrous rise in the number of black
families headed by women in 1965; that rise was continuing steadily. Certainly a program in which there was no financial benefit to division, no
increase in resources available to the female household head, would
change the pattern of incentives and disincentives that seemed to encourage this plague. There was greater concern about the work incentives
problem. Clearly in a situation in which the welfare grant was reduced
dollar for dollar with earnings, the incentive to earn was radically reduced.
But if it was reduced by fifty cents on the dollar, in effect levying a 50
percent tax on earnings, would the incentive to work be much greater?
Nor could the incentive be increased much. If the tax was reduced to, let
us say, 25 percent, the cost of the program would be enormous. This can
be demonstrated simply. Assume that the Family Assistance Plan was to
provide $4,000 for a family of four. Assume a 50 percent "tax." The head
of household would be receiving some grant from FAP until he earned
$8,000, when the FAP grant would be reduced to zero (50 percent of
$8,000, eliminating the $4,000 grant). But if the tax was reduced to 25
percent, he would be eligible for FAP until he earned $16,000. Worse,
everyone earning less than $16,000 for a family of four would be eligible!

Sheldon Danziger has referred to the "iron triangle" which hamstrung
every effort to get FAP passed: the triangle created by the inherent conflicts among the income guarantee level, the work incentive (how much of
an imputed "tax" on earnings), and total costs.[5] This was the problem I
have just illustrated. In theory, the negative income tax approach was ingenious. For conservatives, it introduced work incentives stronger than
existing welfare; for liberals, it reduced the stigma inherent in welfare not
only by a change of name but by a change of rationalization and justification. Income aid was no longer to be seen as a sign of abject failure in

a market economy, but a simple adjustment in the tax system: if you made more than a certain amount, you paid the government (taking into account deductions for family size, and so on); if you made less, the government paid you. In practice, either total costs ballooned to the point where conservatives (and not only conservatives) were frightened, or the FAP allowance was so reduced, and the tax rate so increased, that liberals rebelled. In the first campaigns for the FAP under President Nixon, no settlement of the matter capable of getting a majority of liberals and conservatives in Congress to adopt FAP could be constructed.

But the failure to get the right coalition never led to a challenge to the basic incentive theory. By the time Jimmy Carter was running for office in 1976, family policy had emerged as an issue, not only for poor welfare families, but for all families.[6] It was clear welfare reform would be attempted again. In view of the fact that more or less the same professionals were at work with the same models to create the new program, it would have to be the same program as before. After all, there were no others. The secretary of Health, Education, and Welfare was set to work to construct the new program, now called Program for Better Jobs and Income. Names were crucial: the negative income tax gave the logic for the new program, but that name was too negative and came up against a stubborn insistence on the part of most Americans that welfare *was* charity, not simply negative income. A "guaranteed annual income" also seemed too much like a handout. Nixon's administration came up with the Family Assistance Plan—who could be against family assistance? Carter's administration came up with PBJI. Knowing the suspicion that would accompany a broadening of welfare to families headed by a working male, the emphasis in the program's title was to be on providing jobs.

The new element that now entered an old drama, and wrecked the possibility of adoption of the incentive approach, was publication of the findings of the major social experiments that had been launched in the late 1960s and early 1970s to test the idea of a negative income tax—and that had now come to fruition with unexpected results. The high-riding social scientists of the late 1960s had not only constructed the program and estimated in their models the costs and effects, they had also received millions of dollars to actually test the negative income tax in reality. Thus thousands of families were enrolled in a program, to last three or five years, in which they would be *guaranteed* an annual income, which would be reduced in accordance with their earnings. Perhaps uniquely in the history of social policy (I know of no example from European countries), a major program was to be tested before being launched. The test would of course have to be expensive. For not only would the enrolled families be interviewed at regular intervals, there would have to be additional families not in the experiment to serve as controls, and there would have to be a number of different variants tested. Thus different tax rates would be set for different samples (different rates at which guaranteed income declined with earnings), different guarantee levels would be set—at the poverty level, or below it, or above it. Further, sufficient numbers would have to be enrolled to test responses among key subgroups: whites, blacks, and Hispanic Americans. These experiments would make it possible to test what was seen as the major problem, labor response, the degree to which work effort was reduced by a guaranteed income at different levels.

The first major experiments were started with samples in Pennsylvania and New Jersey in the late 1960s. Early results were gratifying. Yes, there was a slight reduction of work effort, a somewhat greater reduction among secondary earners (wives and older children), but not sufficient to give support to the fear that a negative income tax would undermine the Protestant ethic, or, more pragmatically, that the reduction of earnings in response to an NIT would balloon costs excessively. But a larger experiment, begun in 1970–71 in Seattle, and 1971–72 in Denver, known as the SIME-DIME experiment (Seattle Income Maintenance Experiment, Denver Income Maintenance Experiment) showed more unsettling results. Designed, as was the New Jersey-Pennsylvania experiment, primarily to test for labor response, it showed a remarkable marital instability response. A program that, it was assumed, would keep families together was having the effect of increasing separations!

One can see how unsettling all this was in reading the hearings on Welfare Research and Experimentation conducted by Senator Daniel P. Moynihan in November 1978, where these results were first displayed in the large. The man who had been a chief architect and propagandist for FAP, who had been expected by the administration to be the chief advocate in the Senate for PBJI—no one in that body understood these matters better than he did—was now discovering that the entire enterprise was basically flawed: the incentive theory did not work when it came to family effects. Since for Senator Moynihan family effects were crucial—he had always been most concerned with family changes affecting children, less concerned with labor supply effects—the findings could only be termed explosive. In a program testing an income guarantee level of 90 percent of the poverty level (it was not possible that Congress would ever approve more), the increase in marital dissolutions (as compared to controls) was estimated, over a thirty-six month period, to be 43 percent for blacks, 63 percent for whites, 37 percent for Hispanics.[7] The effects could be estimated in various ways, but in whatever way one did, they stood up.

For the social scientists, the problem was to explain effects so at variance with common sense, and they did. They postulated three effects. Most straightforward was the "income" effect: as income goes up and life becomes more comfortable for a family, the chances of marital breakup decline: it is regularly lower at higher income levels. And indeed, the experiments showed that at higher guarantee levels (for example, 140 percent of poverty), the number of marital breakups compared with controls went up much more moderately, and, in the case of Hispanics, declined. But there is also an "independence" effect: this is the effect created by the fact that the mother knows she will receive income for herself and her children whether the husband-father stays with her or not. This leads to breakup. But why should the breakup be *more* than that in the control group, many of whom are on welfare? For this one must postulate a "welfare discount" effect: The NIT or guaranteed income in the SIME-DIME experiment is more attractive than welfare because there is more information as to one's rights, less stigma, less problem dealing with a suspicious welfare administration.[8]

Our concern here is less with the details of the experiments, which have been analyzed and reanalyzed in many publications, than with their effect on policy: when it turned out that income guarantees would reduce work effort a bit, in line with the common understanding of the effect of guaranteed income, but would increase marital breakups a lot, *against* the common understanding, scholarly, political, and popular, of the effects of the incentive approach to reforming welfare, welfare reform was dead. As Senator Moynihan said, "I am sort of sorry about these hearings. I am certainly sorry about your findings. I wish they had been that everything we thought we should do was what we should do and that would be it. But that is what intellectual work is about. It comes up with things you do not want to hear once in a while."[9]

In any case, by 1978 the crisis of the welfare explosion was past. Welfare was being controlled during the 1970s, and under Reagan it was to be increasingly controlled in the 1980s, not by a subtle arrangement of incentives, as the social policy planners hoped, but by regulatory controls (see Chapter 3). In the big welfare states—New York, California, Massachusetts, and others—costs had become so high that benefits levels were kept down, and applicants for welfare and those on welfare were more closely scrutinized for undeclared resources and earnings. Although the number of those on welfare tripled in the prosperous 1960s, the numbers were kept level in the troubled 1970s. There was no explosion with the increase in unemployment in the early 1980s, though there was some increase. Perhaps the incentive theory was working in one respect: as welfare grants were kept low, and inflation reduced their value, their attractiveness declined. But this disincentive was combined with a new, suspicious regulatory environment, one which only increased in the Reagan administration.

Was there a family crisis that demanded some response in the 1960s and 1970s? And was welfare reform in the shape of an NIT the right response? In one respect, it was clear there was a crisis, one that showed no abatement during the ten years the incentive approach to welfare reform was debated. The figures were startling and sobering. The proportion of husband-wife families—that is, "normal" families—among blacks declined from 66 percent of all black families to 54 percent between 1971 and 1981. There was decline too of this type of family among whites, but it was much slighter—from 88 to 85 percent. The likelihood of divorce or separation among blacks was enormous: from 92 per 1,000 black married persons with spouses present in 1971 to 233 in 1981 (among whites, from 48 to 100). Separations, for blacks, increased from 172 per 1,000 married persons living with their spouse in 1971 to 225 in 1981 (white separations, from 21 to 29). Illegitimacy rose among whites from 6 to 9 percent of all births between 1971 and 1979; among blacks from 41 to 55 percent.[10]

A very sizable proportion of black female-headed families was on welfare, and welfare's role in creating this situation to some degree was clear. The situation that Moynihan had pointed to in 1965, and that had created a storm of attack, had markedly worsened in the years since.

Would an incentive-based NIT guaranteed income have changed matters? The research had shown it would not. Indeed, since the days when we had begun talking about welfare reform in the early 1960s, welfare itself had changed, to become more like the NIT—and produce the same effects of family breakup that the SIME-DIME experiment had shown. The independence effect was at work encouraging women to manage on their own, and their female children to start their own families and become female household heads on their own. The income effect—higher income encouraging the family to stay together—could not operate because welfare became more niggardly in the 1970s. And the welfare discount effect operated less and less as large numbers of female-headed households took welfare for granted and shrugged off the stigma. Indeed, in their communities, the stigma barely operated.[11]

Twenty years after the Moynihan report, this was widely considered a disastrous situation in the black community itself. But no one had any answer to it, and there seemed to be no way of modifying the welfare system to reduce its character as an incentive to family instability and illegitimacy. After all, welfare, and any conceivable replacement, had to respond to need. If "needs" were created in order to induce a larger response, how was one to take care of that? Welfare had in effect created two kinds of relationship of the family to economic support. The basic form of support was earnings, or its replacement by retirement, disability, or unemployment insurance. None of these forms of support were responsive to the size of the family. The other type was residual welfare aid, and this was calculated primarily on the basis of family size. An NIT-type program would have the same character, and, if this was a defect, the same defect. The only solution was to strengthen the family-stabilizing income effect, which meant reducing unemployment and low wages among black males. And that, especially in times of economic sluggishness, was no simple matter.

There had been one other major change affecting the family during the period of debate over welfare reform, and that change inevitably had to affect thinking about welfare. When welfare had been designed, in 1935, it was taken for granted that the task of a mother was to stay home and raise her children. Indeed, welfare permitted just that. There was little concern about any disincentive to work—mothers were not expected to. The concern about disincentive to work that played so substantial a role in the debates over FAP and PBJI were not over disincentives to *mothers* working, but over disincentives to *fathers* working. That mothers reduced their hours of work under the income-maintenance experiments was not seen as undesirable; the issue was whether fathers did.

But in the middle decades of the twentieth century a phenomenal change occurred in this pattern. In 1940, only 8.6 percent of married women with children under seventeen worked. By 1960, no less than 39 percent of women with children aged six to seventeen worked, and even 18.6 percent of women with children under five.[12] By 1980, 61.8 percent of married women with children six to seventeen worked, and 45 percent of married women with children under five. For separated and divorced

women, a majority of those with children under five worked (51.8 percent
for separated, 68.0 percent for divorced).[13] If half of the mothers with
young children worked, this suggested another course for welfare reform,
as did the difficulties of the iron triangle. It will be recalled that this made
it difficult to maintain work incentives for men because earnings remained
impervious to needs as determined by number of children, whereas the
income guarantee of NIT rose with need as determined by children. Perhaps what was needed in the next wave of reform efforts—if there was to
be one—was more attention to low-paid work in America than to welfare.
About welfare there seemed little one could do: about work one could do
a good deal to make it competitive with welfare. It was foolish, if one was
concerned about the attractions of minimal-income dependency, to have a
system in which the welfare poor received free medical care, while those
who worked at low-paying jobs generally did not have medical insurance
and lost their insurance benefits when they lost their jobs. This alone made
welfare more attractive than work. Its attractiveness was increased by the
fact that the United States, alone among major industrial countries, had
no child allowance to compensate for the cost of large families. Both measures—and others that might address the circumstances of the low-income
worker—had more chance of reducing the numbers on welfare than any
attempt to reform welfare directly.[14]

One final reflection on incentive-based welfare reform is warranted, in
view of the family issues that rose to prominence in the early 1980s, such
as the right to abortion and the right of minor females to birth-control
information and materials without the knowledge of their families, and
indeed the whole range of issues that reflected a resurgent, if far from
majority, conservatism in family matters. The incentive-based approach
eschewed moral judgments and eschewed any attempt to support directly
traditional norms of family behavior: the right arrangement of economic
incentives would reduce the costs of family dependency. Direct efforts to
maintain traditional family behavior had been abandoned, under the revolution in morals of the 1960s and 1970s (for example, the rise of the
"counterculture") and under the legal onslaught, through the federal
courts, on state-legislated efforts to maintain traditional family patterns
and practices (for example, the authority of parents over children's behavior). But the question raised was the following: if a society found a certain
kind of behavior morally as well as practically desirable, should it, could
it, induce this behavior primarily through economic incentive? The federal
government wanted to reduce the family instability and illegitimacy that

led to increased welfare costs. It hesitated to demand family stability: that flew in the face of a widespread acceptance of divorce and separation in fulfillment of individual desires. It hesitated to attack illegitimacy: one reason was that such a criticism would directly impinge on behavior particularly widespread in the black community. In the same way, the retreat from any value-based norms and traditional morality meant disaster for President Carter's effort to run a major White House conference on the family: it ran aground on the demands of feminists and gay militants that a variety of family forms be recognized as legitimate.

Social engineering promised that it would achieve what most people wanted without insisting that it was what God wanted, or what religion wanted, or what was best for people and their communities. But the best-designed morally neutral policy could not deliver this. In the next phase, a new president straightforwardly abandoned economic incentives. There would be fewer people on welfare because the rules would be hardened, the benefits reduced, the potential clients required to seek work. Regulation based on traditional morality and demands would replace incentives.

And strangely enough, in some respects that worked better than the incentives. Even in the early days of welfare reform, in the early 1960s, many congressmen asked, why shouldn't fathers pay for their children? The social workers responded that the fathers were poor, they had started new families, they couldn't be found, efforts to find them would harm their relations with their former female partners and their children, and the whole effort couldn't possibly pay. Nevertheless, Congress insisted that stronger efforts be made to find fathers and make them pay. No question of economic incentives here. Fathers had responsibilities: they should be made to fulfill them. And that was one welfare reform that seemed to be working.[15]

3 | The Social Policy of the Reagan Administration

Many hopes and expectations in social policy, among them major welfare reform, came to an end with the election of Ronald Reagan in 1980. The new administration was animated by an approach to social policy that was quite different from what we had seen for twenty years before, whether in Democratic or Republican administrations. The new approach, which I analyze in this chapter, was that desirable social behavior was not a matter to which government could be morally neutral, hoping for economic incentives to encourage it: it was to be required of those who benefited from government programs. That, at least, was the hope and the intention. Of course political realities dictated otherwise. The new approach, however, brought something quite new to the social policy debate.[1]

The Reagan administration was—rare if not unique in American politics—truly an ideological one. One does not expect ideological administrations in the United States. If candidates stray too far from political exigencies, as did Goldwater in 1964 and McGovern in 1972, overwhelming defeat is likely. But the Reagan administration came to office with a program in which barely any element was tailored to what had been considered for decades the necessities of American politics. It promised not to do anything to affect social security benefits—that was all. Beyond that, it committed itself to *reversing* the course in social policy that had been set for almost twenty years.

The Reagan administration campaigned not only against big government, big taxes, big expenditures—all easy to do in general—but also, with more or less specificity, against the innovations in social policy that had characterized the preceding two decades. The only beneficiary group of the past two decades that did not need to tremble was the aged. Everyone else was put on pretty clear notice—the poor, the blacks, the Hispanic

Americans, the handicapped, the college students, the beneficiaries of strong environmental and consumer protection. None of these groups could be in doubt as to where the new administration, if it came to office, would stand. Their votes showed they knew what to expect. And the administration tried to fulfill its promises.

Its proposed actions were not simply a reflection of annoyance with governmental intervention and the size of the tax bill, nor of the self-interest of those who paid it; they rested on fairly coherent ideological themes. The ideology attacked governmental inefficiency and the ineffectiveness of government programs, but its underlying force was given by a vision of how societies grow economically and what makes them strong. Individual action, unhampered by government, spurs an economy. Consideration for the poor in the form of special programs undermines the incentives that drive them into economic action. Government can do little but get out of people's way so they can take care of themselves, and in doing so it can contribute to the economic strength of a society.

Supply-side economics in its nascent stage was seized upon as a more sophisticated rationale for what was basically a simple view of human nature and of society: tax cuts would restore individual and corporate initiative, and a flood of increased economic activity would reduce inflation, take care of the poor, eliminate the heritage of racial discrimination, reduce the deficit, and provide the wherewithal for a huge buildup of national defense.

An ideology can be defined by what it is against. This ideology was against confidence in the capacity of a central human wisdom, expressed in government, to plan for and manage the economy and to solve the problems of the poor and the unfortunates of a complex industrial society. Admittedly, no ideology can escape the reality that governments are now—and have been, since at least the Great Depression—held responsible for the general state of the economy. But this ideology, opposing Keynesian fine-tuning and "social engineering" (leave aside that no administration could escape from both—but I speak of its thrust), said it would strike out on a new course in which human wisdom as embodied in government would recognize its limitations and the arrogance involved in any central directing center dealing with the economic and social problems of a complex society. Corollaries of this approach were greater reliance on the initiatives of private philanthropy, local government, and the states. A commitment to the federalism of the original Constitution buttressed various other reasons for reducing the role of the federal government in social policy. It was symbolic that both the education and energy departments were scheduled to be eliminated. (Neither, of course, was.) Indeed, the ideological fervor of the new administration was marked by the fact that tests of loyalty excluded not only almost all Democrats (except those whose ideology was almost identical with that of the administration) but almost all liberal Republicans.

So much was intended, so much was expected, so much was feared: One must ask, what then ensued? Did we see a revolution in social policy—the first to take us backward rather than forward? How far back, with what effects on its beneficiaries? And with what degree of permanence?

The Scale of Change

The ideology was so clear; the reality is so complex. It is easier to study what the administration *intended* than to study *effects*. To estimate significance is even more difficult.

Much of what was done was done early. The big change was signaled by the budget of 1982 and the legerdemain of the Reconciliation Act of 1981. No subsequent change was as great. Even the last revolutionary burst in social policy, that of Johnson's Great Society, saw all its major legislation passed in a surprising two years. No matter how great an electoral victory, that seems to be the maximum amount of time given to a president to introduce change. After that, and often long before, the powers of inertia and opposition have regrouped to make further change difficult. And so the budget of 1983 did not add much more to what that of 1982 had done in advancing the ideology and program of the Reagan administration; that of 1984 did less.[2]

I must begin with one large statement, which I hope to document: less has happened in the realm of social policy than the amount of anger, resistance, agonizing, newspaper reporting suggests. There *have* been reductions in some key programs, particularly as measured against the size they might have attained in a severe recession. Undoubtedly distress rose, but that was probably to be attributed more to the impact of the severe recession of 1981 and 1982 than to substantial social policy changes, when one considers the actual scale of change. Various authorities who have examined the *annus mirabilis* of substantial social policy cuts and social policy changes summed up in the Reconciliation Act of 1981 agree on the scale: it was not very large.

The Brookings Institution volume *Setting National Priorities, 1983* asserts that the reductions of 1981 imposed on the budget of 1982, the only year in which the Reagan administration was able to get Congress to accept most of what it wanted, was $27.1 billion in outlays—hardly enormous in a budget of $725 billion.[3] John Ellwood, in *Reductions in U.S. Domestic Spending*, gives a somewhat higher estimate: he reports that the Congressional Budget Office estimated cuts of $35.2 billion in outlays, and more than that in budget authority. Richard Nathan, in the same volume, thinks this is too high: "Estimates of the total reductions in the 212 federal budget accounts affected by the reconciliation act range from a high of 51 billion in budget authority and 33 billion in outlays to a low of 37 billion in budget authority and 15 billion in outlays . . . These cuts amount to between 10 percent and 7 percent of current policy budget authority for all spending in fiscal year 1982 aside from defense spending and interest on the national debt, and between 7 percent and 3 percent of all outlays." In his conclusion Nathan writes, "We believe estimates in the lower range should be used in assessing the outlay cuts of 1982," and he points out sensibly that public officials, conservative and liberal alike, have a strong tendency to overstate the size of the cuts—conservatives to demonstrate they are really carrying out their programs, liberals to build up public support against further cuts.[4]

John Palmer and Gregory Mills stand closer to the Brookings figures, estimating nondefense program reductions in outlays of $31.6 billion, 6.4 percent of their baseline expenditures for 1982 (rising to $54.8 billion or 8.2 percent of the baseline expenditure for 1986).[5]

Where Change Occurred

In one sense, all these estimates understate the social policy cuts, insofar as they take as a base nondefense expenditures. But most nondefense expenditures were almost impossible to reduce, for political reasons primarily. Social security was sacrosanct. Proposals that all (all analysts, that is, not politicians) agreed were necessary to reduce the growth of social security expenditures, which had greatly exceeded growth in wages and were tied to an unrealistic measure of cost of living, were met by total resistance from elected officials, Democrats and Republicans alike. The huge Medicare expenditures were very difficult to reduce. Here the problem was not so much massive political resistance but the simple technical difficulties of finding a mode of reimbursement that does not rise very rapidly and does not threaten the quality of health care. Pensions for government servants and the military were as sacrosanct as social security. So the reductions, perhaps a modest 4 percent of the total budget, could rise to a striking percentage overall of the parts of the budget that were not as well defended as social security and pensions and Medicare. Cuts that were small in overall total could amount to very substantial percentages of some programs, and, as it turned out, those programs focused most on the poor. Although AFDC, food stamps, and Medicaid might be considered in some budget accounts entitlements on the same order as social security or Medicare, there was no getting around the fact that the latter were based on taxes and contributions devoted specifically to them. They were "insurance," at least in the public mind, if not in the strict sense, and in the minds of their beneficiaries. The entitlements focused on the poor were not seen as insurance and indeed were not buttressed by the sense that they had been paid for and that people had a right to them. Thus a common sense of justice, combined with simple political reality—the fact that far more people get social security than welfare, far more Medicare than Medicaid, and those who get the insurance-type entitlements participate more actively in politics and carry more political weight than the poor—to focus the cuts on benefits to the poor, whether directly or through state and local government.

In another sense many of the changes in social programs could be said to be more moderate than the uproar over the cuts indicated: many of the proposed and enacted program cuts had been proposed by previous administrations (including Democratic ones) and were seen by independent, or at any rate not sharply partisan, policy analysts as valuable in themselves. And indeed, the growth of entitlement programs and grants to states and localities had already received some check under the Carter administration.[6] With the élan of the Reagan victory and with a stunned Congress, a great deal could be done that earlier administrations, with a more positive outlook on the value of governmental activity, had wished to do but could not. Although the cuts could be attributed to the new ideology of less government, and less government aid to the poor, they were made possible not only by ideology but by the fact that these restructurings and reductions were already part of the potential array of government actions, often proposed and still stacked away hopefully for future use in the Office of Management and Budget. Many of these cuts could not be attributed simply to the Reagan administration and its philosophy but to the ongoing efforts, generally frustrated, to streamline government and make it more efficient, an effort that goes on without great success under *all* administrations. Thus a sober analysis by Palmer and Sawhill asserts:

Some of the program changes proposed by the Reagan administration have long-standing antecedents and were widely considered meritorious. Several had been advocated by earlier administrations, usually for reasons that went beyond simple budgetary considerations. Examples are reductions in the guaranteed student loan subsidy and support for physician education, reduced reliance on new construction in housing assistance programs, and the scaling back of public service employment.

Other proposals, though representing a more marked departure from past presidential policies, were fully developed prior to the Reagan administration and had considerable bipartisan support. Examples . . . are the reduction of direct federal housing finance operations and greater user fees for transportation services.

Several measures reduced or eliminated programs that many policy makers and analysts had criticized as being of dubious effectiveness, although such cutbacks had not been proposed by previous administrations. Examples include the Professional Standards Review Organizations (PSRO's) and certificates of need programs in health, trade adjustment assistance, and several small regional economic programs.

Palmer and Sawhill also looked favorably on some cuts in programs that needed "trimming and restructuring": social security benefit cuts for early and new retirees, the cap on federal Medicaid grants to states (both rejected by Congress), and cuts in CETA training programs.

On the other hand, in their view programs with records of success or strong promise of success were also scheduled for severe cuts. For example: immunization grants; the Job Corps; the nutrition program for low-income pregnant women, infants, and children (WIC); compensatory education for disadvantaged children; and the new child welfare services program.

And some of the program changes they called "gambles that could jeopardize stated purposes": reductions in income-related benefit payments, the most prominent example, will be analyzed further below.[7]

To many, this will be a rather too benign evaluation of the program cuts. Yet it is true that many proposals made and implemented were those of previous administrations and nonpolitical policy analysts, and we must take this into account in estimating the direct impact of the strong ideological character of the new administration in changing the mix in social policy. And yet another factor moderated this impact: both an increase in defense spending and a decrease in the personal tax rate, which was felt to be inhibiting economic recovery, were generally in the cards. The increase in the defense budget was already under way during the Carter administration. To quote Palmer and Sawhill again: "The ratio of federal taxes to GNP had . . . crept up [in the years before 1981]. Another in the series of periodic tax cuts was clearly in order for the early 1980's, but it would have to be accompanied by greater spending restraint if it were not to result in a continued upward drift in the federal tax burden or high risk of large deficits. It was also evident that the burden of any such spending restraint would have to fall primarily on nondefense spending, since Congress (and the Carter administration) had recently initiated a program of real defense growth planned to be sustained well into the 1980's."[8]

Of course this says nothing about the scale of the tax cuts or their type and nothing about the rate of military buildup. The Carter administration projected an increase in defense expenditures, but the rate of increase in the early years of the Reagan administration was larger.[9] And the tax cuts of 1981, already taken back somewhat in 1982, by congressional action, were not exactly what the administration wanted. A riot of tax cuts ensued in Congress, many going beyond administration proposals. The point is that in some considerable measure the social program cuts were based on a continuity of policies and pressures independent of the specific ideology of the administration.

The Eclipse of "Social Engineering"

But even if the overall cuts in social programs were not devastating, even if much of what happened was owing less to specific ideology than to the pressures of economic recession, defense spending increase, and tax cuts reducing government income, the fact remains that the administration, within the limits of freedom that any administration must expect in the American political and economic order, was able to express its view on social policy.

The most striking pattern that emerged was one that I would call the rejection of "social engineering," rejection of the capacity of human foresight, using subtly graduated incentives and disincentives and sharply focused programs, to affect human behavior and to improve the human condition. This was the dominant ideology of the 1960s and 1970s; it was sharply rejected in the 1980s. When the history of American social policy is written, I think the greatest weight will have to be put on this theme: an optimistic evaluation of human and social scientific capacities marked the 1960s and 1970s, with decreasing confidence in the 1970s. This evaluation was rejected by the Reagan administration, apparently without any great (or sufficiently great) movement of resistance by any powerful sector of the American population.

A number of the significant actions of program reduction under the Reagan administration demonstrate this rejection. Perhaps the most striking is the end of the effort of what we might call social science–based welfare reform (AFDC), which had been such an important part of the domestic initiatives of the Nixon and Carter administrations. The approach to welfare reform shaped by economists, on the basis of theories and assumptions by social workers and sociologists, had dominated that period. Economists wanted to simplify the array of aids going to poor families and to modify the incentives to family breakup and to reduction of work effort.

The approach developed was one in which adjustments in the incentives inherent in welfare would bring forth socially desired behavior from men and women and families without resort to direct prohibitions and requirements. It assumed that a high implicit tax on the earnings of those on welfare (imposed by reducing welfare benefits) reduced the incentive to work and that a program aimed at income maintenance for mothers and their children, rather than complete families, reduced incentives for fathers to stay with their families and help support them. Major social experiments were launched to test the effects of this approach on different populations, using different tax rates and different support levels. But it seemed apparent that the current system was an incentive to family breakup and to reduction of work effort and that any change in the direction of more uniform support of working *and* nonworking poor families, those with father present *and* those without, would be for the best. These were the underlying bases of the reforms proposed by the Nixon and Carter administrations, and they were rarely challenged. What was challenged was that sufficiently strong incentives to increased work effort could technically be built into a reform; it was scarcely doubted that positive family effects would follow a reform.[10]

While AFDC is by no means the largest social program, and indeed compared to social security and Medicare is minor, with even food stamps and Medicaid larger, it has always been considered a key program in social policy. It is *the* major basic program for the destitute, it encompasses a substantial proportion of the black population (about a fifth), it is the major means of support for large parts of the population of large central cities, it includes a particularly high proportion of children, and it raises in the sharpest form the fears that many Americans will not be integrated into work and family life and will pass on their dependency to their children. The evidence for these fears is not overwhelming, but the fears exist, and a program that costs $8 billion of federal money, and similar amounts from state and local sources, has received more concentrated and steady attention and analysis than perhaps any other program of its size.

All this analysis was scrapped by the Reagan administration. Welfare would be held down by reverting to earlier patterns in social policy: it would become basic charity and support, with a sufficient degree of harshness in administration and limitation of benefits that people who could work would be happy to get off it, and those who did work would try to stay off, even if working did not provide more than welfare.

Welfare: From Incentives to Norms

This seemed to be the point of view of the administration. The chief example of this point of view, and the factor against which the strongest criticism was directed by almost all policy analysts—and, of course, by all those who benefited from welfare and their supporters—was the change in the treatment of earnings incorporated into the Reconciliation Act of 1981. During the 1970s, the first $30 a month of earnings, and one third of the remaining amount, had been deducted in estimating a person's need. The Reconciliation Act allowed such deductions during the first four months of employment only. It also placed a cap on work expenses that could be disregarded in calculating income and need—for child care $160 per child per month, for work expenses $75 per month. It limited the total income any family could have and qualify for welfare. And there were other changes.[11] There is no question that these changes reduce the incentive to work while on welfare, and this is why they were so fiercely attacked. It was argued that working welfare recipients would cease work to stay on welfare.

And yet one may make three observations. First, substantial incentives to work had already been incorporated into welfare, and it was these substantial benefits that made it so difficult to design an incentive-based welfare reform, a "negative income tax" (NIT) program: someone on welfare *and* working could almost always make more than someone not on welfare working at the kind of low-wage job welfare recipients generally had. If need, as assessed by number of children, was great, income from work and welfare could rise quite high and simply could not compete with income from work alone. This raised the cost of any negative income tax program to a point where it was not fiscally acceptable. Further, the reduction of stigma, which was one objective of NIT welfare reform, always presented the fear that the dependent poor would not be incorporated into the working world, but that instead the working poor would incorporate themselves into the welfare world. Work was still possible while on welfare after the Reagan reforms, but more of the return from work was taken into account in reckoning need.

A second observation: one argument of those who favored a high welfare minimum was that the poor wanted to work and that their behavior in seeking work would not be affected by increasing the minimum support level. The Reagan administration turned this argument on its head: if the poor would not reduce work effort when the minimum support level was high and was only moderately reduced by work earnings, they would *not* reduce work effort if the support level *was* more sharply affected by work earnings. If economic incentives did not outweigh a culturally based desire to work in the first case, they would not reduce it in the second. In the event, some preliminary research did not indicate a rush to leave jobs so as not to lose the benefits of welfare. Thus, Richard Nathan's study of the response of states and localities to budget cuts found "the return rate for families removed from the welfare rolls due to the Reagan changes so far has been low—about 10 percent on average. This estimate is based on information from those states and local jurisdictions that had conducted studies covering the first six months to one year of experience under the new policies." And a widely noted study by the Research Triangle, which compared the behavior of welfare recipients leaving the rolls in forty localities in twenty-seven states, before and after the Reagan changes, from the point of view of finding out whether there was a rush to return to welfare after the changes, found no such effect.[12]

A third observation: all the incentives that had been built into the system to encourage work did not seem to have much effect anyway. This may have been owing to the limited capacity of most adults on welfare (women with poor education) to work, the limited number of jobs, or the simple fact that for mothers without great prospects of earning much from work, welfare was preferable. Perhaps both the liberal and the conservative supporters of the notion that people worked because they *felt* they should were right, and we had exaggerated the significance of work incentives. If this was the case, then a system which took it for granted that people should work and that work income was a desirable substitute for welfare, rather than a reward for trying harder, might encourage the work ethos that most Americans still had, rather than lead to a rush away from work to get the less painful and more desirable benefits from welfare.

One other change in the treatment of earned income should be mentioned: low-income families have been eligible for some years for an Earned Income Tax Credit (EITC) or rebate if they work. This was introduced as one of the incentives to work. Under the Reconciliation Act the tax credit is taken into account in determining income eligibility, whether families apply for it or not. This is one way of reducing the welfare payment, but it reduces it only by taking into account what another benefit of the federal government will provide. With proper education, everyone eligible will certainly apply for the EITC. And this is all to the good. It means the low-income welfare family will learn to make out an income tax return and learn that the federal government will do something *more* for them if they work, which is symbolically rather different from saying "We will not reduce your welfare payment if you work." Getting a government tax credit for earned income assumes that work is the norm; not having your welfare grant reduced because of earned income assumes that welfare is the norm. To an economist, both may be incentives to work and should work the same way. I would argue that an EITC has a different kind of teaching effect.[13]

Various other changes introduced into welfare deserve comment as indicating which way the administration was moving and how it was implementing its ideology. For example, part of a stepparent's income could now be considered as income available for support of AFDC stepchildren. Under previous law, as interpreted by the Supreme Court, a woman with children could live with a man who was not the father of her children, and he would not be responsible for the support of those children. Certainly this encouraged women to take up with other men, and encouraged men to live serially with mothers for whose children's support they would not be held responsible. If limiting the amount of family breakup was one objective of welfare policy, here was one possible approach. But note that the approach was not so much to encourage family stability by an incentive; it was to promote stability by imposing a norm: that a man living with a mother and her children had an obligation, as husband, to support the woman with whom he lived, and as father, the children with whom he lived. (If he didn't act as husband and father because the Supreme Court said he owed them no support, a new law that he did so owe might encourage him to do so).

A social worker might argue that imposing a traditional norm was no way to get traditional behavior: to avoid becoming liable for support for mother and children, the man would just not move in, and there would be more female-headed families, not fewer. Very possibly so: but once again, as in the case of work, the incentive-based approach had been abandoned in favor of what we may well call moralism and traditionalism. The man should contribute to the support of that mother and children, whether he had an economic incentive to do so or not.

A final change deserves notice: if a woman had no previous children, she would not be eligible for welfare benefits until the sixth month of pregnancy. One of the presumed scandals of welfare—we leave aside the question of how widespread the scandal is—was that girls were treated as women, with their own welfare grant for themselves and their child, as soon as they became pregnant. Teenagers could thus achieve independence through their own, pregnancy-generated income. Whether this was a factor in the monstrous illegitimacy rates in poor areas, and in particular in poor black areas, is as debatable as any other kind of incentive analysis. Maybe there are enough other reasons for girls to become pregnant at such a high rate, for example the need to be loved, or to have someone to love. Welfare's nonjudgmental supportive role—which, it seems from this modification of law, could begin at the moment of pregnancy—was now modified. Certainly one effect of the rule is to increase, admittedly by only a few months, the period during which a parent can exercise control over a child. It is worth noting because it not only tells us what welfare had become, it also tells us what the Reagan administration was trying to do with welfare.

All this is to me rather independent of the question of how much money these changes would save. Probably very little. There were some modest savings to the federal government. There were other modest savings to states, which could now provide lesser benefits or, if so inclined, could maintain previous benefits. One must emphasize that what is at stake here is what benefits the federal government would share in funding: states could go far beyond this, and many did. But they indicate a direction, and the direction is against social engineering of the lives of welfare recipients through a subtle pattern of economic incentives, and toward the simple insistence that welfare was only going to take care of the destitute and get them, if possible, to work. But if they did work it would be because they should, not because they would be getting a reward from government for working that was not available to other low-income workers who had not gone on welfare. The traditional incentives to work and to support the family were now assumed rather than paid for. It is in this sense that I say social engineering had been abandoned.

The Withdrawal from Education and Urban Policy

There were other examples of abandonment of the social engineering approach. One of them was the incorporation of twenty-nine educational programs into one consolidated block grant. Many of these programs were pet projects of various congressmen. Others, such as the important grants under the Emergency School Aid Act (ESAA), did represent what I have called the social engineering approach: targeting money to deal with a complex social problem in specified ways, with an underlying assumption that Washington would know better how to deal with it than local officials. ESAA grants were for the purpose of dealing with the problems of desegregation. The idea was that a variety of possible programs would ease its strains and burdens. Many of these programs were designed by professors of education and sociology and communications—and many of them gave consultation and other fees to such professors and other desegregation experts. Perhaps some of this money helped. School districts would take it because they will take money for any purpose, hoping to shift at least some overhead costs to them. Experts would fight for them because they believe they had expert advice and expert training to provide for difficult problems. But the federal government proposed such action because it believed it could deal with difficult social problems with well-targeted money. The fact that no less than twenty-nine programs, with a variety of origins and purposes, were simply bundled into one program for states indicates that the Reagan administration had given up the belief held by five preceding administrations that the feds knew better than the locals. (There was, of course, another reason for the block grants: the commitment to federalism, which is independent of the question of whether the feds knew better than the states and locals or not.) Anyone interested in seeing how far the federal government had gone in trying to guide education—and how far congressmen had gone in imposing their pet ideas—may peruse in amazement the list of programs that the Reagan administration succeeded in combining into one block grant.[14]

And yet a third area of abandonment of social engineering was housing and community development. This is the area to which the word "planning" was most often applied in the past. "Planning," of course, is anathema to those who believe a central intelligence can do no better and indeed will do worse than small units of decision making, from individuals and families to states, operating on their own. Public housing projects were "planned," urban renewal projects were "planned." And the piecemeal planning of major projects occurred within federally supported efforts to plan for the city as a whole. The well-advertised disasters of the great American city—President Carter posing in the ruins of the South Bronx— suggest that here is an area where such an effort is needed. Planning had undergone various transmutations in the course of the 1960s and 1970s, but it was still a central theme of federal policy for the city. The early 1960s saw the multibranched effort to deal with juvenile delinquency in low-income areas of cities by complex urban programs, the poverty program which succeeded it, community participation, which became a major theme of the poverty program and of the Model Cities program which built on it. The provision of low-cost housing for the poor in newly built public developments was a steady accompaniment to this social urban planning, but dismay with large projects led to a shift in 1974 under Nixon, and the subsidization of (mostly) new housing in smaller developments built for the poor by private developers. The Carter administration launched a major urban program, little of which was adopted, but by the end of that administration the analysts of the administration-sponsored *Agenda for the Eighties* were gloomily suggesting that most efforts to shore up jobs and population in older cities be abandoned.

The Reagan administration did not even speak about an urban policy. Apparently it did not think it knew how to help older cities, and because of its dependence on free market mechanisms it wouldn't try even if it knew how. Its major initiative was housing vouchers, which reduce even that modicum of the planning thrust that was still left in subsidized housing. Under a housing voucher plan the poor would find their own housing, and local communities would have no greater control stemming from federal mandates in placing or designing such housing than they have in any other kind of housing development—even less, in view of the fact that housing vouchers are used for existing housing.

The thrust was clear: government was giving up the effort to do better. And it gave up too the effort to complete the pattern of governmental services in a developed welfare state that was so marked a feature of the 1960s and 1970s. If there are gaps in the American welfare state, the administration seemed to be saying, so be it. We have already done more than we should, more than any administration can dismantle, and our only responsibility is a "social safety net" which will deal with the most serious

cases of distress. Income redistribution was of no concern to this government. Quite the contrary: its tax cuts and other measures showed no inhi-
bition about allowing rich people, and more people of any income status,
to retain more of their funds for their own use. This approach is based on
a commitment to individualism and individual economic freedom, not on
any concern for the poor or equality, though when pressed, administration
spokesmen claimed their policies would help the poor through general
prosperity more than any program addressed directly to their needs. But
no one argues it will produce more equality.

The biggest hole in the American system of social policy remains. This
is the absence of a system of medical insurance for the low-income working poor without job-related benefits. With a high unemployment rate, this
gap became more evident. With the pushing down of the income limits at
which poor people can qualify for welfare, and thus for Medicaid, the gap
has been further spotlighted. Indeed, the desire to keep Medicaid benefits
must be a greater incentive to avoid work income which will push one
above the welfare-beneficiary level than the desire for money benefits
from welfare itself.

The Significance of Federalism

A second ideological theme, closely related to the first, is strongly in
evidence in the administration's social policy: returning programs to the
states and restricting federal controls. This was also a theme of the Nixon
administration, where many block grants were proposed and some were
created. The Reagan administration was more successful, though hardly
as successful as it wished.

Does this have the further effect of hurting the black and the poor? Their
advocates think so. They are used to dealing with Washington and prefer
Washington controls on social programs, which they believe they can influence, to state controls. No easy answer is possible. Now that blacks can
elect mayors in Chicago, Philadelphia, and most other big cities, now that
increased registration and voting by blacks is making their power evident
in many states, it is hard to believe that the results of such turnbacks will
not be various—depending on the political situation in each state—rather
than uniform, in favor of white and middle-class groups. Close federal
control over welfare, with sympathetic administrators monitoring each
state, has not prevented huge disparities in benefits, coverage, and regulations. If Texas can run the kind of welfare system it has under federal

tutelage, it is hardly likely that it will run a harsher one with fewer federal controls. And it is likely that a a growing Mexican-American political presence will do more to change the Texas welfare system—if it changes at all—than close federal control. I would argue similarly for education, housing, and other programs.

Even after a period of enormous growth of federal power, we are still a federal system, with more of our taxes raised by independent state and local authorities than any other developed industrial nation. There is no question that ideology drives a return to states' rights in the Republican administration and that in the past this has been associated with conservatism and racism. But we have always had states like Wisconsin and New York and Massachusetts, and now we have North Carolina and Georgia, which in their politics on race and poverty are not very different. A slogan changes its concrete meaning with social change. Federalism happens to be written into the Constitution, which still shows remarkable vitality and arouses an almost mystical commitment. A return to federalism will of course focus more attention on the states, will require the building and rebuilding of new connections between interest groups and state capitals. But in a large and heterogeneous country, with varied ethnic and racial groups, striking regional differences, different codes of morality dominant in different sections, it is a good thing that a substantial degree of power remains in the states and cities.

The major contemporary argument against the federalism and state power built into the Constitution, power that the Reagan administration wished to reinvigorate through federal withdrawal from policy areas staked out in the 1960s and 1970s, is that certain social problems must be dealt with at the national level. One major reason is that they affect different parts of the country differently. If a section is burdened with poverty and has limited resources, its effort to deal with poverty on its own, without transfers from wealthier parts of the country, will mean raising its tax rates, driving away industry, further reducing the tax base necessary to deal with problems of povery. This is an economic argument for "nationalizing" the problem of poverty, or welfare, or elementary education, and it is in principle a good argument. Just as important in the federal government's intervention in sectional issues was the aim of freeing large minorities from prejudice and discrimination institutionalized in that section. The federal power intervened massively in the South through the Civil Rights Act and Voting Rights Act to ensure equality in political power and in access to jobs and education and public facilities for blacks, and only this intervention permitted the revolution in the political and civic position of blacks that has occurred in the South in the past twenty years. Thus an emphasis on federalism appears to be an action not only against the poor, but against blacks and other minorities.

But I would argue that in making these arguments we are anchored in analyses that no longer hold. We have seen a sharp reduction in regional disparities in income in recent decades. Along with this reduction in disparity has come increasing difficulty in deciding which section is "poor" and which is "rich." Were New York and Michigan still "rich" when they showed high unemployment rates, declining populations, the migration of job-seekers to South and West? Were southern states "poor" when the numbers of jobs there increased, their population grew through migration of those seeking work, their unemployment rates were low? The difficulty of relying on traditional measures of which section deserves help and which does not is illustrated by the fierce fights over funding formulas in federal programs in Congress and in the claims of states such as New York, through its articulate Senator Daniel P. Moynihan, that it is discriminated against in getting its proper share of federal funds, though by certain measures its need is great.

I would not dismiss the logic of the economic and political arguments for a federal role in social programs from which the Reagan administration withdrew or would have liked to withdraw. But two changes undermine the force of this logic. One is that measures of sectional poverty and wealth become increasingly ambiguous as sections draw closer to each other in wealth and income. The second is that the civil rights revolution has succeeded in creating a measure of minority political power that, as the constitutional argument which gave first priority to achieving political equality hoped would happen, ensures minority participation in state and local decisions.

Yet another point may be made about regional differences and their implications for a federal role: many of these differences are created by regional choices. Welfare is high in New York and low in Texas. Undoubtedly, for this reason alone, industry seeking low-wage labor will find a more favorable climate in Texas than in New York. But this is New York's choice, and Texas's. (I do not underestimate the political realities that make for both those choices.) Is it up to the federal government to "equalize" or "make good" the effect of these choices through federal aid formulas?

These two points—the growing economic equality among the states and the increasing political power of minorities—argue forcefully for a lesser federal role in equalization of income, wealth, and political power than prevailed in the 1960s and 1970s.

And these developments are relevant to the role of the Reagan administration in enforcement of the civil rights laws. There is much cant in the argument over civil rights enforcement, on both sides. Civil rights advocates insist that support of busing of schoolchildren, for example, is a key measure of commitment to equality. By this measure the Reagan administration fails. But it is arguable whether busing today is anything more than an expensive and ineffective token, irrelevant to the improvement of the education of black children. Similarly, there is no question that the Reagan administration is unsympathetic to goals and quotas as techniques for enforcing equality in economic opportunity. Undoubtedly these techniques have had some effect in getting jobs, and better jobs, for blacks. Yet there are grave issues of law and principle over institutionalizing measures which allocate jobs and scarce places in educational institutions on the basis of race and national origin. The administration wavers between defending the principle and insisting it is doing "as much" to promote civil rights as the Carter administration. Of course it is not, if the measures are lawsuits for school busing or for goals and quotas; but it is not politically helpful to argue that there are reasons of effectiveness and reasons of principle for its withdrawal from advocacy of such measures. And it would be politically disastrous to make the key argument that the economic and educational level of the black population *now* has very little to do with the level of enforcement of laws against discriminatory practices, which have in any case declined sharply in the past twenty years, and much more to do with other factors that seem almost impervious to intelligent governmental intervention. After all, the hue and cry over the inadequacies of American and black education today come after twenty years of unparalleled federal intervention. Which brings us back to the initial point: social engineering is out of favor with this administration and with the American people largely because the promises and hopes of twenty years of activist federal government have not been fulfilled.

But beyond all arguments as to when and whether the federal government should intervene in dealing with social problems is the master vision of the Reagan administration as to how societies overcome poverty, to which I pointed earlier: they do it on their own, and people do it on their own, and help from government is likely to do more harm than good. That after twenty years of major social programs the black underclass seems as badly off as ever—and possibly not even proportionately much smaller—and that American education seems to do no better—these give a certain plausibility to the view. If this is the master vision, then an argument that demonstrates on the basis of welfare economics or equity that the federal government should act on this or that problem is likely to be met with skepticism. Yes, the poor states deserve more, and the poor deserve more, but if government tries to provide that more it will do them no good.

And it is this skepticism with government, as well as the desire to save money, that leads to the encouragement of private philanthropy and charity to deal with the problems of the poor, as well as with problems in other sectors of society—education, health, culture—in which the federal contribution is being cut back. With what effect? It is no easy matter to encourage private philanthropy, which already exists on a greater scale in the United States than elsewhere. And reducing the rate of taxation is, as was widely pointed out, an "incentive" to provide less for charity, since the value of the tax exemption declines. But in this area, as in so many, economic arguments have been undermined. People made contributions to hospitals, universities, social agencies long before there were income taxes and thus an "incentive" to contribute. The economic analysis goes only part of the way. Need also induces contributions, and the cutback of federal funds has increased the needs of many institutions. The effect of Reagan administration policies on private giving—reducing the incentive on the one hand, increasing the exhortation to give on the other—will be one of the most interesting parts of a full evaluation of the Reagan administration.[15] But the main effect has been an increase in private giving.

The Impact on the Poor

Most criticism of the Reagan social policy changes has emphasized one theme, and one alone. Independent policy analysts and partisans alike have again and again pointed out that the budget cuts have fallen on the poor. The government has tried to counter. I think there is no way of escaping this overall charge. It is hardly necessary to quote all the summary judgments which tell us this.

Nathan: "The cuts that we made in Federal domestic spending in fiscal year 1982 affected poor people—especially the working poor—more than they affected the treasuries of state and local governments." Palmer and Sawhill: "The net effect of these tax and social program cuts through 1984 will be to provide no significant overall change in the purchasing power of those with incomes below $15,000, modest increases for the broad middle class, and substantial gains for higher-income families. Within the bottom group those receiving benefit payments of one sort or another are likely to find themselves worse off."[16]

One way of interpreting this pattern of social policy is to look at who supported the Reagan administration, who runs it. While we can exaggerate, and many do, the differences in education and occupation of Republicans and Democrats, and even of Right Republicans and Left Democrats, undoubtedly these differences are an element. The advocates of the poor play no role in this administration. On this fact, one can conclude that blindness to their problems, at best, and positive malice, at worst, animates the administration's policies.

I have suggested something else: ideology animates the policies, but it is an ideology that operates under constraint. Part of the ideology dictates steps that in practical effect are no different from legislating selfishness. If the economic problem of America (including America's poor) is seen as insufficient savings for investment, if that is combined with a conviction that government cannot plan investment as well as a multitude of actors in the private sector can, then one has an argument for cuts that help high-income people more than low-income people. I would fault the administration less on its ideology—in view of the difficulties modern welfare states were suffering, this was not unreasonable—than on its lack of political courage in trying to implement the measures that were necessary to accompany that ideology. If taxes were to be cut and defense was to be raised—issues on which in general, if not in scale, there was bipartisan consensus during the early Reagan years—then there would be huge deficits unless nondefense expenditure was brought under control. And here, although the administration tried, it achieved very little in bringing the most rapidly growing domestic programs under control. These are, of course, social security, Medicare, and government and military pensions.

Perhaps it is simply the better or necessary part of political wisdom to give up on these huge big-ticket items and to concentrate on those programs that are less well defended and more easily cut. In any case, that is what the administration did. Reviewing the income security area, James R. Storey pointed out, "The expected outlay savings in 1984 arising from 1981 actions . . . are about 4 percent of projected income security spending under previous policies . . . Nearly 60 percent occurred in low-income assistance programs, though these account for only 18 percent of income security outlays." Program savings as percentage of baseline amount are

1.6 percent for OASDI [social security], 0.8 percent for federal employee retirement and disability, as against 16.3 percent for AFDC, 18.6 percent for food stamps, 34.5 percent for low-income energy assistance.[17] One can make a case for this pattern, of course. But the main explanation was inevitably political. Against political realities, what could be done? Perhaps nothing, if one expected to govern and win elections. But I would argue that a greater degree of effort and education was needed to explain where the problems lie. The issue of selfishness was often raised, and many middle-income people thought they could smugly raise it because they were not that rich. Yet the selfishness was also at work in vast stretches of the middle class, who resisted well-argued reductions in the rate of increase in social security and government and government and military pensions and in aid to students in higher education from middle-income families. There is no question their resistance was rather more effective than that of the advocates of the poor.[18]

There were two good arguments for cuts in such programs: (1) equity—equal sharing of pain—and (2) effectiveness—cutting big programs is far more effective in bringing the budget under control than cutting small ones. An estimated 1.6 percent reduction in OASDI produced 25.2 percent of the savings in Storey's analysis. And if, as all agree, the enormous deficits are a problem, a willingness to reduce one's take in government benefits must be spread through the wide middle- and upper-middle-income sections of the population who now receive those benefits.

Conclusion

The Reagan administration represented the coming to power of a government with a coherent ideology guiding its actions in social policy. It believed people could manage by themselves and had no need of sophisticated federal government interventions to deal with their problems of poverty, inadequate training for jobs, urban decline, poor education, and the like. Insofar as governmental intervention was necessary or desirable, it should take place on the state and local level. And many of the needs of the poor and the needs and desires of society concerning health, education, welfare, and culture should be met at that level too, and through private philanthropy.

The administration made no head-on assault on the idea, established in the United States as far back as the 1930s, that government had the responsibility to maintain a safety net of basic social programs to provide for the income needs of the destitute, and it announced its complete commitment to social security to provide for the aged and disabled, unemployment insurance for the unemployed, health insurance for the aged and destitute. The major programs of the 1930s and 1960s would, it asserted, remain intact. The Reagan administration thus represented the complete acceptance of the New Deal welfare state, as supplemented in the Johnson administration. Reagan was neither the Goldwater of 1964 nor the Reagan of earlier campaigns, and his victory was that of a conservatism that accepted the major lineaments of the welfare state. That was not where the main dispute with his opponents lay.

Rather, the originality of the administration lay in its conviction that the way to wealth and national income growth and the way out of poverty for the poor could not be designed by government and implemented by programs keyed to specific problems. Thus almost all such programs came under attack, through efforts to eliminate them, to reduce them, or to package them in general block grants. If people could manage by themselves, what need for the hundreds of federal programs directed at specific targets—food supplements for poor mothers-to-be, work training for dropouts, decay of inner-city housing stocks? It may be argued that the Reagan administration did believe in central intelligence guiding society, for how else can one explain its conviction that tax cuts would lead to saving, encourage investment, and the like? But this, from the Reagan administration's point of view, is what people do naturally—they see their opportunities and seize them. The only role of government is to stay out of their way, and that was the point of the tax cuts. And once again, it should be clear I speak of *intentions:* in the event, the tax reduction was riddled with exemptions and incentives designed to do this or that, or to reward the earning of income in one way rather than another. But that is what happens when a general philosophy meets the specific and concrete interests represented in government, whether in the executive or in the legislative branch.

The tax cut was to be across the board, with no sophisticated effort to point it to the well-off and the rich: that would happen naturally when a progressive tax system was cut across the board. Again, in the event, many special interests came into play, it ended up being less fair than it would have been in its pure form, and it ended up larger than anticipated. Combined with a recession and a substantial increase in the rate of growth of the military buildup, the result was huge deficits, never before seen in peacetime, sustained even after the recession was overcome, and with potential effects on the economy that were frightening.

Ideological commitments were reinforced by necessity as the deficits ballooned, and further pressure was put on that part of the nondefense budget that had the least political support. Inevitably, these were programs focused on the poor, even though the major causes of growth in the budget were to be found in the growth of benefits which went mostly to the middle classes. But in time pressure to reduce the growth of these benefits must come.

There is no escape in a modern developed nation from the major social programs that were developed under Franklin D. Roosevelt and expanded in the years since—social security, unemployment insurance, some form of health insurance, which will undoubtedly be expanded to cover populations not yet served. Nor did the Reagan administration wish to move in on these programs. But the programs based on discrete and sophisticated interventions, and on assumptions as to the effectiveness of certain kinds of incentives, detailed planning, sharply targeted expenditures on specific problems, have been cut. Undoubtedly a general disillusionment with such programs, not justified in all cases, assists in the dismantling of a good part of the newer social policy thrusts of the 1960s and 1970s.

Nor does one see any support for such programs in the campaign rhetoric of opponents of the Reagan administration. The day of the "laundry list"—the array of new programs for all possible problems and constituencies—seems gone, whether in the campaigns of 1984 or in that for 1988. And its demise must be attributed in good part to the failure of laundry lists to do what they promised to do. The programs grew in number and scale, the problems remained. A time of respite was due, and it has come with the Reagan administration. Perhaps our confidence in our ability to understand our social problems and attack them with specially designed scalpels will return. But as of this writing, nothing suggests that that confidence will come soon.

Education, Training, and Poverty: What Worked? | 4

In 1974, at a conference sponsored by the Institute for Research on Poverty, Henry Levin analyzed what he called "A Decade of Policy Developments in Improving Education and Training for Low-Income Populations." The examination was thorough and extensive: a great many programs were described, and knowledge of their effectiveness discussed: Head Start, Title I of the Elementary and Secondary Education Act of 1965, Upward Bound, School Lunch Program, School Breakfast Program, Vocational Education, Teachers Corps, Neighborhood Youth Corps, Job Corps, Educational Opportunity Grants, Guaranteed Student Loans, Work Study, Talent Search, Adult Education Act of 1966, Migrant Workers, Work Experience, Job Opportunities in the Business Sector, and Manpower Development Training Act. Even so, Levin was hardly exhaustive: "We have selected only the principal federal activities, and the reader should be aware there are others that we have not reviewed because they were short-lived, or modest in scope, or primarily designed to serve functions other than antipoverty ones." Bilingual programs, also directed in large measure against poverty, though mentioned, received no great attention, and state and local efforts, not insubstantial, were also outside the scope of the examination.

In 1974 the judgment, not Levin's alone, as to the effectiveness of such programs in combating poverty was gloomy: "There are few who would deny the basic failure of existing approaches toward education and training for alleviating poverty." And he went on to quote the negative assessment of two such different analysts as David Gordon and Arthur Jensen. The general position was that schooling did not improve achievement, achievement did not improve economic circumstances.

What I am describing, of course, is the common wisdom of the mid-

1970s. The report *Equality of Educational Opportunity,* whose chief author was James Coleman, had appeared in 1966, at the beginning of a period of great ferment in programs addressed to poverty, but its impact on the academic community was expanded by the reanalyses of its data in Frederick Mosteller and Daniel P. Moynihan's *On Equality of Educational Opportunity* in 1972. Christopher Jencks's *Inequality* also appeared in that year. While it would be unfair to summarize the message of these major works as saying "nothing worked," that is certainly how the message came across. And indeed, sophisticated analysis of the effects of intelligence or educational skills or schooling, isolated from other factors, on inequality or earnings, came closer to sending that message than any other. The evaluations of specific programs that were available during the first ten years after the launching of the poverty program confirmed the verdict: nothing worked, and, in particular, nothing that one did in education worked. If one wanted to redistribute income, one should redistribute it directly. And if one wanted to reduce poverty, that strategy was far more efficient than any other.

The negative assessment went further than an evaluation of the ineffectiveness of programs. Even if the programs worked in terms of their immediate objectives (improving educational skills, lengthening schooling, providing job skills), there were insufficient jobs, or insufficient good jobs: "Increasing educational attainments of the existing poor would [not] have reduced substantially the poverty class in a society where there are simply an inadequate number of jobs at wages above the poverty level to absorb all job seekers . . . Large changes in the number of years of schooling attained would likely secure nonpoverty status only at the expense of persons with less schooling who have been filling those positions."[1]

Two highly qualified discussants did not dispute Levin's findings. Burton Weisbrod pondered the ten-year-old assertions in the 1964 *Economic Report of the President,* one of the opening guns in the war on poverty, that "universal education has been the greatest single force contributing both to social mobility and to general economic growth," and that "if children of poor families can be given skills and motivation, they will not become poor adults." Can we still believe that? he asked. He did not dispute the findings on the weak relationship between "learning, as measured, and earnings." But he was definitely uncomfortable, and he suggested a variety of hypotheses that might mitigate this disastrous lack of connection. Perhaps education does teach people more, but they don't use it to increase earnings; perhaps certain types of education don't work with the poor, but other types would work; perhaps we are not measuring the correct variables ("years of schooling" may not equal "amount of education"). He commented further that it is odd that "when we study, econometrically and statistically, the effects of some policy instrument on some dependent variable, the result is that it does not make any difference, . . . our measurements or our theory or the truth somehow all conspired to lead us to the conclusion that nothing makes a difference." Weisbrod resisted that conclusion: "Our measures may be bad, our theories may be bad, our specification of relationships may be bad."

And finally he pointed out that even if education didn't make a difference, the American people would prefer to educate people out of poverty or train them out of poverty to simply redistributing income to the poor.

The second discussant, Wilbur J. Cohen, made the point more resoundingly: "The evidence shown by these papers is that there is no concrete way to prove that money spent on these educational programs leads to specific IQ, cognitive, or affective improvement. Yet, the amazing thing is that the Americans today are still as convinced as ever by every public opinion poll I have studied that one of the primary ways to overcome poverty is to invest more money in education. So, there is obviously a great gap between research knowledge and conventional wisdom." Could the gap be closed (naturally, by imposing research knowledge on conventional wisdom)? Cohen considered the possibilities for the negative income tax, direct redistribution of income to the poor, and judged that its prospects were not good.[2]

Since that time the American people have not changed their mind—certainly not on direct income redistribution, and certainly not on the efficacy of education for some things, if we take their continued and extraordinary interest in educational reform seriously. But something else has happened: the direction in which the evaluations pointed has begun to turn. Evaluations are technically better, bigger, and more numerous. They are less ambitious in assuming any direct link between education and reduction of poverty. There was always the realization on the part of economists and sociologists that as they analyzed these relationships, they were ignoring the "black box" of education and training, the box into which inputs were fed and from which outputs were measured. It seemed to be the case in the early 1970s that great increases in input had little effect on output. In some degree, what has happened has been a closer examination of the black box, a more sober assessment of what is possible, such that disappointment does not come as easily as it did in 1974; but most important, there is some evidence as to real effects and real changes—wispy, limited, on the horizon, and only doubtfully owing to direct policy efforts, but still quite clear.

Will this matter for the distribution of income? Or the percentage of those in poverty? The modest signs of change in the educational achievement of the poor that I will discuss, which some analysts attribute to the effectiveness of expenditures on education for the poor, may or may not have effects on inequality and on the proportion in poverty. It is possible that improvement in the educational achievement of the poor results in no improvement in their economic position if all others improve at the same rate, even if one accepts the model that achievement increases economic effectiveness. Indeed, it is even possible that a narrowing of the difference in achievement between poor and nonpoor—and I will give some evidence of that effect—has no influence on numbers in poverty or inequality; one can envisage a system of queuing for good positions such that each group maintains its own position, with educational achievement that was once considered a qualification for a certain kind of job now discounted and used only to admit one to a lesser-paying job.[3] Today it is even possible to argue—and not without some good reasoning and strong evidence—that directly redistributing income to the poor, the alternative that Jencks and Levin once favored, does not improve their relative economic position.[4]

But I will not consider directly the effects of an improvement in the educational achievement of the poor on income distribution or on the reduction of poverty. I will simply take the common wisdom that was so battered during the 1970s for granted: improvements in educational achievement and in the amount of schooling will help poor children. That is what their parents believe, what the neighbors believe, what the children believe, what Congress believes, and what beleaguered educationists believe. I am convinced there is some merit to that position when I read of tests in which large numbers of young people cannot distinguish between doors marked "cafeteria," "library," "nurse," and "principal" when asked "Which door would you go in for lunch?" It was on the basis of such questions, asked by the National Assessment of Educational Progress in 1978, that 13 percent of seventeen-year-olds—and 56 percent of black, 44 percent of Hispanics in that age group—were judged functionally illiterate.[5] I have the impression, along with all the nonauthorities I have mentioned above, that it would do some good if the young people could answer the question, and I feel that is reason enough to explore the nearer end of the chain that in our models leads from education to earnings.

The position, I hope, will not be taken as indicating disrespect for the subtle and elegant work that has gone into analyzing these relationships. The elements that go into educational achievement, measured in scores on specific tests or in amount of schooling, can be decomposed into many prior, interacting effects. But numerous and complex as the effects are, as Jencks's work has shown, the fact is that even this scholar, most notorious among educationists for having argued that "nothing works," points out in a work subsequent to *Inequality* that "when an individual first enters the labor market, the highest grade of school or college he has completed is the best single predictor of his occupational status." There are similar effects on earnings: "Years of education correlated .38 to .49 with ln [log normal] earnings in our four large national surveys." "The best readily observable predictor of a young man's eventual status or earnings is the amount of schooling he has had. This could be because schooling is an arbitrary rationing device for allocating scarce jobs; or because schooling imparts skills, knowledge, or attitudes that employers value; or because schooling alters men's aspirations." That has seemed good enough for most people and most policy makers. It is true there is a "substantial reduction in the apparent effect of schooling when we control causally prior traits," which "suggests only part of the association between schooling and success can be due to what students actually learn from year to year in school."[6] But perhaps one reason for the common belief is that it has appeared to be easier to change schooling than the causally prior factors.

Which raises the second difficulty: research also showed that interventions didn't seem to produce more educational achievement or persistence. Jencks, in *Who Gets Ahead?*, modifies his argument in *Inequality* that "if personal characteristics were equalized, this would have very marginal effects on the distribution of income. This conclusion, while still plausible, may have been premature. But *Inequality* also argued that past efforts at equalizing characteristics known to affect income had been relatively ineffective. This assertion, sad to say, remains as true as ever."[7] It is this second difficulty, on which we now have new evidence, which gives us reason to believe that some differences in characteristics can be, if not removed, reduced.

The perspective of today is thus somewhat different from that of the 1970s. The difference is created not only by new studies and new results. It is well known that neither opinion nor policy is moved much by studies and results. There is also a shift in opinion; the once simple and thus desirable approach to overcoming poverty by redistribution and transfer payments has run into overwhelming opposition (it was always consider-able, as the quote above from Wilbur Cohen shows), and even into some considerable argument as to its effectiveness in reaching simple redistri-bution objectives, owing to its effects on work effort and family composi-ton. And so back to the common man's view: education is the best single available route to overcoming poverty.

The common man, of course, is not simply rooted in ignorance in hold-ing to this position. At a macroeconomic level it has long been maintained that education is a means to overcoming the poverty of nations. And there is even an argument that education is a means to leveling earnings differ-ences. The example of Japan, which has perhaps been the single most important motivator of the current wave of education reform in the United States, is often considered preeminent evidence for both effects.

The econometric mind remains skeptical but grudgingly admits some evi-dence. Stephen P. Mullin and Anita A. Summers have conducted a major review of evaluations of the effectiveness of spending on compensatory education. Most of these evaluations are of Title I programs. Title I of the Elementary and Secondary Education Act of 1965, the largest educational effort launched under the poverty program, was the basic effort to provide federal assistance for the education of poor children. The mechanism that was devised and that has been endlessly fiddled with consisted of first selecting educational districts that had high proportions of children in pov-erty and then, within districts, selecting target schools on the basis of children who did poorly educationally. Just what was to be done for these children was left up to local school districts and schools. Targeted for sharp reductions by the early Reagan administration, the program has sur-vived quite well: its support in Congress and in the local school districts is strong. Retitled Chapter I of the Educational Consolidation and Im-provement Act of 1981, it spent $3,376,000,000 in 1984, and that was scheduled to rise to more than $4 billion by 1989. Fourteen thousand school districts get some funds, almost five million children get services providing supplements to their education, at a cost of about $700 per child.

With what effects? This is the objective of the Mullin-Summers roundup. In a field in which so many evaluations are conducted, to select a group for meta-evaluation is no simple task. It seems to have been done carefully, and forty-two studies, some of which were themselves aggregations of a substantial group of primary evaluations, were selected. The major conclusions:

> The programs have a positive, though small, effect on the achievement of disadvantaged students.
>
> The results of most studies are overstated because of the upward biases inherent in several statistical procedures.
>
> The gains appear to be greater in earlier years, and the evidence is fairly strong that early gains are not sustained.
>
> No significant association exists between dollars spent and achievement gains.
>
> No approach or program characteristic was consistently found to be effective.[8]

This cautious and hard-headed summary suggests something can be done. In its modesty it seems to me to understate what is still overall an achievement. It also neglects to note that the more recent studies—and, one suspects, the better ones, since early evaluation efforts under Title I were subjected to fierce criticism—seem to show results, while the early ones don't. Thus, the average year of publication of fifteen studies that showed no result—one must realize the programs evaluated were being conducted a few years before this generally—was 1973; the average year of publication of the thirty-two studies that showed some result was 1975. Some of these studies are substantially bigger and better than others, and two seem as decisive as studies on the effects of educational intervention can be. In both cases, when one goes beyond the meta-evaluation to the studies themselves, one finds perhaps more than Mullin and Stephens are willing to grant.

Thus, consider the ingenious study titled *Lasting Effects after Preschool.*[9] (The principal investigators challenged Mullin and Summers's account as depreciating the quality and importance of the study.)[10] The Lasting Effects Studies group went back to eleven preschool intervention programs of various types from the early 1960s and followed up the subjects in these programs in 1976 and 1977. The studies had all had control groups of various types, and follow-up data had been collected on both experimentals and controls. Ten years after these studies had been completed, the investigators discovered some substantial differences between the experimentals and controls. There were no lasting differences of significance in IQ or achievement test scores, but there were substantial differences in the degree to which the children who had received some special programs were "retained in grade"—held back—or were assigned to special education classes. One of these studies, that conducted in Ypsilanti, has been the subject of considerable publicity, but the others show the same effects. What is interesting is the consistency of results. The median rate of failure (that is, failing a grade or being assigned to special education) was 45 percent for the controls, 24 percent for the experimental subjects. One must be impressed at the enterprise of the investigators: they were able to find 1,599 of the 2,700 children who originally participated in the eleven programs. The only study for which follow-up failed to the point where analysis of lasting effects was pointless was that conducted in New York City. The subjects were low-income and disadvantaged: 92 percent were black, 40 percent had no father at home. The methods used in the preschool programs varied substantially: traditional nursery preschool, emphasis on language development, cognitive development and self-concept, work at home with mothers of children along with the children's attendance at a center, different kinds of Head Start curricula, indeed the whole gamut of ideas of the 1960s. The length of time in which children were involved ranged from one to five years. As against the view that nothing works, the lasting effects group claimed everything worked, to some extent, if one used the measure of not failing a grade and not being required to attend special classes.

Clearly this is not the kind of study which will satisfy purists. Each of the original enterprises was based on faith that something would help these children do better educationally. Each involved, one suspects, the kinds of teachers and child workers drawn to academic and experimental enterprises, whose quality is probably higher than the quality of those who would be available if an effort were made to make preschool opportunities universal. But a number of features of this study warrant attention. One is that it seems to coincide with the judgment of increasing numbers of Americans as to what is good for their children, as we see from the rising numbers of children from middle-class families now attending preschool. It coincides with the positive evaluation steadily given to Head Start, both by those who participate in it and by policy makers, who refused to accept the "no effects" results of the early Westinghouse study.[11] Admittedly common sense is no guide to effective policy, nor is the judgment of elected policy makers (except that there is no other way to get policy). But more technical evaluations also have their problems, and one would hesitate to challenge the judgment of parents that preschool is good for their children, when so many who can choose it do so, and when so many who cannot would like to. Enrollment of three- and four-year-olds in pre-primary education increased between 1968 and 1980 from 15.7 percent to 36.7 percent; among five-year-olds we are reaching close to the entire group, with an increase from 66 percent in 1968 to 84.7 percent in 1980.[12]

Finally, the kinds of programs examined in this study, despite their ex-perimental character and the involvement of academic social scientists in designing and evaluating them, seem very similar, in their variety and type, to the kinds of preschool programs that Head Start makes possible. Head Start remains the most popular of the efforts launched under the poverty program; more than any other, it sustains a substantial degree of parent and local community involvement. Among social programs that the Reagan administration hoped to cut, it was the least threatened and it survived the best. In 1984, 430,000 children were included in it, and it spent almost $1 billion. The cost is not minor (more than $2,200 a child), yet does not reach anywhere near the awesome costs of intensive work-training programs for teenagers and young adults.

I begin with this study, modest as the conclusions are that can be drawn from it, for a number of reasons. First, it permits us to begin at the begin-ning—or at least as much of a beginning as we may expect from public efforts in education and training—with preschool education. It suggests that something can be done, and even suggests, at a time when little more in the way of effort is being considered, what more may be done: the expansion of preschool education in recent decades still leaves large num-bers of children from poor families unaffected. The study also demon-strates sharply the difference in evaluations by econometricians, who are not overly impressed, and those by the softer social scientists and educa-tionists, who are. But there is harder evidence as to early school effects, evidence which is by now generally accepted. The largest evaluation ever conducted of Title I can be found, in some form, in the Mullin-Summers summary, but nestled rather inconspicuously among the other studies. It is known as the Sustaining Effects Study of Compensatory and Elemen-tary Education and was funded by the Department of Education under a mandate from Congress in 1975. It involved many subparts and many reports, and it took some time for any substantial presentations of its find-ings to reach the educational community. It had many objectives, the most important being to conduct a longitudinal study over a period of three years of children receiving Title I services and those who did not. As is the inevitable nature of a massive study in real school districts and real schools, the "controls" do not satisfy the strict methodological requirements for controls, but are in this case poor children ("needy") who do not receive Title I services. The process involved in the distribution of Title I funds to final recipients of services ensures there will be many "controls," for there are poor children in districts and schools that do not qualify for funds on the basis of district poverty, as well as nonpoor students in poor districts and schools that do qualify for funds. No less than 120,000 students were tested, in a representative sample of more than 300 schools, drawn from a survey of principals of more than 5,000 schools.

Such a massive undertaking also made it possible to determine how effective the complex formulas, regulations, and intradistrict and intra-school decisions are in targeting the Title I funds on poor and low-achieving children. The results display the difficulty of distributing federal funds to 14,000 districts under the guidelines set by a Congress determined that each congressman's district will not be short-changed. It appears that 60 percent of economically poor children, using the Orshansky Index, receive Title I services, 40 percent do not. In 1976–77, of 2,923,000 children receiving Title I services, a minority—1,230,000—were poor. Among low-achieving students (one or more years behind grade level), a minority—46 percent—received Title I services, while 19 percent of children who were not low-achieving received them. The children receiving such services, compared to all poor or low-achieving, were disproportionately Hispanic and black, in large cities and in rural areas.

In such a massive study even small effects are convincing. They exist: "Statistical analysis showed significant gains for Title I students, relative to needy students [who qualified for but did not receive Title I services], for the Mathematics section of the Comprehensive Tests of Basic Skills. This was true for grades 1 to 6. For the reading section . . . , significant reading gains were found for grades 1 to 3, but not for grades 4, 5, and 6."

The chief investigator points out that the largest relative gains are in first grade. But the rate of gain for Title I students in all three grades is at least equal to that for regular students, while the gains for those without Title I services are not as great. The other major finding of interest is that students who received these services for one year did better than those who received them for all three years of the study. The explanation is that those in the first group were not so far behind, extra teaching improved them, and they "graduated" from Title I eligibility. Those who were far behind to begin with and who qualified for Title I each year showed no improvement: "Title I was effective for students who were only moderately disadvantaged, but it did not improve the educational achievement of the most disadvantaged part of the school population."

Gains were not lost over the summer, but by the time the students reached junior high there was no evidence of sustained or delayed effects, and Title I students took more remedial courses in junior high than others. Fifty-five high-poverty schools were studied in depth to find "successful practices": the results are too complex for easy reproduction or dissemination. "We had hoped to find instructional programs that were particularly effective with disadvantaged students, but we did not find them."

The study considers the problem with which we began: do schools have effects on the achievement of children independently of background? Path diagrams relate background, school characteristics, and initial achievement to a school composite measure and final achievement. Since students were followed for three years, and cohorts were initially selected from grades one to four, it was possible to study the effects of these interactions for children of different ages. The results are sobering. The path coefficients between school learning experiences and final achievement decline from the first cohort to the fourth: "These figures are very important. They imply that in the beginning grades, School Learning Experiences are almost as effective as Initial Achievement and perhaps as important as Background. But as grade progresses, the influence of School Learning Experiences seems to exert little influence on Final Achievement."[13]

And these results are confirmed more generally by analyses of the National Assessment of Educational Progress. Progress has been noted in the early grades; less progress or decline has been evident for junior high school and high school. The NAEP has tested large samples at ages nine, thirteen, and seventeen. Black nine-year-olds and thirteen-year-olds showed a better rate of improvement than whites on reading performance between 1971 and 1980. Black seventeen-year-olds showed slight improvement, whites declined. On mathematics, between 1973 and 1978 there was a decline for white nine-year-olds and an improvement for blacks; a more modest improvement was recorded for black thirteen-year-olds, and a white decline for the same age grade. For seventeen-year-olds, declines were recorded for both groups, somewhat less for blacks than for whites.[14]

A full analysis of all areas in which tests have been given twice (writing, science, and social studies, in addition to reading and mathematics), for nine- and thirteen-year-olds, shows a remarkably steady rate of reduction of the black-white disparity for all fields and for all students, regardless of year of birth back to 1956. But this same analysis does not include the seventeen-year-olds' results because, as it points out, by this year the number of dropouts means that the population is much less completely covered. However, as we have seen, where we have data for seventeen-year-olds it is not good.[15] And trying to reach the dropouts for testing will hardly improve matters. Indeed, they might make the seventeen-year-old showing even worse, for since the 1970s there seems to have been a decline in the percentage of youths, particularly males, finishing high school.

I have described improvements for low-income students in the lower grades, related to Title I compensatory education expenditures, and improvements for black students in the lower grades, not related to specific expenditures for compensatory education. Yet we know that the Title I expenditures manage to reach, somewhat erratically, it is true, substantial numbers of low-income and black students. The pattern in both the Sustaining Effects Study and the NAEP assessments is consistent: more improvement at earlier grades, extending into later elementary grades for mathematics but not for reading.

Some of the evidence above relates to groups defined by income, some to groups defined by minority, specifically black, status. There is of course some overlap among "low-income," "black," "minority," but they are hardly synonyms.

Educational failure in this country, however, insofar as it is a problem of public consciousness, of politics, of social policy, of the attainment of social harmony, is predominantly, I would argue, a problem of failure with and among blacks. The term "minority" is overbroad: some of the most rapidly growing minority groups, such as Asians, show no general problem of educational (or for that matter, economic), backwardness, despite substantial differences from group to group and within groups. Note, for example, to take one key figure, dropout rates for 1980 high school sophomores by the spring of 1982: the white non-Hispanic rate is 12.2 percent, the black non-Hispanic rate is 17.0 percent, the Hispanic rate 18 percent, the Asian rate 3.0.[16] Low achievement of Hispanics, as the figures cited show, and of the low-income group, as other figures in the same source indicate (the dropout rate for low-income students is 17.4 percent, the same as that for blacks), should be properly a matter of great concern. But as a *political* issue blacks dominate the discussion of poverty because they are by far the largest minority, because they are the most politically active and effective of the deprived minorities, and because no additional com-plications relating to language problems, recency of immigration, or legal status in this country can be brought forward to explain or excuse the situation. In this country low-income or working-class status as such has not been a force in the push to improve education as a means of overcom-ing poverty: it is well known, for example, that low-income whites in urban high schools have been on the whole content with their achievement and their prospects and have not been very active in pushing for greater expenditures on education. If such expenditures have been conditioned on integration with blacks, indeed, they have often been opposed vigorously. It is not low-income or working-class groups as such that are the main force pushing for educational improvement.

Despite the increase in numbers of Hispanics and in the degree to which they are becoming politically mobilized, the problem of poor education as a barrier to economic advancement influences them less than blacks, and thus affects public policy less than the parallel problem among blacks. I have indicated above some reasons for this: that substantial numbers of Hispanics are recent immigrants and have language problems, and it is taken for granted by Americans in general—and perhaps by the group in question, if not by its leaders—that these factors understandably will take time to overcome and that they offer plausible explanations for educational backwardness. A second factor reducing the impact of this problem is that among the various Hispanic groups, some do not have special problems in education that mark them out as a group requiring long-term and serious concern. This is certainly true of the Cubans, may well be true of recent immigrants from Central America and some countries of South America, who may indeed come as immigrants primarily to take advantage of edu-cational opportunities in the United States or to enable their children to take advantage of such opportunities. And finally, the special problem we have flagged for blacks, that of the increasing ineffectiveness of educa-tional programs with advancing grade in school, may not be a problem of the same severity for Hispanics. Thus in comparisons of reading perform-ance, nine-year-old Hispanics made the same progress as blacks (and thus more than whites) between 1975 and 1980; thirteen-year-old Hispanics made somewhat less progress than blacks but more than whites; and for the key seventeen-year-old group, the Hispanics showed progress where the blacks showed none and the whites retrogressed. On mathematics test scores of high school seniors, related to number of years of mathematics taken, Hispanics regularly perform slightly better than blacks, far worse than whites (who perform of course worse than Asians). Where we have data for American Indians, we also find better performance than for blacks, if lower than for whites.[17] This pattern was evident as far back as *Equality of Educational Opportunity* and has not changed.

We have problems in education in this country across the board, as the movement for educational reform which has been under way for some years indicates. We must of course be concerned with the fairly regular association of low levels of education and low income. The problem of black achievement in education is more than this, however. It is, first, analytically more than a matter of low income: controlling for poverty reduces the relationship between minority status and low achievement, but it still remains substantial.[18] We must be concerned as a matter of social policy and politics, because it is here that the demand for improvement is concentrated, here that the moral and constitutional commitment is greatest, and here that the results of failure are most serious.

Can we understand the successes at the lower grades, and does that suggest any hope for the upper grades or any course for policy? When one looks at what was concretely involved in compensatory education under Title I in the mid-1970s, it would appear the effort was a concentrated one. At that time, class sizes for Title I education were small, averaging nine students in reading and twelve in mathematics, compared with twenty-seven in homeroom classes. Students spent an average of five and a half hours a week in special instruction. This amounted to 29 percent of total instruction time for students in reading and mathematics. Forty-six percent of the students in Title I were minority, despite, as I have noted, the difficulty under the formula, regulations, and local practices of ensuring that poor students and educationally disadvantaged students were the only ones to receive services. The services were almost entirely devoted to elementary school students—more than 99 percent—even though there was no such limitation in the legislation.[19] Under these circumstances it would have been discouraging indeed if the result were no effect, or, as a more complex cost-benefit analysis might well conclude, insufficient effect.

A consensus has emerged on the educational changes of the 1970s and early 1980s which presents some modest encouragement for those who believe that "something can be done," but also raises some very serious questions when we consider what more can be done, particularly for students at the age when preparation for transition to work or college is being completed, where we have done so badly. First, it is likely that it is easier in principle to improve achievement at the lower grade levels, where a minimal mechanical ability in reading and mathematics is being attempted, than at higher grades. This is what the improvement at these levels and the narrowing of the white-black gap seem to show, according to a number of analysts. For example:

> Since the greatest declines [in high school mathematics tests] were in such higher-level skills as inferencing, analyzing, interpreting, or solving problems, it is possible that one of the most popular policies of the times—some have called it a general minimalist policy—was partly responsible for drawing attention and resources away from more difficult-to-teach skills and more challenging subjects. Minimalist policies had many facets and spawned many different state and local school district programs, but they shared an emphasis on "basics" and a focus on minimum achievement standards. "Basics" . . . more often than not . . . translated into a concentration upon surface reading skills, sentence-oriented writing instruction, and computation with whole numbers.[20]

This writer is concerned particularly with the decline in achievement for the higher-achieving half of students, who showed a greater decline than the others. The fact that blacks made no progress in closing the black-white gap at the seventeen-year-old level at a time when scores for upper-level and middle-level whites were declining makes the picture for blacks all the worse and should lead us not to overestimate the significance of a small gain among blacks in recent years in closing the large gap with whites in SAT scores.

Jeanne Chall, one of our wisest scholars of reading, suggests that the improvement at the earliest ages was also owing to a change in methods of instruction of reading in the early years and that the younger cohorts tested benefited from this change. But she also raises cautions as to whether we can expect improvement among older cohorts who have received better early reading instruction. She notes that reading changes its character after fourth grade: it is there that the influence of differential family background becomes apparent. In a study she conducted with Catherine Snow, the second-year low-SES students had scores generally equal to those of middle-class students, they dropped behind at grade four, and by grade six there was a considerable drop, all of which remains consistent with findings as far back as *Equality of Educational Opportunity.* And her explanation for this shows how formidable our efforts will have to be to overcome it:

Pre–Grade 4 reading can be said to represent the oral tradition, in that text rarely goes beyond the language and knowledge that the reader already has through listening, direct experience, TV, and so forth. We can view reading beyond Grade 4 as comprising the literary tradition—when the reading matter goes beyond what is already known. Thus, Grade 4 can be seen as the beginning of a long progression in the reading of texts that are ever more complicated, literary, abstract, and technical, and that require more world knowledge and ever more sophisticated language and cognitive abilities to engage in the interpretations and critical reactions required. The materials that are typically read at Grade 4 and beyond change in content, in linguistic complexities, and in cognitive demands.[21]

An education journalist, cautioning on overinterpreting the improvement on tests in large cities such as New York, Los Angeles, Atlanta, and Washington, in addition to pointing out problems in the reuse of the same tests, quotes other authorities to the same effect:

> Some education professors who have followed testing trends argue that the narrow focus on the basics in the elementary grades causes an increase in the scores at the lower grades but then results in a decrease in scores at the upper grades. "To read for comprehension and inference, you need broad, general knowledge," says Harry Singer, an education professor at the University of California at Riverside. "Schools have narrowed their curriculum to fit the tests. But they have ignored the general knowledge that makes you a good reader." . . .
> Stanford University Professor Robert Calfee agrees: "If you concentrate on simple passages in a workbook format, you can get test scores up."[22]

I feel these professors of education do have something to offer beyond the analysis of inputs and outputs by economists and sociologists.

A full analysis of the relationship between low SES and educational achievement would have to deal with three other policies of the 1970s, two highly controversial, the other less controversial but much more expensive. The first was the substantial effort to bring black children and white children together in the same schools and in the same classrooms. The educational effects of integration per se have been much disputed. The authorities agree it has not hurt black achievement and has modestly increased skills, by a fraction of one standard deviation, amounting to between two and six weeks of gain; the more optimistic (or liberal), looking at longer-range effects, particularly those on children all of whose education has taken place in integrated settings, argue for a more substantial effect, amounting to a third of a standard deviation, which is not insignificant.[23] Desegregation went on apace with federal expenditures for low-income students, expenditures which were greatest in the South, where desegregation went furthest. The gap between the Southeast and the rest of the country in educational achievement closed considerably during the 1970s, and one would be hard put to separate out the effects of federal programs targeted on low-income groups from the effects of desegregation.

The educational achievement effects of a second controversial program of the 1970s that was focused on low-income groups—bilingual education—have also been much disputed. One cannot find even the minimal agreement that exists for the effects of desegregation. The costs of the bilingual education program were modest at the federal and state level, but with growing numbers of children from non-English-speaking homes, costs and controversy will undoubtedly grow.

The third major program with some impact on children from low-income families and black children was special education. The costs of the great expansion of special education for the handicapped, driven by court decisions, state legislation, and federal legislation, have been enormous. An informed observer asserts that "an educated guess would be that it has been, after inflation, the most important factor in school budget increases between 1973 and 1980."[24] The rate of growth of this program was the fastest of any major federal education program. The burden was substantial at the local and state level. In New York City, for example, the costs rose from $213 million in 1978 to $576 million in 1984, more than 17 percent of the education budget.[25]

At the same time, the numbers of such children—who include the "learning retarded," the mentally retarded, and the emotionally disturbed, among the largest categories—have grown rapidly to include in 1982–83 4.3 million children, or almost 10 percent of all. Any full analysis of the effects on poverty of governmental intervention in education would have to consider this program. But as a preliminary judgment, one could not expect, despite the great expenditures, substantial improvement as measured by the tests of graduating from high school or getting a stable job. For most of these children the aim is to have them enter regular classes, generally at low achieving levels, in other words, to become like the students whose achievement we have been discussing above.

The connection between education and training is unbreakably close: if more students managed to graduate from high school, if they did better at the skills taught in school, the problems of employment and jobs would be much reduced. I realize this may be disputed. Thus, one can argue that the number of good jobs would not necessarily increase. But consider only the problem of the black minority: even if the number of good jobs did not increase, a group that represents only 12 percent of high school youth could see its economic status improve considerably if it did better at these educational tasks, with only a moderate reduction for all the rest.

Unemployment declines and wages rise as young people move to higher and higher steps in the educational ladder: we need not enter into the complex question of just what permits them more easily to avoid unemployment and to get higher wages if they successfully earn high school diplomas and college degrees. Our system of work training is in very large part devoted to making up for educational failure. Its chief clients are high school dropouts. There has been, against all expectations, a steady drop overall in the number of youths who get high school diplomas over the past dozen years. Between 1972 and 1982, for the country as a whole the graduation rate, according to a set of figures compiled by the secretary of education, declined from 77.2 to 72.8 percent, a drop of 4.4 percentage points. The decline was sharpest in the big industrial states, though not all fared equally badly. On the other hand, southern states showed an increase or only small declines. It is impossible to make any clear pattern from this, except that regional differences, in this area as in others, are closing somewhat, and that at least some of the states known for high expenditure on education and social needs have shown remarkably poor records.[26] Within this overall situation, it appears that the decline has been concentrated among white males, with a small decline among white females and an actual decrease in high school dropouts among black males and females.[27]

The secretary of education's figures seem inconsistent with other figures as to high school completion rates among the population aged twenty-five to twenty-nine: the percentage of whites with four years of high school education or more rose from 77.8 percent in March 1970 to 86.9 percent in March 1982; among blacks and other races, it rose from 58.4 to 82.2.[28] One explanation for this inconsistency is that dropouts can get General Equivalency Diplomas on the basis of a test.

Whatever the explanation, it is clear that the most serious problems of youth are disproportionately concentrated among dropouts and, in that group, among minority youth. If one wishes to penetrate the connection between education, training, and poverty, it is there that our attention must be concentrated. If young blacks are doing somewhat better at completing their high school education, they are doing much worse at gaining employment. Despite the substantial expansion of expenditures for education and for training, and their concentration on poor and minority youth, in the past two decades we have seen a disturbing increase in unemployment among minority youth. In 1954 the percentages of unemployed black and white teenagers were about the same. By 1964 the disparity had increased considerably, and by 1983 it had increased much more. These unemployment rates understate the situation because they are based on numbers looking for work. When we consider the percentage of the population employed, the situation can only be described as disastrous (see Table 4-1). Thirty-one percent of black eighteen- and nineteen-year-olds were employed, compared with 58 percent of white youths in that age group. Disproportionate school attendance does not explain this: 32 percent of black and other youths aged sixteen–twenty-four are neither in school nor employed, compared to 18 percent of whites. That discrimination exists cannot be denied: that it can explain such a change goes against all reason. A National Bureau of Economic Research survey, concentrating on inner-city black males in Boston, Philadelphia, and Chicago, analyzed by Rich-

Table 4.1.
Employment and unemployment rates, 1951–1983.

Age group and race	Percentage unemployed					Percentage employed				
	1954	1964	1969	1977	1983	1954	1964	1969	1977	1983
16–17										
Black, other	13.4	25.9	24.7	38.7	47.3	40.4	27.6	28.4	18.9	13.7
White	14.0	16.1	12.5	17.6	22.6	40.6	36.5	42.7	44.3	36.2
18–19										
Black, other	14.7	23.1	19.0	36.1	43.8	66.5	51.8	51.1	36.9	31.3
White	13.0	13.4	7.9	13.0	18.7	61.3	57.7	61.8	65.2	58.0
20–24										
Black, other	16.9	12.6	8.4	21.7	27.2	75.9	78.1	77.3	61.2	57.2
White	9.8	7.4	4.6	9.3	13.8	77.9	79.3	78.8	80.5	74.2

Source: Richard B. Freeman and Harry J. Holzer, "Young Blacks and Jobs: What We Now Know," *The Public Interest* 78 (Winter, 1985): 19; from U.S. Department of Labor, *Employment and Training Report of the President, 1982; Employment and Earnings,* January 1984.

ard Freeman and Harry Holzer, throws some light on the situation. This group of youths is of course worse off than all black youth; fewer are in the labor force (80 percent against 90 percent), more are unemployed (41 against 33 percent), only 28 percent come from a household with a man in it, as against 51 percent for all black youth, 45 percent come from families on welfare, and 32 percent live in public housing.

Many explanations of the growing gap in employment between black and white youths do not hold up in their analysis. It would be hard to maintain that discrimination has gotten worse. Unemployment has gotten worse both in good times and bad, so overall poorer performance of the economy does not explain it, nor is the matter explained by the entry of more women and immigrants into the labor force. Nor is it, surprisingly, explained by inaccessibility of jobs in the suburbs. Big city areas with easy access to suburban jobs do as badly as those without. On the "supply side," one of the most striking factors that helps black youths get employment is attending church; staying in school longer and getting better grades also help. One of the most harmful factors is being involved with the welfare system: "Youths from welfare homes, with the same family income and the same other attributes as from non-welfare homes, do much worse in the job market. Youths living in public housing also do less well than youths living in private housing."[29]

Another analysis of these data comes up with an even more surprising finding. There should be an incentive for young persons on welfare to work and attend school since benefits are not reduced for the earnings of dependent children who are students and not holding a full-time job. Further, owing to variations in the definition of a household, in many states until 1981 children aged eighteen to twenty-one were not included in estimating household benefits, and their earned income was therefore not deducted from the welfare grant. Despite this apparent incentive, fewer youths in welfare families worked.[30]

To concentrate on males, as the NBER survey analyzed by Freeman and Holzer and by Lerman does, is reasonable. Yet as more and more young women enter the labor force and the general social norm shifts to expecting them to be part of the labor force, it is worth noting how the transition from school to work is managed by young minority females. The situation here is particularly disastrous because so many bear children so young. A study of reasons why high school dropouts aged fourteen–twenty-one left school shows that 41 percent of black, 15 percent of Hispanic, 14 percent of white females left because of pregnancy. Nearly three in ten black women aged sixteen to twenty-one are unmarried mothers, compared to one in ten Hispanics, three in one hundred whites.[31] And one of the major reasons for dropping out of training programs is pregnancy. Pregnancy among young women, in particular blacks, has recently become a matter of great concern, though the problem has been evident for at least twenty-five years. Substantial efforts are now made to keep pregnant girls in school, either mainstreamed or in special classes adapted to their situation, to reduce the number of dropouts.

But after dropping out, one must count on work-training programs, and major efforts of the post-1964 policy explosion were directed to creating new types of work training and education outside formal school settings. Since, it was argued, the schools did not seem to know what to do with sixteen- and seventeen-year-olds who were not interested, something new was needed. The thrust of the past twenty years seems to have been to accept the fact that school will fail to prepare many for work and to create new institutions for the purpose. But after having done badly in schooling, we do not do well at making up for the failure through work-training programs, though we have certainly tried.

When it comes to what works in work training for the inadequately educated, for the despairing or dulled or drugged or vicious or those frustrated by their lack of crucially necessary minimal skills, the situation is far more complicated than even the discussion of what works in the education of the children of the poor and of minorities in school programs. There the objective is simpler. Despite the substantial differences among schools, programs, teachers, there is a surprising uniformity in American schooling. If we say this works but that doesn't, we have a sense of what is happening in schools and what can continue to happen if we do the right thing: spend more time on reading or arithmetic, or use a phonic instead of a whole word approach, or whatever. Just as the difficulty of achieving better results increases in high school, with a more differentiated curriculum and with the need to develop more abstract skills and higher processes of reasoning and inference, so we find an additional quantum jump of complexity if we consider the kinds of programs that have been attempted with the high school dropout or the high school graduate with minimal skills. The objective is more difficult and ambitious: not only to improve very often minimal academic skills (reading, calculating), but also to teach work skills related to a specific occupation and social forms related to work (dress, appearance, speech, demeanor). The approaches to doing this are also far more varied than in the elementary and secondary schools: counseling, classroom training, part-time or full-time work, long term or short, training on the job, residential training, various mixes of all the above, with or without stipends for support, with different kinds of reward and punishment mechanisms, or with none at all.

It is understandable that it is very hard to come to conclusions, and if we could say little in 1974, we can say little more today, despite a great expansion in the scale and sophistication of evaluations of work-training programs. The most extensive effort to evaluate the evaluations, by an advocate of the programs who is a social scientist and an administrator, communicates a sense of the difficulty of the task and the near-despair that must overwhelm the person who tries to make sense of what has been done. A mere rollcall of the initials of different programs, each of which has had its own evaluations in number, reduces one to dumbness: ARA, MDTA, JC, NYC, WIN, JOBS, CEP, PEP, CETA, PSE, STIP, HIRE, YEDPA, PSIP, PIC's, YCCIP, YIEPP. They all stand for something, and none stands for something that is not substantial and of some consequence. All once excited enthusiasm as one approach to our problem. But very little emerges that can be asserted with confidence. Robert Taggart writes, in his attempt to draw lessons:

> Even the most detailed analysis will not yield unequivocal proof of what has worked and why . . . Employment and training activities attracted legions of social scientists using their most refined methods to measure every aspect of manpower programs and their impacts . . . There is so much information that it overwhelms policymakers and managers, as well as undermining public understanding and support. Every finding is equivocated or contradicted by an array of competing facts and figures . . .
>
> I have tried to wrestle this welter of information into submission, not to discover new truths or to grind any axes, but rather to make sense out of the confusion and to return to the zone of diminishing rather than negative returns. It is a heroic undertaking.

Taggart applies the term "heroic" to his own activities. Anyone reviewing the area will grant him that license. And what does he conclude, after his service in the Carter administration, where training and employment activities reached a peak of $10 billion a year?

> Income maintenance should be deemphasized. Allowances and wages in training and subsidized jobs are in some cases more than is justified by need or productivity; they attract and hold some participants who have limited interest in improving employability. Reduced allowances and wages would encourage transition into subsidized employment and would leave room for incentives to reward participant performance.
>
> More intensive investments are needed. A second tier should be built

on the short-duration training and remediation efforts which now predomi-
nate . . .

Sorting the performers from nonperformers among participants should
be an objective rather than a taboo, as long as remediation and training is
focussed on those who need it most. The "winners" among the disadvantaged can be rewarded without punishing the "losers." . . .

Training for the disadvantaged should utilize mainstream institutions
wherever possible, providing participants with greater choice and applying
stricter standards of individual performance.[32]

These bare bones of suggestion have to be translated and interpreted.
The first point is clear enough: we don't pay youth to go to school, and
we shouldn't pay them to attend the training and remediation programs
which are required by their failure. This kind of incentive to undergo
training, which in some ways seems reasonable enough, raises the problem of a disincentive to go out and seek unsubsidized work. This is not
unfamiliar from other areas of social policy.

Taggart's second point reflects the research finding that the most intensive programs have done best. The most intensive, and expensive, is Job
Corps, a generally residential program for the most disadvantaged, for
"the hardest of the hard core." In a major evaluation, only half of the
participants came from two-parent families, their average family size was
6.4 persons, average reading and math performance was below the sixth-
grade level, one fourth had applied for and been rejected by the military,
a third had never held a job for more than a month, two-fifths had been
arrested, and three in ten had been convicted. More than two-thirds were
minority, 86 percent were dropouts. The 1980 cost per service year is
$13,193, as against $8,046 for classroom training, $6,088 for on-the-job
training (OJT). The cost of a service year is the cost for one person for
one year in the specified type of training, but Job Corps members spend
on average only six months in the program, and those in classroom training or OJT are in these programs for much shorter periods, so costs per
participant were $6,706 for Job Corps, $2,481 for classroom training,
$1,638 for OJT. The cost-benefit ratios are best for Job Corps, despite the
fact that its ambition is not excessive and its success appears modest:
"1977 corps members were employed two-fifths of the weeks in the first
post-termination year. Just half were employed 18 months after termination and only a fourth were employed full-time . . . Because less than a
third of entrants completed training, while only a proportion of these
found employment and a small proportion found training-related jobs, just

one in seven entrants completed a full vocational program and was sub-sequently employed in a training-related job."[33]

One important reason why the Job Corps comes out well in cost-benefit analyses, despite this less than sterling record, is that criminal activity is reduced, and this means a reduction in criminal justice system costs, personal injury and property damage, and stolen property costs. The Job Corps does better, according to Taggart, than Supported Work, one of the most carefully designed demonstrations, and one of the most carefully evaluated, by the highly respected Manpower Development Research Corporation (MDRC). Although this program tried to reduce dependency and social costs among welfare mothers as well as among ex-addicts, school dropouts, and ex-offenders, it was only among the first group that it showed any success: "During the period 19–27 months after enrollment . . . the average employment rates of the ex-addict, youth, and ex-offender groups were all below those of carefully matched support groups."[34]

Taggart's third conclusion reflects his discontent with the degree to which training programs are not like school, where some students fail and others are promoted. Although he would have services for all, he believes there should be some way for these programs to reward success. And his fourth point again favors the model of schooling and the reality of schooling as the means by which to achieve the objectives of work training. Schoolmen will be pleased by the positive assessment of some of the aspects of schooling by an analyst who had been immersed in the hard-headed and hard-objectives world of work training:

> The mainstream system of preparation for work [by which he means vocational training, secondary education, and college] . . . maintains standards at each level, for the quantity and diversity as well as the quality of inputs. Second, it . . . maintains standards for individual progression through the system, with minimum requirements for graduation from any level, and more refined measures of performance that can be used in assessing qualifications for movement to the next level. Third, the system is self-contained, with built-in ladders and pathways so that performance at one level determines the probability and direction of transition to the next . . . Fourth, the system sorts individuals so that, on average, those who advance are better able to meet the requirements of the next level . . . Fifth, there are . . . second-chance options . . . Finally, the system provides credentials which are recognized in the labor market . . . The local training and remediation system for those failing in or who have been failed by these mainstream institutions operates by a completely different set of principles.[35]

It is startling to discover at the end of this massive evaluation of work-training programs that there is something in school—which failed these youths to begin with—that the enormous and in large measure ad hoc and free-standing work-training system we have created might emulate. Targeted to immediate need, with short courses, with current incentives to maintain attendance, and with promises of immediate jobs at the end, the system, for all sorts of reasons, fails.

It was therefore not surprising that one of the largest experimental efforts ever undertaken in work training during the Carter administration, as part of our last burst of optimism, or at least dogged hope, that we could do something about these matters, was a program that tried to use the provision of guaranteed work as an incentive to maintain attendance in school. The Youth Incentive Entitlement Pilot Project was "the nation's largest demonstration to test the feasibility and effectiveness of a new approach to solving the employment problems of disadvantaged youth . . . a bold $240 million experiment in which 76,000 youths were employed in a research study to determine whether this new idea would correct what seemed an irreversible deterioration in the employment position of poor youths." The approach: "16- to 19-year-old youths from low-income or welfare households who had not yet graduated from high school were offered minimum-wage jobs, part-time during the school year and full-time during the summer, on the condition that they remain in high school (or its equivalent) and meet academic and job standards."[36]

The research could not be faulted: it was conducted by the Manpower Development Research Corporation. As is common in such enormous enterprises, the incidental learning in carrying it out often tells us as much as the direct test of hypothesis by the experimental design. Thus, one thing learned was that black youths responded in much greater numbers than white. No less than 73 percent of the youths applying were black, 18 percent Hispanic; 63 percent of black eligible youths participated, but only 22 percent of whites, 38 percent of Hispanics. (For what reason? Probably because the whites have other channels to other jobs.) Forty-three percent were from families receiving cash welfare, 23 percent had previously participated in a CETA employment program. We have already referred to the impact of youthful pregnancy: "In the fall of 1977 (just before Youth Entitlement began), under 10 per cent of the young women who were 15 or 16 years old at program start-up had a child. By fall, 1981, however, 45 per cent of these same young women, who were now 18 and 19 years old (and mostly unmarried), had at least one child."[37]

The cost of keeping a participant in the program for one year averaged

$4,382. And what did we get for it? We eliminated the gap in employment between black and white youths while the program was in effect, demonstrating that black youths will work at the minimum rate. But during the brief postprogram period this advantage was reduced. There was a large percentage increase in earnings among the youths participating, compared to those in the control cities. This advantage declined but was still substantial in the year after the program. As for school, dropouts were not brought back into school or kept there by the job offer. There was no effect in reducing dropouts or increasing school attendance or graduation rates. By the time the participants were nineteen, in the fall of 1981, only half had graduated and almost two-fifths were dropouts.

There have been more optimistic evaluations of this program than mine, based on the greater earnings of the program participants. But one does not have the impression that much had been done to make a long-range difference.

I do not expect that another review of what we have learned from schooling and training as means to overcome the disadvantages of poor and black youth would give us the answer or answers. We know a bit more, far from enough. We know enough, I would hazard, to suggest that greater resources would be most usefully spent in preschools and elementary schools. There we have evidence that improvement is possible. If that improvement is broadened and sustained, more poor, minority youth should be able to get through high school. It is likely that the still inadequate educational base laid down in elementary school is what makes so many students so unreachable by so much of the high school curriculum, leading to high dropout rates and poor job prospects. (Of course, it may be the curriculum itself, but there are limits to how much that can be bent without making it a travesty, signaling to employers that a high school diploma does not mean what they think it means.) If this is the case, much of the present spate of reform, which emphasizes competency tests for exit from high school, stiffer academic requirements in high school and for college entry, is, I believe, irrelevant to the problems of poor and black youth. If they are not able to reach present standards, why should they be expected to reach higher standards?[38] It is not easy to deal with this educational failure by means of remedial work training and education programs specially designed for the failures: few manage to get much from these programs, as the Job Corps experience demonstrates, not that anyone has anything better in the same line to offer. We cannot induce these children to stay in school with a job offer, and it is doubtful that the job experience combined with the requirement to stay in school will have more than very minimal effects in improving their prospects. There is sufficient evidence that the welfare culture itself, or, more cautiously, the experience of living in poor female-headed families dependent on income transfers and living in concentrations of such people, serves independently to damage the children in these settings. This much we have learned. It is a sober and minimal level from which to continue.

5 | Universal and Income-Tested Social Programs

Welfare is an "income-tested" program: one condition for getting it is not having enough money in either savings or earnings. Public housing is income-tested, as is much middle-income housing in programs such as the Mitchell-Lama in New York: one cannot get such an apartment if one's income is too high, and one must reveal one's income to become eligible. Medicaid is income-tested—it is medical care for the poor. Income-tested programs have always borne a stigma among theorists of social policy. They divide the population into those eligible and those not eligible. They can have perverse effects: people may restrict their income so as to become or remain eligible. They encourage fraud. They increase administrative costs.

By contrast, "universal" programs eliminate these dangers. Everyone is eligible. The British National Health Service is the best example: everyone is eligible, so no examination of anyone's status is necessary. Even foreigners and tourists are eligible.

Was there any way of eliminating welfare, with all its faults, through a universal program? In 1972, running for the presidency, Senator George McGovern was intrigued by proposals by economists and social policy analysts who thought they had a way to do this: the "demogrant." Each person would get a minimal sum from the government for maintenance. It would be returned by way of taxation if that person earned enough from work not to need it. That was the principle. There would be no "welfare" recipients as such: there would merely be people who, because of insufficient earnings, did not have their demogrants fully or partially taxed away.

Would it work? The enthusiasm for universal as against income-tested programs reminded me of a story and induced in me a certain skepticism.

Forty years ago or so, I participated in a small conference on housing problems. Paul and Percival Goodman, who had just written their fascinating book *Communitas,* suggesting and analyzing utopian answers to city problems, were there. Charles Abrams, the housing expert, was also there. The Goodmans made an argument that they also make in their book: why shouldn't expensive items of equipment that are used only an hour or two a day be shared? Take a dishwasher in an apartment. Why couldn't all the apartments on a floor or in a small apartment house share it? Charles Abrams pondered that possibility, and then said: "I don't think Mrs. Goldberg is going to be very happy when Mrs. Murphy puts her nonkosher dishes in the communal dishwasher." Our little story can be put into the terms of our problem: the universal dishwasher does have some benefits, but irrational factors restrain it. And thus back to the income-tested, private dishwasher.

Or consider a more current proposal for applying the principle of universalism. In 1979 *Newsweek* carried a proposal that might lead to $8.8 billion of savings in unnecessary doctors' bills in the next fifteen years: that we pay, out of public funds, the full cost of doctors' education—a mere $200,000,000 a year. This was an alternative to the then-existing situation, in which medical students took out loans at 12 percent interest to cover their medical education. Dick Martz, who made this proposal, argued its virtues. The doctors wouldn't have to pay interest, and thus their fees would be lower. Doctors wouldn't be forced to go into high-paying specialties to pay off debts. With more freedom of choice, "doctors could follow their idealistic impulses to small towns and rural areas where they are desperately needed." And he pointed to the savings in administrative costs: "One check to each of 125 medical schools would replace the current structure of 33,000 individual loans a year. Loan defaults, bankruptcies and collection problems would vanish. And perhaps most important, a medical education would be available to the best-qualified applicants regardless of their parents' wealth—perhaps the most affirmative action possible toward equal opportunity."[1]

This rather intriguing proposal is certainly not income-tested. It was, as I hardly need say, never adopted. Was it pure irrationality that prevented us from gaining the benefits it promised? I think not, and I will explain why a certain skepticism was warranted.

One archetypal universal program, the British National Health Service, comes as close to universal as one can imagine, and it has spurred social policy analysts to think of ways of applying its principles to other kinds of social programs. Another archetypal program, the American Aid to

Families with Dependent Children (AFDC), seems so badly affected by income testing, that it too has spurred on social policy analysts to ponder whether it can be replaced totally by something that approximates the universality of the British National Health Service, with all its advantages. The defects of income-tested welfare have long been familiar. The litany runs that it encourages work avoidance and family splitting, it imposes a stigma which has many other unfortunate effects, it weakens social cohesion, and it is expensive to administer. In contrast, the British National Health Service avoids all of these defects: It is neutral to work behavior or family composition, there is no stigma, and administratively, because it is universal, it is amazingly cheap to run.

Clearly there is much that is attractive in the vision of universality, much that is unpleasant in the reality of income testing. Yet as one ponders alternatives, one begins to waver in one's faith that the National Health case is an example of what can be done to universalize other spheres of income transfer and service provision: perhaps it is the only workable example. The National Health Service, admirable as I believe it to be, and attractive as I find the archetype of universality, cannot easily be adapted to other programs. Yet another conclusion suggests itself: the American welfare program, unattractive as it is in detail, probably has to be, with only modest variations, more or less what it is. The British National Health Service does not provide a model for universalization, and the American welfare program is not a very good candidate for universalization, because the kinds of social policy that modern governments are engaged in, I will argue, are so varied and complex that no single model will work across the broad range of income transfers and provision of goods and services.

The most substantial effort to show how a universal income maintenance program would work was undertaken during the heady days of welfare reform in the 1970s. A number of scholars proposed and analyzed a "Credit Income Tax."[2] The CIT, like the proposal to pay every medical student's tuition, does eliminate a lot of unpleasant side effects and, in its breathtaking simplification of a complex system of taxes and benefits, is extremely attractive. I have no reason (or capacity) to doubt the case made in various analyses that it would get as much money to the poor (or could be made to get as much money to the poor) as welfare and its associated programs. But there are other features of the CIT—aside from its target efficiency, its economic efficiency, or its administrative efficiency— that do not seem to me to have been given enough attention and that, to my mind, make the analyses a contribution more to theory than to living policy.

Kesselman and Garfinkel, in their original article explaining the virtues of the CIT, quoted Milton Friedman's early commonsensical dismissal of providing a universal subsidy, which is the basic CIT proposal as I see it: "In principle there always exists a universal subsidy . . . plus a tax system that would produce identically the same result as a negative income tax . . . The problem in practice is that this system involves mailing out checks to 200 million people in order to help 20 or 40 million, and then having 160 or 180 million others mail back checks." I think he has a point there, and there are other points I will make. But, attracted by what they see as the efficiency of the universal subsidy, as well as by its virtues in overcoming work effects, stigma, and other effects of income testing, Kesselman and Garfinkel see no good reason, apparently, why vast additional shares of personal income should not be taxed away for purposes of transfer to provide the universal subsidy, as long as they can prove that most people will, after the operation, be no worse off, and indeed may be better off by saving the costs of more complicated administration of welfare programs. "Rational individuals who understand what they would lose from a transfer program should be indifferent as to whether or not programs are income-tested, if their net loss is identical." The example they give is elegant: "Imagine a two-man economy with one rich man and one poor man . . . Suppose that the government decided to increase the poor man's income by $1,000. The government could tax the rich man $1,000 and transfer this sum to the poor man. Alternatively the government could tax the rich man $2,000 and transfer $1,000 to each man. Benefits would be income-tested in the former program but not in the latter."[3]

Now I can see many reasons why the rational man—not the economic rational man, perhaps, but the rational man nevertheless—would prefer the first arrangement to the second.

First of all, his tax bill becomes very much larger, even if he gets a check every month or two weeks from the government for his universal subsidy. The taxes will be deducted at the source with unvarying efficiency. His subsidy check may be fouled up by the computer, or lost in the mail, or filched from his mailbox. If we "net out" his gain (or loss) from a CIT, we reduce mailing costs, but other objections (see below) still hold.

Second, the government is not going to make a fine distinction between what it collects in taxes for general government functions and what it collects for transfer—it doesn't now. When the IRS examines his tax bill for error or fraud, the taxpayer will become potentially liable for a much larger amount.

Third, since it all goes to the government, there is no reason to believe that an impregnable line will divide what government does with the vast additional amount it has taxed away for universal transfer and the rest of the money it has taxed away for government functions. Perhaps the taxpayer won't get back what the original arrangement calls for. Government can change tax rates as well as subsidies. It does so all the time. What is to keep the government from using the money taxed for transfer for other government functions—functions the citizen would prefer not to tempt government into performing by providing it with all that additional money? CIT seems to require a remarkable degree of self-denial by government in order to attain all its objectives—for example, the same subsidy regardless of need, the same tax regardless of income. It is hard to see any but a government of rational economists (and even they might disagree) submitting themselves to this discipline.

Fourth, will the rational man value what has been gained? There may be a lesser disincentive to work than that imposed by the high implicit tax rate on earnings that comes with welfare payments. But there is still—to the uninstructed rational man who thinks it is good to work and good for others to work—the disincentive to work for a minimum income, *tout court,* provided (as the program hopes) without stigma.

Fifth, there remains the question whether the CIT really does away with income-tested public assistance, with all its evil effects—and how much it does do away with. Undoubtedly for many present welfare recipients the CIT solves the problem. But everywhere in the administration of welfare there are those for whom basic payments are a floor from which they move on to get additional assistance on what seem to be perfectly sound bases. The apartment has burned down. Furniture and clothes have been stolen. They have used up the rent allotment on food—and are about to be ejected. Or on heat—and are about starve. Or the children are not being fed, and the neighbors complain. In every state the "extra" payments are always a problem. Welfare departments will not be, cannot be, disbanded. At first, with the coming of CIT, they will, one hopes, not have much to do, but will deal only with the 10 or 20 percent (pure guesses) of unfortunates or incorrigibles who have money problems even after the CIT subsidy. One has the strong feeling that in this country, with its litigious traditions, its public interest law firms, its racial antagonisms dividing recipients from providers, that percentage will rise. In time the CIT will be seen as a floor above which other kinds of income-tested provision will have to be made. It will be income-tested because the first question the welfare worker asks will be, what have you done with your universal subsidy?

Finally, there are some considerations James Coleman raises.[4] The more government does, the less social cohesion there is. People become less dependent on nongovernmental structures of support, more dependent on government. This undermines those perhaps vestigial sources of support which still operate—family, neighborhood, church, ethnic group. Further, there remains the problem of increasing the power of government. One assumes and hopes that the CIT subsidy will be distributed with absolute neutrality and that it will not contribute to greater government power. And yet, how can this be? Congress has cut off social security to Communists in the past. Dissidents of one sort or another, if public passions are great enough, may find they are not eligible for their subsidies.

This leaves aside some more legitimate considerations that may limit the universality of the subsidy: for example, does the undocumented alien get it? The long-term visitor? Once again, one thinks enviously of the true universality of the National Health Service. But there is a difference between providing a service that anyone who walks in off the street may use and sending out a check at regular intervals. And thus we have other considerations raised by Coleman's paper: whether it is the IRS or the Social Security Administration that deals with the CIT, the numbers of people involved will be vast, and their chances of being treated as individuals by government and its agents (and undoubtedly there will be the need to occasionally deal with government) will be correspondingly reduced. Experience with any government bureaucracy does not encourage placing the entire population, many of whom after all do escape dealings with government, in the position of dependency on monthly or biweekly checks.

Having considered some of the reasons the rational man might look skeptically on the CIT, I will give some of those that might appear irrational to the rational economist.

It's *my* money, people will say. Why should the government take it, even if it promises, cross its heart, to give it all back? I think people don't want the government messing with their money in general, and they would resent the government engaging in a massive transfer simply to solve some imputed problems of the 10 or 15 percent who are poor and now getting income-tested transfers from the government. If you tell them that the new approach will solve nonpoor people's problems, too, by encouraging low-income people to take paying jobs, the average person—or many average people—is likely to say, force them to work. If you tell them that the CIT will reduce stigma, they are likely to say, why shouldn't poor people know it's charity? *I* see the chain of reasoning which goes from stigma and work avoidance encouraged by income testing to juvenile delinquency and an awful urban environment—or rather, I see the chain which *may* lead from one to the other. But I doubt we will be able to convince many congressmen and their constituents that it is worth handing over an additional and very substantial part of their income to the government for a beneficial (one hopes) massive transfer.

After all this is said, there is still the vision of universality, of all treated alike, and it is a vision which, despite what I have said, moves me as well as those who argue for the CIT. Is any part of the vision salvageable when we deal with the issue of income transfers? The part that has always seemed to me most salvageable is children's allowances. This is a viable form of universal income transfer. It already exists in many countries, so there would be in most people's minds better reasons for this kind of income transfer than for universal allowances. Children involve expense, they are the future of society, people deserve help with children. Such a first, modest approach to universality has much to commend it. Some of the arguments I have made against the CIT would apply to the children's allowance, but two features would help it: it would not require anything like the massive income transfer of the CIT, and it would go to assist children rather than people in general. Obviously its "target efficiency" in reaching the children of the poor would be low. But the poor do have more children, and many people are poor because of the number of children they have. Some part of the welfare population, which as we know moves into and out of welfare and is often just above or just below the line of eligibility, would be relieved of the need for applying for income-tested benefits by a children's allowance.

Another approach to universality would have a good deal of attractiveness as a viable political possibility: free health care for children. The poor already have free health care, but the near-poor are denied it if they don't qualify for Medicaid. The same arguments that could be made for children's allowances can be made for government-paid health care for children. There are also administrative efficiency arguments, since public health services for children, limited generally to diagnosis, are already provided without income testing under various public health and educational programs. Since the poor already get free health care, the "target efficiency" is low, but one objective of universality is gained—a single health system for children, poor and nonpoor.

Nor is it only in the case of children's programs that one sees possible approaches to universalism. Non-income-tested insurance for catastrophic costs of medical care is another real possibility, in the real world, for another modest foray away from the income-tested, and toward the universal, that would have much to commend it.

But as I suggested in the beginning, the spread of universalism seems to me to have limits, and these limits are reached quite early. They are reached not only for political reasons but for economic reasons and for reasons of values that are strongly held.

The larger political context today is one in which, as we all know, for a variety of reasons, large new social programs are not attractive politically—which means not attractive to the people that elected government represents. However far we are from a Swedish level of taxation, people feel taxation severely and don't want to pay more, even if it is explained that the "more" goes to give them services. Perhaps they can be convinced that these services are *really* for them—as in children's allowances and child health and catastrophic insurance—but they are clearly not eager to accept new programs that are really for people they think of as "them." The tide is running against universalism.

But aside from the strong antitax and anti-big-government mood, which may be temporary, there is a strong tide against the kinds of values which are necessary if we are to maintain or expand universal programs. We see a number of shifts in opinion and in values that do not favor the universal. Thus, in one area, Arnold Heidenheimer and John Layson tell us, the United States has led the world in approaching universality, in education.[5] Yet in just that area we see a withdrawal of support for universality. People want more and more to select the specific kind of education they want for their children, and large numbers of them don't think they can get it in the public education system. Those who use private education do so mostly for religious reasons, and they have been demanding relief. Whether this comes in the form of tax deductibility or tax credits, it will introduce a degree of what we have been calling income testing into public education. Depending on the mechanism, it will make it less onerous for people to opt out of the universal system of public education, because it will give them some relief in doing so.

One could say—and this indicates the slippery meanings of our terms—that because such a program expands the opportunity of lower-income groups to select private education and gives them a more equal chance to opt out of the public education system, it increases "universality." If we take the identifying feature of universality to mean each one gets the same, then facilitating choice of private education through the tax system reduces universality. If we take it to mean a universal freedom to choose, then it increases it.

Yet another problem for universalism: one of the most passionate arguments in public policy today is over free abortion for Medicaid recipients. Medicaid is of course an income-tested program, but within it there was no income testing for specific medical services. Now abortion has been withdrawn. However minor the degree of universalism paid abortions within Medicaid represented, clearly its withdrawal suggests the strength of opposition to an effort initiated by the Supreme Court to impose a universal standard for abortions. Once again, people are saying, we want our distinctive values to be given some support, as in the case of private religious education.

The withdrawal from universalism is not only a matter of the traditional Catholic resistance to universal programs which do not recognize distinctively Catholic values. As we know, Catholics are supported in the case of education and abortion by many Jews and Protestants, too. Nor is it simply a matter of more traditional elements defending their values against a wave of modernizing universalism. One also finds resistance to universalism on the left. Note what little support we find among liberals and college students for the universal service of youth in the armed forces. Indeed, perhaps the greatest example of an increase in income testing in social programs (I realize national defense is not a "social program," but every program has a social aspect) has been the replacement of the draft by a volunteer army; as a result, it is the poorer who enlist in the armed forces, while those with greater opportunities need not.

In yet another area we find a withdrawal from universalism: in affirmative action in employment and promotion, and in admissions to selective professional programs. It is particularly tricky to apply our terms in this context. Affirmative action is in one sense an effort to achieve universalism: all groups should be included. In yet another sense it reduces (or may reduce) implicit income testing: less emphasis on merit and test scores and achievement may favor lower-income groups. But it is also a withdrawal from universalistic values. Universalism in transfer programs means that we can be blind to individual traits, we don't have to examine how much money and assets an individual or family has. Such programs seem to me close relatives to the kinds of programs in which we don't have to examine the individual to find out what race or ethnic group he or she belongs to. Universalism in transfer programs shares with universalism in employment and education programs the same quality of salutory blindness.

This retreat from universalism, to my mind, stems from a weakening of commonly held values as to the good society. We once seemed to agree that the same public education for all, limits on abortion, all youth serving in the armed forces, and merit as the test for employment and higher education represented the good society, or at least a very large number of us seemed to agree. We don't any longer. We no longer sense that we share commonly held values. I cautiously use the word "sense" instead of saying forthrightly we don't hold common values any longer, because I think there is a greater degree of commonality in our values than one might guess from the tenor of public discussion. And indeed, one of the causes of suspicion, I believe, of such a proposal as the CIT, and its distant ancestor, the demogrant proposal of Senator McGovern in the 1972 campaign, is that those who uphold what were once generally and widely accepted values feel that such a proposal is yet another attack on the values they think good and which they see weakening. While one can argue that this is not the effect of a CIT, the proposal will be seen as undermining the desirability of work for all, of the two-parent family, of father support for children.

Universal social programs have virtues. They can help create a common society and a common nation. But if they are seen as attacking widely held, once-universal values, then rather than contributing to the creation of a common society and a common nation, they further divide it. Under those circumstances, one sees a withdrawal of support for universality, both from right and left, with the varying rallying cries of "liberty," "freedom," or "do your own thing."

One must ask, then, about universal programs, to what end? What behavior do they encourage? And we can adapt the principles of universalism to encourage the responsible behavior most people want to support. Consider the argument of Harold Watts and his colleagues.[6] Yes, they say, income transfer programs of a universal type are good, but they penalize the one-parent household. What to do? Surprisingly, in the literature of econometric analysis of alternative programs, they propose filling the gap with a very different kind of universalism, one economists generally don't talk about—the universal requirement for income support by two parents, strongly enforced. In other words, they acknowledge a widely held value which many of the proposals for NIT and CIT and the like have not acknowledged. They would combine a universal transfer program, with its practical and pragmatic benefits, with the support of a universally held value, that is, the requirement that fathers support their children financially, whether they are present or absent. In the past many social workers and social policy analysts have spoken as if such a demand were malicious persecution of the poor. But the expectation of support by two parents is as near universal as anything in our society.

Other possibilities exist for a kind of universalism that advances widely held values. One example was given earlier: free health care for all children. Yet another field for universalism is little explored: social benefits attached to jobs, all jobs. They could be child benefits, they could be health insurance. One of the problems that proponents of a CIT are trying to deal with is the work disincentive of welfare. Rather than a universal CIT, why not attach the benefits of welfare—health insurance or Medicaid, vacations—universally to jobs?[7]

It becomes clear that there is no universal rule that can settle, for all kinds of social services and money transfers, the question whether benefits and services should be income-tested or not. The story will appear quite different whether we talk about housing, health, or education, and whether we talk about preschool, elementary and secondary, higher, or postsecondary education. And when we talk of direct money benefits for single-parent households, for the destitute, for the aged, for the chronically sick, and for other categories, and allowances for children, matters get even more complicated.

What I have suggested, and I believe it is more than a play on the word "universal," is that we should be concerned with universal or near-universal values as well as universal programs. In any case, if programs are to become reality, attention to these values and to whether programs are seen as validating or negating them will be crucial. There are certain values which we would all want to see supported that a universal program would harm. Thus many people believe the CIT would damage a commitment to work and to the responsibility to maintain oneself, and these values are not so strong or so useless that we would want to see them weakened. On the other hand, a common, non-means-tested provision of health care has many arguments in its favor and does not seem to harm any values we want to support. Thus, in a universal health service the individual still retains responsibility for his or her own care. After all, one must get up and go to see the doctor, which makes health care very different from a universal income transfer, in which one waits for a check which comes whether one stirs oneself or not. And in going to see the doctor, one puts oneself within range of influences which will encourage one to take better care of oneself. In other cases, values we want to support seem to be ranged on both sides. Thus, I do not like the stigma and the division between "them" and "us" that welfare imposes. But I do not like the costs, as I have described them, of programs which claim they would make welfare unnecessary. Nor do I believe the claim that we can design a program that dispenses with the need to distinguish between those who truly need a benefit and those who do not, no matter how ingenious the policies we construct.

6 | Crisis and Redirection in Social Policy

It was only in the late 1970s that discontent with the growth of social programs—with the overall level of expenditures, the range of services provided, the number of areas within which governmental social policy replaced private action or provided a service that had not hitherto been a public responsibility—became widespread in the United States and in other countries, including leaders in the development of the welfare state. Was there some desirable "limit" to the growth of social programs?

The notion of limit had many meanings. But the essential core of this growing conviction was that the straight-line growth of social policy that was evident in the seventies should change direction. Perhaps no one was so simple-minded as to extrapolate the developments of the past in a straight-line fashion to predict the future of social policy. But it was certainly true that ten years ago those countries that spent less on social policy and provided insurance for a narrower range of accidents and disabilities and conditions saw their future as one in which they would approximate ever more closely the more advanced welfare states. The United States and Japan were seen as backward, Sweden and England as advanced, and it was generally agreed that the United States and Japan should try to become more like England and Sweden.

Replacing a simpleminded faith in growth is a widening expectation that social policy will increasingly supplement central governmental insurance and other policies with programs and policies that in some way try to respond to complexity. One reason for increased complexity is the diversity of populations, in ethnic origins, in cultural style, and in voluntarily chosen life-styles—a diversity that either is actually increasing or is seen as something to which a response in the form of more differentiated policies is necessary. A second reason for complexity is the recognition of certain issues as intractable and thus requiring a wider range of policies, many clearly experimental. A third reason for complexity is the increasing insistence of those who are the beneficiaries of social policy on participating in shaping and administering it.

While each country will show a different pattern of response, I believe large comprehensive programs will develop more and more variants, and, where the political or social system makes it possible, we will see a larger role for various kinds of quasi-governmental and nongovernmental smaller-scale institutions and communities in social policy.

The development of social policy will undoubtedly be affected by what kind of dissatisfactions exist, and how the notion of limits and the subsequent idea that a change is necessary develop in various countries. But I believe the idea that some kind of turning point in social policy has been reached is near-universal in advanced industrial societies. The idea of a limit or a turning point in social policy breaks down into four separate and distinct elements, present both in the United States and in the more advanced welfare states.

The first of these is the growing sense in many countries that they have reached a limit in what can be raised in taxation for social policy. There is no clearly fixed figure which tells us that when government takes 40 or 50 or 60 or more percent of the gross national product for public purposes, and in increasing measure for social purposes (rather than for such traditional state aims as war, internal peace, and roads), we must have some kind of reaction in which the majority of the electors cry "too much." Sweden and Germany may wonder why relatively lightly taxed California (by European standards) revolts against a property tax and radically cuts public services, and Americans may wonder why California, more lightly taxed than Massachusetts, precedes Massachusetts in rebelling. And yet, whether the country in question is Denmark, with its remarkably elaborate social programs, or the United Kingdom, which despite its primacy has not gone as far, the discontent is seen everywhere.

The crude resistance to taxation increasingly finds sophisticated support from supply-side economics, which argues that the disincentive in high progressive income and capital taxation to investment and greater work effort actually hurts the poor, by imposing a brake on economic growth, more than the direct benefits of the social programs made possible by this taxation aid them. Interestingly enough, this approach—whatever its economic force, which I leave to others—seems to provide one way of overcoming John Rawls's powerful argument in his *Theory of Justice* for a thorough egalitarianism, for his general formula for justice reads: "All social values—liberty and opportunity, income and wealth, and the bases of self-respect—are to be distributed equally unless an unequal distribution of any, or all, of these values is to everyone's advantage."[1] Rawlsians in the first instance would argue against tax cuts in which savings to the wealthier and to business are greater than savings to the poorer and to individuals—but the supply-side economists can argue that the benefits to investment, productivity, and economic growth would indeed be "to everyone's advantage."

Of course, public response to the pressure of taxation has little to do with abstract Rawlsian principles or the sophistication of supply-side economics. Harold Wilensky, who believes that the United States is a welfare state "laggard," presumably doomed (or blessed) to proceed along the road to greater expenditure and more extensive programs, resists the common view that "cultural values—our economic individualism, our unusual emphasis on private property, the free market, and minimum government" explain the American resistance to public spending and taxing. He points to a more interesting feature of the United States: the high proportion of taxes that are visible (income and property taxes). A second feature that explains tax revolt is very rapid increase in taxes, as in Denmark between 1965 and 1971. The same phenomenon sparked the California revolt.[2] Conceivably we will see increasing resort to indirect taxes.

A second sense of limits, more closely related to the issue of changes in roles and responsibilities in social policy, is a sense of limits to *effectiveness*. Once again, variations in such a sense, between kinds of services and different countries, are very great. The largest element in social policy, old-age pensions, is exempt from concern about effectiveness: their objective is met by the very act of transfer, for it is to provide income to the nonworking on the basis of previous contribution, whether strict insurance principles apply or they are modified by some skewing for the benefit of low earners (as in American social security). Universal child allowances are also exempt from concern about effectiveness; their aim, as in the case of old-age pensions, is to simply provide the income.

But in all other branches, issues of effectiveness arise and have become more urgent. Thus, the enormous increases in expenditure for health costs raise questions of effectiveness. To what extent does the availability of services increase use and cost without an additional improvement in health? Can the pattern of expenditure be shifted to less expensive services? To what extent does expensive intervention really add to overall health as against prevention or changes in diet and patterns of exercise? And so on. The issue of effectiveness comes up, too, in housing policy, certainly in the United States. Here the objective is not only to transfer income for purposes of providing good housing but also to directly provide such housing for the poor; thus questions of design and planning come up, and it may turn out that the housing and developments provided are unattractive, and great sums must be spent to remodel them or, in the worst cases, great sums are lost when they are demolished because tenants cannot be attracted to them. Wherever large public decisions on housing are made, the question comes up whether these housing services might not have provided more satisfaction if different policies had been developed—either different sites, or lower densities, or different patterns of tenure, or greater freedom to choose facilities provided by a market response.

But effectiveness was most deeply challenged by developments and thinking in the 1970s in those areas of public policy where services and expenditure are expected to produce a fairly complex response. In the United States there are two striking examples: welfare (income-tested support for the poor), and work training. In both cases the objective is not simply money transfer (though to a large extent this is all we expect or should expect when we support an abandoned mother and her children). For those who are neither aged nor handicapped, welfare is still considered "temporary" assistance, which should be accompanied by efforts by social agencies as well as recipients to find basic support through work. The debate over welfare has been intense and continuous for twenty-five years, and the programs that we have adopted to modify or accompany basic support for the poor are legion. Yet in common (and scholarly) belief, a basic aim of this program eludes us, that is, aiding people out of dependency rather than encouraging them to enter into dependency and stay there. The dissatisfaction with work-training programs, which are also legion, is also great. They are expected to take persons who have not established a steady relationship with the labor market and do so. The reasons why, after many years of effort and very substantial expenditures, such great numbers of persons, particularly youths, cannot establish such a relationship, defies easy explanation.[3] There are mysteries in these programs. Focused on black youth, of whom 400,000 are unemployed, they provided half a million jobs for young people in 1979 (aside from 800,000 summer jobs). The problem of black youth unemployment was nevertheless worse than before these programs started.[4]

Ineffectiveness is bad enough, but a third source of the sense of limits is the conviction among both ordinary citizens and experts that some programs are perverse and produce the effects they are meant to cure. Once again old-age pensions are exempt: no one becomes old to get a pension. Assistance to the handicapped was once exempt, but in the 1970s surprising increases in the numbers who get social security payments on the basis of disability suggested that not all disability is beyond control of the disabled, or incapable of being affected by incentives and disincentives. But again, the key example of a program which creates the effects it is meant to cure is welfare, where policy makers and analysts believed that family breakup was being encouraged by the availability of welfare payments and that payments reduced in accord with earned income discouraged adult persons on welfare from taking paying jobs.

Perverse effects are not limited to welfare. In work training, there is fear not only of ineffectiveness but of teaching how to avoid work: "Some learn the wrong thing: that they can be paid without doing any productive work."[5] Of course, this is a matter of good administration. But how many administrators of competence and commitment can we expect when we try to put 800,000 youths, many troubled, to work every summer?

And a final source of the concern for limits. As I have suggested above in speaking of resistance to high taxes for transfer and social programs, some economists suggest that sums now spent on social policy and transfer might do more good if they were directed into productive investment. Reduced taxes might allow more of these funds to be invested by the private sector, or, even if taxes were not reduced, more of the funds collected by government could be used for public investment in productive resources rather than for consumption and various kinds of social policy. This also certainly reflects doubt as to the effectiveness of many of our investments in human resources.

One of the major responses to dissatisfaction with social policy, whatever its sources, has been exploration of somewhat different roles for central government, for local government, for voluntary organizations, and for the private sector. Basically I will argue that the answer to the sense of limits and to growing dissatisfaction with social policy is not major reform at the center but a growing acceptance of diversity and variety in programs. Many developments of the 1970s already portend such developments: the movement toward participation, with its multiple tendencies and meanings; the movement toward decentralization; the tendency to make greater use of market-type incentives in social policy; the movement

toward deinstitutionalization, which inevitably means large institutions replaced by none or by much smaller ones; and the rise of respect for ethnic
and racial diversity which again, I believe, must lead to greater diversity,
decentralization, and the use of nongovernmental actors in social policy.

For certain programs—old-age pensions, child allowances—there is no
good substitute for centralization in policy. Simple demographic reality
triggers the program; the range of discretion of low-level administrators is
narrow; for old-age pensions perverse consequences are not possible, and
most agree modest child allowances are not a significant incentive to a
higher birth rate. But in most other programs, one has to deal with individual cases of great variety; and while central government provision of
funds is crucial and one sees no substitute for it, central government de-
termination of policy raises questions of how far down the line to the
decision made by an individual government worker providing a service to
an individual or family central policy determinations should extend. A
uniform provision for a uniform mass should increasingly give way to
differentiated provision. The theme was indicated by Sidney Webb more
than seventy-five years ago, when he presented the problem of social policy in a society rising above destitution for the masses in a striking image:

> A regiment of naked men needs clothing too urgently to allow us to
> grumble that the standard sizes of the regimental contractor makes all the
> uniforms nothing better than misfits. The early Victorian community, bare
> of schools, or drains, or Factory Acts, had to get itself supplied with the
> common article of standard pattern. The most important business of twen-
> tieth century governments must be to provide not only for minorities but
> even for quite small minorities, and actually for individuals. Every minority,
> every citizen, in fact, has to be supplied just as every soldier in the regiment
> has to have his pair of marching boots.[6]

While appreciating the truth in this image, we must modify it, because
the issue is not only provision—getting more and more refined subdivi-
sions in the kind of services provided. The issue indeed is governmental
provision itself, and the degree to which it can be replaced by other mechanisms which utilize more of the fine grain of society: its voluntary organizations, its ethnic and religious groupings, its neighborhoods, its small
businesses. Peter Berger and Richard Neuhaus have argued for the role of
"mediating structures" in social policy, those subgroupings in society that
stand between the state and the individual. They may be in principle more
effective agents in providing social services, and further worthy of the
support of the state because of all the other benefits they provide to soci-

ety, as in maintaining a democratic polity by giving greater strength to the individual.[7]

Obviously, we must be aware in considering alternate sources for social policy of the dangers both of nostalgia (hoping for a past which we cannot find a way back to, and which in any case did not manage social problems effectively) and of utopia (hoping for ideal circumstances which cannot be created). Guarding as best we can against these dangers, we can nevertheless see, both in the discontents that presently exist and in the experiences with social policy of the last decade, tendencies to disaggregation, decentralization, and the use of nongovernmental actors that will continue to expand. For even in the most advanced and most successful welfare states, one can detect hints of the dissatisfactions I have described, and suggestions that the course of social policy will follow this disaggregated and differentiated pattern I have suggested.

Thus, Hans Zetterberg reports from surveys of the Swedish Institute of Public Opinion that "increased investments in welfare institutions and longer experience with them has not led to a greater appreciation of them. In fact, there has been some decline." Thus, between 1972 and 1978, those who thought health care was getting better declined from 72 percent to 65 percent; those who thought child care was getting better declined from 65 percent to 60 percent; and there was an even more substantial decline in people's judgments of youth care ("better," 49 percent to 29 percent), and care of the aged ("better," 82 percent to 62 percent). Of course these should not be taken as objective judgments. Zetterberg's own explanation is as follows:

> The decline in appreciation can partly be explained by rising expectations, but there is another factor that is even more important. The expansion of social welfare since World War II has largely segregated the consumers of social welfare from normal, everyday life. Children are sent to day nurseries, the unemployed to training centers, sick people to hospitals, and the aged to old people's homes or facilities for the chronically ill. As a rule, where welfare policy has intervened, normal social contacts have been broken up. This is a cruel role for a humanitarian activity. Certainly, people say, we receive help, but do the welfare institutions really care about us? A large number feel negatively about this today . . . In the 1980s, it seems clear that Sweden will have to search for programs that reintegrate care with areas of residence and places of work, strengthening the natural social network of care for others.[8]

There is much here that reminds us of the "mediating structures" perspective of Berger and Neuhaus. But how will it work? How can it work?

I will trace this tendency to what I have called disaggregation or differentiation through four phases. Each is an expression of this desire to break up the large divisions.

The first phase in this development was "participation": that is, the direct involvement of beneficiaries or supposed beneficiaries of policies in shaping them. Beginning with the programs of the Office of Economic Opportunity (the "poverty program") of 1964 and the Model Cities program a few years later, we have seen a remarkable expansion of participation in social programs by beneficiaries of all types.

In each case the argument was put forward by beneficiaries, or rather their representatives, that professionals—whether they were social workers, or city planners, or educators, or doctors, or administrators of institutions for the mentally ill and the mentally retarded—were inadequate in their understanding and should submit to some degree of participation and involvement by beneficiaries or those who spoke for or claimed to speak for them. Increasingly, the right to participation was written into the federal laws under which various programs were set up. Clearly there were some types of service in which the claim to professionalism was so well grounded that the degree of participation had to be limited, and the best example of this is health services. But even here there were spontaneous examples of clinics in which lay people played active roles, even in medical decisions,[9] and there were some federally funded health-care programs which required lay participation in decision making on the choosing of administrators, provision of services, and the like.

Those who claimed participation were many: poor people in areas in which community organizations distributing federal funds were set up, who voted, on the basis of residence or income, for boards; neighborhood residents opposing or urging a road or park or housing; welfare recipients, who created a short-lived Welfare Rights Organization, which was consulted on welfare reform and welfare policy and which, together with other activists, gained a wide range of new rights for welfare recipients; public-housing tenants, who set up organizations and, depending on their effectiveness, were consulted. Some participatory rights were granted in statutory law, some were gained in litigation by public-interest lawyers (lawyers, funded by government or foundations, active in the defense of the rights of a given group of beneficiaries), some were gained through local agitation, some became institutionalized, and some fell by the way.

It is very hard to sum up the extent and effects of participation. It took many forms: the right to be heard, to be informed, to receive notice, to speak at public hearings, to be consulted on budgets, to sit as representatives on boards, to hold a certain percentage of seats on boards. Even without formal rights to participation, movements of the formerly unorganized or if organized not influential—such as the handicapped—have become influential in participating in the shaping of policies that affect them, by appeal to public opinion and, at the extremes, by demonstrations blocking public offices. A separate issue was who in any group of beneficiaries were the proper participants. Thus, it became common for students (or rather, a single student) to become a member of a commission dealing with an educational issue. But the rights of participation in education were primarily defined as parents' rights. In mental hospitals and institutions for the mentally retarded these were again parents' or guardians' rights, though there is an incipient movement claiming that even the mentally retarded can participate, and meetings of the mentally retarded demanding participation have been organized.

But when one reads that such a meeting has been held under the slogan, "Yes, we can!" one must ask, who organized the meeting? and who sustains the movement? and who, indeed, will do the participating? We have seen in the United States a shift from community organizers (with or without larger political objectives), dominant in the later 1960s, to lawyers, increasingly dominant in the later 1970s and the 1980s. Whether lawyers are properly participants when they represent welfare recipients, students, the mentally ill, tenants, prisoners, or the like may be questioned, but in theory a lawyer can only act as the representative of a client. When, then, lawyers for a class that they have gained the right to represent by application to a judge, and on the basis of some evidence that they do represent individual members of the class, negotiate an agreement with the state providers of a service which changes the pattern of provision and in addition gives rights to recipients (which again will be exercised primarily by lawyers), do we indeed have an extension of participation—and by whom?

The issue of course is not completely new. After all, even before the beginning of the movement for participation, individual citizens "participated" in social services by the election of representatives who formulated statutes and approved budgets. But this type of participation hardly helped the individual claimant for a benefit or recipient of a service, dealing with a "street-level bureaucrat" (as the lesser officialdom is now called) applying regulations written by higher-level bureaucrats, all far from the ken of elected representatives.

There is apparently an irrepressible tendency for participation to move from those directly affected to some kind of representative. The elected representative was too distant as we pondered social policy in the mid-1960s. So we had a spurt of participatory provisions in law and regulation, and then, in time, the new representatives, community activists and organizers, began to seem too remote. Now the task of participation is in the hands of lawyers operating under the loose provisions of American law which enable a lawyer to represent a huge class, and to gain victories for that class, often unbeknownst to most of them. There is no escape from the iron law of representation, in which the representative becomes more distant—for one reason, because the represented, having gained some of their ends, become less interested in keeping tabs on the representative.

The original participants in the movement for participation are not happy over these developments. Michael Walzer in a revealing article describes the evolution of the movement for participation initiated by young radical organizers into a pattern of legal representation:

> The peculiar difficulties of participatory democracy as an organizing strategy were much discussed in the 60s and are well known today, certainly to contemporary organizers. Their own commitment is made in the teeth of their knowledge, with considerable sophistication, and they meet the difficulties, I think, with more grace and less hypocrisy than their predecessors. I remember attending a meeting of the Newark Community Union with an SDS organizer in the mid-60s. "Local people" presided; the organizer, resolutely self-effacing, placed himself in the back row; and the participants had to sit sideways on their chairs so that they could make sure of the reactions and opinions of the real chairman of the meeting. No doubt, the problems are the same today . . .
>
> Hence [the organizations] drift, inexorably though always reluctantly, toward a kind of advocacy politics. They are more likely to identify and represent a constituency than to mobilize its members for active struggle. Or, they mobilize a relatively small group of men and women who then provide them with a kind of warrant to act on behalf of similar people in a particular neighborhood or city . . .
>
> What happens is simple enough. Social conflict in the U.S. today has few direct forms. Everywhere, it is mediated by the state. Municipal housing codes, rent control, affirmative action, NLRB regulations: all these shape the course of particular struggles, and they shape it in ways that make advocacy and legal representation as important or more important than political mobilization. Anyone trying to work with tenants, for example, quickly finds himself entangled in the rules that govern the repairs that land-

lords have to make and the rent that tenants can withhold. The rules are complex, and they require interpretation. Soon the organizer is negotiating with city officials; soon he has to bring in lawyers. It will sometimes be useful to organize a demonstration at a city council meeting. Equally often, it will be useful to go to court. And a single tenant withholding rent makes as good a court case as a thousand tenants withholding rent. Once the negotiations and the litigations begin, there is little, in any case, that the tenants can do for themselves.[10]

And yet there are successes of participation, in all its various forms, from outside pressure to sitting as representatives on boards and committees, and this can mold services so they are better adapted to the needs and tastes of specific groups. But it is no easy task striking a balance between the dominance of central and local governments and an anarchic diffusion of power in which representation shifts to those who have less legitimacy than the elected representatives of formal democracy.

Quite different from various forms of beneficiary and client participation, and yet overlapping with it, is decentralization of social services. Once again, the issue of decentralization affects least national schemes of social security—old-age pensions, unemployment compensation, and the like—based on large pools of the insured. Typically, in these cases, a national scheme prevails, and the virtues of centralized administration seem overwhelming.

Decentralization, like participation, is a means of adapting social services to different needs and tastes of beneficiaries and clients, in this case less by the direct route of participation than by the route of bringing authority closer to those upon whom or for whose benefit it is exercised. In the case of a federal state, decentralization can be to states, to cities and smaller communities, or even to nongovernmental or quasi-governmental organizations carrying out functions that public bodies might exercise. The forms of decentralization are so many that no general overview can be given. In addition, they must differ vastly from country to country, depending on the constitutional and legal powers of central government, state or province, city and community, and the degree to which mixed public-private institutions are possible.

Decentralization can be independent of or connected with some degree of participation. In the major conflict over administration of the schools of New York City in 1968, resulting in the decentralization of the school system in 1969, there was administrative decentralization to districts (each of which, however, was of the scale of a city school system in its own right), combined with participation by parents in the election of local boards.[11] The social turmoil of the late 1960s led to other kinds of decentralization: neighborhood city halls, which shortened the distance geographically (and, it was hoped, administratively) between the citizen and city services.

Another form decentralization has taken in the United States stems from a source very different from the racial and ethnic conflicts of the late 1960s which created the decentralized New York City school system. The Republican administrations of Richard Nixon and Ronald Reagan argued that states and communities should have a larger control over the funds that flowed to them for defined and narrow purposes from the federal government. They hoped to replace discrete programs with broad "block grants" which states and cities could use with more freedom. Each program had its defenders and adherents, in Congress and outside, and despite the fact that cities groaned under the administrative task of manipulating scores of programs in the field of children's services, or planning and housing, or health, in order to achieve a given objective, the replacement of so-called categorical programs with block grants did not proceed easily.

Has the attempt to decentralize programs to local levels by means of less burdened and restrictive federal grants improved efficiency and effectiveness? No simple answer, as usual, is possible. Undoubtedly in some fields we see adaptation to local differences that might not have been as easy before. Thus, the cities of the Sunbelt spent their community development funds more for new infrastructure and new recreational facilities, those of the aging Northeast spent more of theirs on rehabilitation. Questions remain. Do those at lower levels of government know better what local needs are than people at higher levels? Even if they know, are they not more subject to powerful local pressures than the national federal level, where a large national interest may be discerned? Does the proportion of funds going to the poorer decline as local power structures gain more authority in expenditure? Are racial and ethnic minorities locked out, and would they do better with national administration? These are some of the questions that arise in our experiments with decentralization.

Yet a third means of disaggregating and differentiating social services may be seen: greater dependence on the free market or on principles derived from the free market. The issue here is not the disbanding of social services and return to the condition that preceded them, in which the market provided income through jobs, and those who could not gain sufficient income this way fended for themselves or resorted to private and community charity. Rather, the objective of this approach is to introduce market-like principles in social services so that a greater degree of choice is possible, a measure of competition is introduced into public monopolies, and a greater degree of efficiency and effectiveness is gained.

One example of a remarkably influential proposal that has only been implemented experimentally but which will not die and which may lead to major changes is that of "vouchers" for public education. First proposed by a great advocate of the efficiency of the market, Milton Friedman, and by a left-wing social analyst concerned with improving the effectiveness of education for poor children and minorities, Christopher Jencks, the proposal continues to have support from both political wings, but now more from the right than from the left. The most sustained argument for educational vouchers has been made by two law professors in California.[12] One proposal reached the level of a statewide referendum in Michigan. (It failed.) Ronald Reagan's administration has consistently supported some kind of voucher.

The educational voucher proposal, which has been explored in some depth, and in part tested, forms the basis for proposals for the use of market principles in other areas. Clearly it does not return education fully to the free market, since public taxation would be used to raise funds for education vouchers, but subsequently choice and competition would be introduced because these publicly provided vouchers could be spent for education in private as well as public schools.

In housing one can see the possibility of vouchers replacing the provision of housing built specifically for the poor, and in some measure this has happened, as housing authorities get out of the business of building in favor of signing contracts to subsidize the rent of low-income tenants in developments built by nonprofit or limited-profit corporations. A kind of limited market is here introduced, as the degree of choice of the low-income family is widened. The spread of small developments widens the locations and type of developments within which low-income families can live with public subsidy. The extensive rent-allowance experiments point to a policy that would widen choice even more.[13]

Both in education and in housing, one key issue is what kind of school or housing would qualify for the public voucher (for the state would not want to underwrite either inadequate schools or slum housing), and what would happen to the stock of public schools and public housing in competition with the schools and housing that would enter the market for government vouchers. Two special issues limit the attractiveness of voucher proposals: first, the problem of relations between church and state—for most private schools are religious schools, sharply restricted in their ability to get public funds by Supreme Court decisions based on the Constitution. And second, the problem of racial segregation, which might be worsened with the freer choice provided by vouchers.

In a limited way, market principles might be considered to prevail in work-training programs. Thousands of different community groups conduct these programs with public funds. There is of course a "political market" determining who gets such funds, but further, one could speculate that programs would be more or less successful in getting trainees depending on how successful they were in placing them in good jobs. One hears little about such an informed choice affecting the future of such projects: it seems the income they provide their trainees is sufficient to get trainees regardless of later job success. On the other hand, vocational schools, for which students pay, are affected by their differential success in getting jobs for their students.

A final example of differentiation and diversification of social services is to be seen in the strong trend to deinstitutionalization. As Zetterberg wrote in commenting on an increase in dissatisfaction with social services in Sweden, "As a rule, where welfare policy has intervened, normal social contacts have been broken up . . . In the 1980s, it seems clear that Sweden will have to search for programs that reintegrate care with areas of residence and places of work, strengthening the natural social network of care for others."[14]

Deinstitutionalization in the United States may be seen as part of this tendency. Deinstitutionalization means taking people out of institutions— whether for children, for the handicapped, for the mentally ill or mentally retarded, for prisoners—and bringing them into closer regular contact with their families, communities of origin, and persons not in need of the special services the institutionalized require. The impact of deinstitutionalization has been greatest on handicapped (mentally or physically) children who, under both federal statute and many legal decisions, are now increasingly "mainstreamed"—put into schools and classes of children without these handicaps. Similarly, children in trouble, whether because of family neglect or their own antisocial actions, are increasingly deinstitutionalized and placed in community settings, houses in normal neighborhoods, where they are to receive treatment in settings approximating everyday life. The movement stems from a change of attitude and belief on the part of theorists and experts affecting programs and legislation, as well as from the powerful role of the courts in requiring more humane treatment, as defined by the public legal advocates and experts.[15] The mentally retarded and the mentally ill are also increasingly placed in "community treatment facilities," ordinary houses, or even apartments or are released into the community.

Something of the same sort may be seen in public housing, where the building of large projects has ceased since the early 1970s; indeed, some large projects have been demolished or reduced in size. New subsidized housing now goes up in small developments, scattered among nonsubsidized populations, and we experiment in reducing the scale of such projects even further in "rent allowance" programs, in which each family or individual is free to seek housing wherever they prefer, which will be subsidized on the basis of income. The push to health maintenance organizations (HMOs), supported by the federal government because they are expected to reduce health costs, may be considered yet another example of deinstitutionalization, in that the poor would receive their health care not in huge charity hospitals, but in smaller settings which we can hope are better attuned to individual needs.

Deinstitutionalization and "strengthening the natural social network" will mean different things in different countries. Thus American social services (leaving aside the major insurance programs of social security, unemployment insurance, and Medicare) are for the poor and those in trouble, while Swedish social services in contrast are in greater degree for "everyone." Thus Swedes may be expected to be uncomfortable over the fact that services to those they consider (or feel they should consider) close to them, part of them, as members of their families or their communities, are provided in segregated settings. On the contrary, the average American feels services are "for them" and is upset when the delinquent youth, the mentally retarded, the mentally ill appear in the house or apartment next door, or when the subsidized development for the poor appears on the next block.

There are many forces leading to deinstitutionalization. On occasion it is cheaper. This may be the case when the mentally ill or retarded are released into the community without sufficient services, though when they are provided with appropriate services community treatment may be more expensive than institutionalization. In certain fields reformers have made powerful arguments for the ineffectiveness of institutions, as in the case of very large housing projects, often running enormous costs for vandalism, security, and vacancies, or institutions for delinquent youth, which may teach crime rather than cure it. Sometimes the parents or the guardians of those incarcerated (the mentally ill or prisoners) demand forms of treatment that take these persons out of institutions. As often, they only demand better facilities within institutions. Whatever the source, public-interest lawyers play an important role in bringing cases leading to large-scale judgments requiring reform.

Deinstitutionalization, it must be pointed out, is a means—just as are participation, decentralization, and resort to the market—of giving important roles to voluntary organizations, often of a religious or ethnic character. If hundreds of small community settings must be created to accommodate thousands of the retarded being released from institutions, then the state prefers to subcontract the management of these houses and apartments to voluntary organizations. If delinquent youth are to be released from institutions, once again voluntary organizations seem ideal for the creation of "halfway houses" and other substitutes. If large numbers of the institutionalized are black or Puerto Rican or Mexican, then new treatment settings drawing upon the cultural and human resources of the group may be more effective in dealing with these youths than state agencies, which must be culturally neutral. The state is suited for the management of institutions, with their huge populations and staffs. It is less suited to handle a house for a dozen youths. This development is all the more likely because institutions for children in trouble or need or for the aged are often run by religious and ethnic groups. Thus the pattern is set, as the state adopts deinstitutionalization, for continuing or revivifying religious and ethnic-group social welfare institutions, now working on contract from the state.

Participation, decentralization, the market, and deinstitutionalization are all ways of *breaking up* large, uniform, national schemes. Indeed, there is only one area of social policy in which the attempt to break up the national schemes to permit more participation, a greater measure of local government control, and more individual choice, is not likely to happen, and this is social security and employment insurance in the United States and its equivalents in other countries. Here there are virtues to national (or statewide) uniformity that seem to outweigh the advantages of small-group participation, local government control, and market principles.

The effect of such changes in social policy is to strengthen "mediating structures," or what Burke called the "small platoons" in society. The local community or neighborhood may find itself running services, building houses, managing planning, overseeing a local health center, or doing more of these than it used to. One may find, depending on the composition and history of a nation, that churches and religious groups undertake these functions. Or organized ethnic and racial groups may do so.

Just as such developments to break up and "devolve" social policy on smaller units might serve to improve the effectiveness and acceptability of social policy, they might also serve—and this is one intention in pressing for such developments—to strengthen mediating structures directly. One could therefore urge such steps in social policy on the ground that inter-mediate sectors in society—neighborhoods, churches, ethnic groups, and trade unions—should be strong and so limit the power of the state, in-crease the felt sense of power of individuals, and in general help create a healthier and more varied social environment.

If these new approaches to diversification of social policy remain pop-ular, as I believe they will, what issues are likely to come up and how can they be dealt with?

The major issue is that of equity—or equality. A national and uniform system can provide the same for everyone. If there is to be participation, local governmental input, market principles, deinstitutionalization, it is in order to adapt services better to the tastes and desires of given groups of beneficiaries, communities, individuals. Inevitably programs will be *different*. Indeed, the entire point of these developments is that they *should* be different. If local governments handle the money for community devel-opment, some of them will put it into low-cost housing, some into parks and playgrounds, some into urban renewal to tempt large industrial or commercial enterprises to relocate into the city. The poor will be better served in one community than another. If there is participation in local child care centers, some will be "progressive" and some will be "tradi-tional." Even if they each spend the same amount per child, the working-class parents may complain about the progressive center, and the middle-class parents about the traditional center. If parents have vouchers and send their children to schools very different from the local public school, the children may get equally expensive educations, but will get very dif-ferent educations. Money alone is not the measure of equality, and yet that is the only thing that can be equalized.

The more we diversify services, the less likely it is that outcomes will be the same, even if services are funded at the same level. This is best seen in education, where different ethnic and racial groups achieve differ-ently even in the same school, and very likely even more differently if the schools begin to reflect specific communities. One may expect the same from child care services. One of the arguments against educational vouchers is that with very different schools chosen by very different groups of parents, the differences in educational achievement among socioeconomic and racial-ethnic (and regional) groups may be greater than if they are in a uniform system. How do we manage conflict over such differences when they can no longer be attributed to underfunded services or unsympathetic government officials and employees?

In ethnically and religiously diverse societies such as ours, there will inevitably be questions of the degree to which public funds may be used for propagation or implementation of ethnic and religious values. Our strictly interpreted constitutional division between church and state leads to a hodgepodge of decisions as to what type of social services conducted by religious groups may receive support, and what may not. Thus, child care centers may be conducted by churches and receive public funds, but elementary and secondary schools may not. And there are other anomalies. But if one deficiency of national and uniform services in a heterogeneous society is that they cannot press a distinctive, consistent, and uniform set of values upon recipients, a weakness of publicly supported, privately provided services is that they may press values repugnant to others. Thus, should a black-studies program, created with local participation, also be a nationalist, separatist, and anti-American program? This is an issue that arose in the late 1960s. As social policy tries to take account of the increasingly diverse societies of the West, issues of this type may be expected to arise in other countries.

For example, in time Germany may feel it should fund social services conducted by minority communities for their children. But consider the following report about Turks in West Berlin: "Because West German schools do not provide what they deem proper religious instruction, Turks have set up 133 Islamic centers that offer prayer meetings and teach the Koran. It is at these Koran schools some Germans contend that Turkish children are taught to hate nonbelievers."[16] In time, as the Turkish population is more permanently established and substantial numbers become citizens, public policy may well have to deal with the issue of whether such schools, and perhaps other social welfare institutions the Turkish community may create, will be better adapted to and more effective in meeting the needs of the Turkish population than public institutions. Should they then be publicly funded in whole or in part? And if they are, with what control over what is taught and what values are spread? This is one of the dilemmas of the types of differentiation we have discussed.

Such schools cannot be expected, to the same degree as a national public system, to inculcate common values and attitudes; but at the same time, they may be expected to be more effective than the common national system. If the effectiveness is measured in a common accepted coin—educational achievement, let us say—no problem may arise. If the measure is inculcation of distinctive and separate values, problems cannot be avoided. Inevitably, devolving to smaller public units or private groups means they will act with the load of values, prejudices, and tastes that derive from a distinctive group experience.

National responses will be differentiated by the degree to which traditions of strong centralization persist and are accepted, and by the degree to which professionalization and respect for professionals and professional judgment are institutionalized. Another important line of differentiation is likely to be the degree of ethnic differentiation and diversity and its legal status. In the United States and in England, minorities are part of the polity, internal to it. They are, in a word, citizens, with citizens' rights. This also means there is a strong basis for the demand for differentiation, participation, and local control, so as to express the different cultures, values, tastes of different groups. In other countries (Germany or France) minorities tend to be considered outsiders, and citizenship means complete identification with the status of Frenchman or German, with no lingering attachments to subnational identities expected. In others, of course (for example, Italy), there are no large groups of minorities or foreigners, but there we have a strong internal differentiation by region which may have some potential consequences for the character of social policy and social services.

In certain respects the United States is unique: in the variety of its ethnic and racial groups, the scale of current permanent immigration, the still-continuing strength of federalism, the diverse arrangements for local government, and the still-strong position of the ideology of the free market. And yet I do not think these differences are so great as to make our developments unique and without interest to other nations. The forces leading to these developments may be seen in some measure everywhere: rising expenditures for social programs, recently arousing more or less disgruntlement and opposition; concern over the effectiveness of some programs (for example, youth employment); concern with perverse effects (particularly on work behavior). Another underlying condition leading to these developments—ethnic and racial diversity—is one which in lesser degree can be found in many economically advanced countries, and these countries must now resign themselves to permanent large populations of different ethnic background and culture.

Nor have these developments run their course in the United States, despite some checks. Participation in some of its variants has lost much of its appeal, but it is far more strongly institutionalized than it was in the 1960s, and in addition it now spreads to the middle classes, which is increasingly effective in overruling professionals in various policy areas. The age of the quiescent consumer, client, beneficiary, inmate is over, and we will see in the future forms of participation (a somewhat benign way of describing what to professionals and experts will appear sabotage of programs) that we have not yet envisaged. Decentralization in the United States, checked by President Nixon's Watergate disaster, resumed under President Reagan. Market and marketlike principles in guiding social policy also expanded under Reagan, though they would have had considerable life even under a Democratic presidency. Deinstitutionalization is a most powerful trend. We will scarcely see its end in the 1980s, and we may yet see forms that are surprising.

But what we will not see is a return to more centralized and uniform schemes of social policy.

7 | Toward a Self-Service Society

Nothing so clearly indicated the future shape of the welfare society as the surprising convergence, in one respect, of the proposals of two such disparate regimes as the new Socialist government of France and the new right-wing Republican government of the United States in 1981. Both committed themselves to a substantial degree of decentralization or devolution of central governmental powers. The hallowed tradition of prefectoral government in France was due for substantial overhaul and change, giving greater powers to locally elected executives and legislatures. The enormous structure of central government grants to state and local government in the United States was also slated for substantial overhaul.

The most radical proposals of the Reagan administration to return social programs to the states remained only proposals. Thus the suggestion in the 1982 State of the Union message that Aid to Families with Dependent Children (welfare), food stamps, social services—all involving some mix of federal and state and local powers, whether in source of funds, in law and regulation, or administration—become strictly state programs, went nowhere.

Nor was there a smooth course for the proposals of France's Socialist government for decentralization. Nevertheless, the fact that such proposals were made, both in the United States and in France, tells us something, and it is not minor. The decentralization proposed by the Reagan administration in its first budget that was solely the product of the new administration was matched in weight by the proposals of the Mitterand government. As a correspondent of the *New York Times* wrote: "If nationalization has attracted the controversies and the headlines, the biggest potential change that the Socialists aim to introduce is to bring about decentralization, giving to local elected officials and assemblies a portion of the polit-

ical and economic power that flowed to Paris over the centuries. The de-
concentration of power in France, in fact, may be the most fundamental
and paradoxical impulse in the political current that won last Spring's
election."[1]

These proposals tell us something, but what that something is will be
disputed. One thing is clear: the new decentralization proposals have little
to do with any drive for simple *administrative* efficiency. This has been
one argument for decentralization, both of government and of major corporate enterprises, for a long time: give the administrator close to the
scene of operations greater freedom, and he will work more effectively;
the overall aims of the organization will be better accomplished if administrators down the line are given greater authority. This purely administrative objective of decentralization has little to do with present-day proposals: their aim is not to increase the authority of lesser, centrally appointed
administrators, but to reduce it, and to increase the power and weight of
people outside the administrative chain altogether, those on whom administrators operate: beneficiaries, clients, and people, the public, the taxpayers. This distinction should be clear.

And whatever the fate of these large-scale proposals, one thing we were
being told is that, at the crudest level, such proposals were seen as politically popular. From the point of view of the future of social policy, they
suggest a good deal of discomfort with the long-received idea that central
administration, national rules are in various ways more desirable than local variation. At the level of political philosophy, they suggest growing
discontent with the capacities of a centralized government to manage effectively, efficiently, or equitably the vast range of social services that have
become a major—indeed *the* major—part of the activities of government.

Clearly there is little discontent evidenced with certain traditional functions of central government. No one is suggesting that the armed forces
be decentralized, that the central bank be disestablished, that management
of customs and tariffs be decentralized. The thrust toward decentralization
affects for the most part the greatly expanded *newer* functions of central
government, its social policies.

Admittedly one will find very different ideological backgrounds to the
similar movements in the United States and France. But both have much
in common in rejecting arguments, from different sources, for the efficiency and justice of centralized government ruling over local powers. In
France we have the Jacobin and plebiscitarian traditions, according to
which, in one central action of revolution or assent, the people's will is

enthroned. In this tradition one does not argue with the fact that the people's will, centralized in government, happens to express itself through bureaucracy and prefects distant from the people. But now this argument is made. As Richard Eder argues, there is now a split, among Socialists and among the French as a whole, between

> the impulse to centralize and concentrate, and the longing to decentralize and escape concentration . . . One part of the Socialist tradition, the older, thinks in terms of using concentrated government power to break up big private interests and impose a change of society. But the millions of young Socialist voters, and the school teachers and bank clerks they sent to fill the benches of the National Assembly . . . , think in quite different terms.
>
> They belong to the generation that took to the streets in 1968. Their lives, or at least their heads, have been nurtured on social and personal experiment, the ecology movement, and community action, emerging—in approximately equal measure—libertarian, intolerant and with a rooted distrust of bigness.[2]

The thrust toward decentralization in the United States draws from other roots, much deeper in American political traditions, the federal origins of the American commonwealth, but it gets occasional, grudging, partial approval from the rebels of the 1960s and 1970s, who were no part of the Reagan coalition. The United States has had no experience of revolutionary and plebiscitarian traditions arguing for strong centralized government. In contrast, the support for the development of strong central government came from the progressive reform movement of the last decades of the nineteenth century and the first half of the twentieth. This progressive reform movement turned against the exotic efflorescences that had been thrust up in American local government—the various elected boards, the numerous wards electing their own representatives, the excessively large local councils—and demanded simplification along the lines of the efficient American corporation. In many cities all lesser elected authorities were swept away, to be replaced by one small elected board which appointed a city manager to manage, in corporation style, the affairs of the city. In other cities they were replaced by a strong mayor with one council. All during the twentieth century, indeed until the mid-1960s, proposals for city reform generally followed this progressive tradition: make the mayor or the board of supervisors stronger. Let the people's will be expressed by electing executives *with power*—and then let the executives act. The strong mayor, elected by the people, will have the power to implement the people's will, as against the independent school, police, health, and other independent boards operating specific city functions. If he failed, he could be turned out. If he succeeded, he could be rewarded by reelection. Power being centralized, responsibility would be centralized. Similarly, the federal government was favored by reformers over the states. This was the modest American equivalent of revolutionary democratic plebiscitarianism, and progressive reformers saw little virtue in maintaining the separation of powers called for in our national conservative Constitution.

Thus both in France and the United States there were arguments that defended centralization, even if the political history that had led to them, and the ideological origins of the arguments defending them, were quite different.

The 1960s brought a change in the United States on the local level; in the 1980s it spread to the national level. At the local level, in the 1960s for the first time the intellectual elite and the liberal national media abandoned the argument of progressive reformers and supported demands for *decentralization* of city functions. No, it was now argued, in favor of abandoning sixty-year-old positions, the education of city children was *not* best accomplished by a strong central board of education, appointing, in corporate management style, a strong superintendent. The specific interests of black children and other poor children required an input from parents, from community leaders, from children themselves. The experts of centralized local government could not be trusted. Decentralization schemes of one sort or another were put into effect in various cities; advisory boards of parents, community leaders, students flourished. And similarly with other functions of city government: one big city hall was to be replaced by many little city halls.

This development was encouraged by the ferment of the poverty programs, in which federal government reformers in the Johnson administration combined with local groups of the black and the poor to undermine the powers of mayors, city councils, and state governors and legislatures by creating new elected bodies for the communities, disposing of money that came to them from the federal government directly, rather than through city hall and state capital. Almost every piece of federal legislation that provided for specific social services during the 1960s and 1970s—and the legislative machine of central government did not stop grinding out new programs until well into the 1970s, regardless of the skepticism of Republican presidents—required the setting up of advisory groups which included beneficiaries of these programs or their representatives. The progressive reform impulse which had tried to create an independent and powerful executive responsible to the elected officials, and only through them to the electorate, withered; the restrictions on executives became more and more complex, owing in large measure to the desire to "empower" clients and beneficiaries. Public executives were continuously challenged by beneficiaries and clients, and, with the support of the courts, hobbled.

When in the late 1960s the slogans of "black power" and "power to the people" were raised in the United States and were in large measure implemented, as the poverty program and the model cities program required elected bodies representing the poor to be created in the large cities as a condition for receiving federal grants, they represented a radical demand. The rhetoric of black power borrowed from the movements against imperialism and, through them, from traditional socialist and communist denunciations of a central power that was seen as dominated by capitalists and capitalism. The more moderate slogan used to demand local control of schools, "community control," was also seen as coming from the left. And yet there was always an ambiguity in the slogan "community control." It was, after all, community control that the South fought for when it defended segregated schools, that the North defended in opposing busing for desegregation, and it was community control that well-to-do suburbs in the United States possessed, and retained. People aside from those black and poor found attractive the concept of "power to the people," if not the specific slogan. By the second half of the 1970s, the notion of power to the people no longer could be characterized as "left" or "right." It represented a generalized disillusionment with big government that encompassed all parts of the political spectrum. Peter Berger and Richard Neuhaus appropriated the concept of power to the people in their pamphlet, *To Empower People,* published by the conservative American Enterprise Institute. Like the earlier black power and community control advocates, they argued against unresponsive and inflexible central governmental bureaucracies. They were as critical of them as the earlier critics from the left had been, and they were able to transfer the emotional charge in the notion of people's power so that it could now be used by the right—and as effectively as the left had used it in the 1960s. It is an intriguing development, and not a matter of the inappropriate capture of a term by those who mean the opposite, as in the case of the expropriation of "democracy" by undemocratic communist regimes through sheer weight of rhetoric and propaganda. For the discontent with powerful government is felt by people of every status, of all degrees of wealth and power. What they would concretely want to do to lift this weight does vary considerably, for of course people's interests depend on their circumstances. But almost all feel the problem of big government and at least nourish the hope that it can be brought closer to people and made more responsive.

In the 1960s the formal aspect of democracy—elections, representation, the judiciary—was attacked by those on the left under the slogans of power to the people, or black power, or community control, as inadequate to guarantee people's rights. By the late 1970s they were joined by groups on the right, who also wanted to get out from under the one big system, the one big program, to pursue diverse individual and community goals. It would appear that it is generally recognized now that elections are no longer sufficient to recognize a popular role in government. When government does so much to affect lives and livelihoods, people demand a more continuous representation and influence, and this can be wielded in many ways.

Those who demanded power to the people did not necessarily represent those for whom they claimed to be demanding power. Nor did the fact of the devolution of power to lower levels automatically provide greater satisfaction or a better solution to the problems for which power was being wielded. The arguments over community control and community participation became quite complex. The experience was so varied that it was not possible to pronounce any overall judgment as to the success of the new wind. But one thing was clear: whatever the failures of community control and community participation, whatever the modification of the new procedures built on the slogan of more power to the people, the thesis that had characterized the old progressivism, with its enthronement of the strong mayor, the single powerful board, the strong federal government, and the wisdom of the experts they selected, a thesis that had been dominant for sixty years or more among liberal experts on government, never returned. Community control and participation may not have been a great success, but it led to no desire to return to a situation that was seen as even less desirable.

And so the superintendent of schools is no longer seen primarily as a nonpolitical expert to whom deference is owed. He has to satisfy his constituency—a difficult matter when it is generally so fiercely divided on questions of progressive versus traditional educational techniques, sex education, and racial integration. His life is harder, and he lasts for a shorter time. He was always a politician, someone who had to make use of available people and resources to achieve an end, but he once did so with the aura of the nonpartisan professional expert. No longer.

In the field of health, although doctors still receive respect for their skills, they are no longer dominant in the argument over the management of health resources. Indeed, even their skills in achieving health are now subjected to sophisticated criticism, as we find out how much illness is caused by doctors, drugs, and hospitals, and how much good health and care can be ascribed to strong families, friendships, and traditional networks generally.[3]

The decline of perfect faith in experts in education and health is matched by a decline of faith in experts in the third great branch of social policy, welfare. In the United States in the early 1960s, policies on welfare assistance—public assistance to the destitute—were dominated by experts. The first major reform of welfare, instituted in the administration of President Kennedy, was entirely dominated by social worker experts, who urged increased services. A new wave of experts dominated the proposed reforms of the early Nixon administration, and of the Carter administration, as the social workers were thrust aside by the economists, who wanted to change a system based on assessment of resources and needs to an income-maintenance program, with subtly graduated incentives that would encourage work and discourage family abandonment. When the Reagan administration took office, as I have indicated, no expert advice, whether from social workers, economists, or sociologists, was called upon. Cuts in levels of support and increased compulsion to work, either by lowered benefits or direct requirements, were now favored.[4]

In each area, admittedly, disillusion with experts takes different forms. In education it takes the form of a distrust of the professionally qualified teacher or principal, a greater willingness to entrust education to schools that represent the values of distinctive cultural, ethnic, religious, and geographic communities, even if their administrators and teachers are less well qualified, or the physical facilities are not as extensive and well equipped as those of the public facilities. Indeed, there is a movement to return decisions over education to the individual parents of individual children. Thus there are now organizations that assist parents in educating their children at home, even though this gets parents into difficulty with laws requiring school attendance. There is a more widely based movement, drawing support from various parts of the political spectrum, for education vouchers, with which parents would be able to use public funds to finance their child's education in any school, public or nonpublic. And there has been a recent and surprising growth of a variety of private schools.[5]

In the field of health care, distrust of experts leads to a great range of self-help groups for various ailments (alcoholism, obesity, mental health problems), and the greater involvement of parents, lay practitioners, and midwives in childbirth, as well as a burst of litigation charging malpractice. In the field of welfare, distrust of experts takes the form of abandoning reform and returning more powers to the states.

Decentralization or devolution is of course only one of the themes which reflect a surprising disillusionment, discussed in Chapter 6, with the capacities of a central state, utilizing experts and advanced techniques, to provide satisfactorily the range of social services to its citizens that it has taken on. Everywhere we find a growing demand for "accountability," a term that is itself fairly new in its application to social services. There was a time when only the elected official was expected to be accountable. It is now the teacher, the policeman, the doctor, the social worker who must be accountable. The mechanisms of accountability have created endless difficulties as they confront the realities of professionalization and the need for many social service professionals working directly with ordinary people to exercise a vast range of discretion.[6]

Another new term in discussion of social services is "privatization," which means the use of the market and market-disciplined services (in other words, profit-making services) to take up functions in health, housing, and education in competition with public services formerly seen as more appropriate and efficient as providers in these areas for a number of reasons ("spillover" or "neighborhood" effects, the ignorance of consumers, and so on).[7]

Clearly one reason there is so much interest in new approaches to social policy is the seemingly unmanageable growth in cost of public social services. If the costs of pensions for the aged threaten to become an unmanageable burden, perhaps one can make better use of the private sector for pension plans to supplement a more modest government minimum, with the additional advantage of encouraging an increase in savings, seen as necessary in the United States and the United Kingdom, because savings are too low to support the proper level of investment for modernization of the economy.[8] If subsidies for publicly built housing become enormous, perhaps a rent supplement, leaving the poor free to seek the housing that satisfies them, might reduce costs and provide as much or more satisfaction. If health costs become frightening, perhaps competition can be arranged among health maintenance organizations or proprietary (for-profit) hospitals, or other for-profit health services may provide some services more economically than public agencies (though on that score there is much skepticism). Market-oriented thinking, driven by concern for public costs, proceeds apace and has even gone so far as to spawn a proposal for private prisons: imprisonment is enormously expensive, and there is a strong need for the building of new prisons at great capital costs. Would private prisons help? Perhaps.[9]

But I would like to emphasize two other reasons for this discontent with centralized government social services which have been less noted. One is, in a word, the growing personal affluence that has paradoxically accompanied growing pressure on public funds. This leads many to believe they could manage the education of their children, or their own health, more effectively and with greater satisfaction—and perhaps with a better return for their expenditure—by allocating their own funds to a range of competing organizations, public and private, rather than by paying taxes. This is the interest argument of, among others, Arthur Seldon, of the Institute for Economic Affairs in London. He emphasizes the growing economic capacity of a substantial number of citizens, so that in contrast to the period of the origins of the welfare state, when only the rich could protect themselves from the accidents and disasters of an industrial society, and the great masses needed state insurance or a basic minimum of protection provided by the state, now increasing numbers can manage for themselves. He summarizes his argument by asserting that the "welfare state is withering away because it is being undermined by market forces in changing conditions of supply and demand for education, medicine, housing, pensions, and lesser components of 'welfare.'" And he adds further, as a "proposition from everyday empirical observation, . . . that consumers are increasingly able to pay for, and will therefore demand, better education, medicine, housing and pensions than the state supplies, and that suppliers are increasingly able to provide alternatives in the market."[10]

He points, for example, to the fact that there is an increasing shift in England to home ownership, now widely seen as more desirable than council tenancy in subsidized public housing. In the United Kingdom, as in the United States, there is an increasing problem of filling housing designed for the poor: much well-built, subsidized housing now stands empty.[11] The United Kingdom led Europe and the United States, perhaps led the world, in providing a high standard of housing in the postwar period. Thus it may be in the vanguard of a development that may affect vast quantities of postwar housing built on the Continent as standards rise and people demand more space and more ground. It is also true that more than simple demands for better amenities have led to the abandonment of housing in the United Kingdom and the United States: there has been poor planning, unexpected migrations. In the United States, in particular, crime, changing ethnic composition, and many other issues have led to this phenomenon. But one factor that facilitates it is the availability of better housing in the private sector.

Seldon's argument is made generally, but most strongly in connection with two major state services, health and education. He argues that the fact that Britain spends a smaller percentage of its GNP on health than those countries that have better-developed private health insurance systems and a greater range of nonstate health services does not indicate efficiency and avoidance of waste, which is the common interpretation of the low British expenditure for health. Seldon argues that third-party payments always inflate costs. Lower expenditure in Britain merely indicates a lower quality and volume of health services, lower than people would buy if they had a free market. He makes comparisons with the United States, that, to the surprise of this American, favor the United States, despite its enormous health costs, because by certain indices better service is provided.[12]

He also argues, based on the interesting studies of E. G. West, that a nonstate system would have led to greater expenditure by individuals for the education of their children than is the case in a tax-supported system, and to better education as well, because of the benefits of competition and individual choice.[13]

One need not take the argument whole to see that in a society where the poor are only the bottom 10 or 20 percent of the population, tastes in public policy will change. And these tastes may tend toward diversity and variety and a degree of individual tailoring that it will be increasingly difficult for state services to satisfy.

One effect of the welfare state is that people will increasingly have to provide common labor services for themselves: wages will have risen too high, because the level of minimum state provision is high, to permit a large servant class, a large class of handymen, helpers, babysitters. This is the argument of Assar Lindbeck as to what is happening in Sweden. He writes that the effect of high state expenditures and high marginal tax rates is that "public authorities increasingly take care of *intimate personal services,* while households increasingly take care of *things* like gardening and the repair of houses, durable consumer goods, and the like."[14] But perhaps technological advance will permit in time the management within the family of some social services that are now the province of the welfare state. Consider the argument of Jonathan Gershuny, who notes the increasing incorporation of personal services into the household by means of investment in durable consumer goods such as automobiles, washing machines, tools, television sets. One wonders whether this domestication of services such as entertainment and household management may not spread (perhaps by way of computers?) to education and health and social services. This is one implication of Gershuny's work.[15]

We may point more briefly to a second unnoted development which encourages the kind of changes we are seeing in the welfare state. This is the demand of more people for more participation in government generally, owing to a higher level of education. Daniel P. Moynihan pointed out with prescience twenty years ago that political scientists who suggested there was "too much" government in the United States—too many states, counties, cities and towns, special districts for all sorts of functions—and American government would have to be and would indeed be increasingly simplified by centralization, were wrong. There was no feeling in those parts of the United States where the best-educated lived, the new middle-class suburbs, that there was "too much" government: they participated actively and had no desire for a lesser role in government or for fewer forums in which to exercise citizenship. At the time this went against the thinking of the experts who examined American government. But it turned out Moynihan was right: and as education spread, as the average American saw himself as being as good as or better than the average social worker, teacher, policeman, or government administrator, it was inevitable that he (and increasingly she) would demand a greater role in government and in management of the services government provided. This meant, when it came to social services, a taste for less central government and for more local government, which competent citizens could influence. I believe this is an important underlying factor in what is happening in the social services. And thus the new demand for accountability. This is the background against which we should view the development of social services in the 1980s.

Central government today believes it should be capable of satisfying all human needs and all public demands, even the demand for less central government, more power to local government, local communities. Decentralization proposals are one such example. But perhaps the easiest way for government to satisfy the demand for less central government is to stay out of the way of those services and programs that arise without governmental assistance to satisfy some need of individuals or communities, and that manage well enough without the assistance of government. This would appear to be easy for government to do at a time (and what time is different?) of increasing pressure on governmental resources. But there are all too many cases in which such activities have attracted governmental subsidy—and have suffered thereby. In part this is a matter of government seeking to do more because legislators want to show enterprise, because government executives like larger budgets, staffs, functions. But of course it is also true that at a time when government does so much, those who carry on important functions without governmental assistance, and with the use of volunteers and contributed funds, look enviously at the opportunity to attract government funds, provided effortlessly (to the agency and the recipient) through the tax levy and providing professional staff instead of volunteers' time. One prefers to have a ready source of funds and staff rather than to scrounge for them, understandably. But some case studies and comments as to what happens when government funds and staff replace voluntary funds and staff suggest that an increase in resources is accompanied by a decline in the ability of the service to fill needs satisfactorily. Consider these three examples from the United States and Canada.

1. For some twenty-five years or more, old people limited in their ability to cook for themselves or go out for meals have been benefiting from "meals-on-wheels" programs in the United States, and undoubtedly elsewhere. The need for these programs has expanded not only because the numbers of the old have risen, but because more of them can now afford to live alone in their own homes and apartments, rather than with children or in institutions. (Thus we see how an improvement in one area, the financial circumstances of the old, creates a need in another.) There are hundreds, perhaps thousands, of such programs in the United States. They are small, they rely on volunteers to cook and deliver the meals (often using their own cars and their own gasoline), they are sponsored by churches and other voluntary organizations, they depend on local contributions for the cost of food and whatever paid staff they use, they generally charge for the meals but provide them free for those who cannot afford to pay. All in all, a useful and economical service.

In 1978 Congress voted amendments that would provide such programs with federal assistance. The federal government already funded "congregate nutrition services" (meals provided in a central place) for the elderly; it would now add meals-on-wheels. Michael P. Balzano has analyzed Congress's action and has pointed to a host of potential difficulties for the meals-on-wheels programs. There are already a mass of regulations that apply to congregate nutrition services, which are much larger than meals-on-wheels programs; the same or very similar regulations will undoubtedly apply to meals-on-wheels. These regulations require, among other things, that each service must provide more than one hundred meals daily, that they provide auxiliary social services to meals recipients, that they cooperate with area-wide comprehensive planning agencies for the elderly, that they train their staffs and send them to seminars provided by the Administration on Aging, that they provide evidence the areas they work in have suitable concentrations of the aged poor, that they have full-time directors. When one realizes that meals-on-wheels programs are small, use volunteers, are unacquainted with elaborate paperwork and regulations involved in qualifying for federal assistance, one sees the difficulties they will have in satisfying government regulations and in also remaining what they are.

One notes other requirements that prelude difficulty: for example, nutrition education must be provided—this to persons who have been used to cooking and providing for themselves all their lives. A project council must be organized, and there are elaborate regulations as to how it must be constituted and what its powers will be. The project must favor for employment persons over sixty and those from minority groups. Projects "must be located in facilities where the eligible individuals will feel free to visit," so as "not to offend the cultural and ethnic preferences" of eligible individuals. Yet many of the meals-on-wheels programs are centered on a Catholic church, or a Jewish synagogue, or an ethnic community organization, and are designed for the people of that community. Another regulation specifies in detail what a government-funded meal must consist of, which can scarcely take into account regional or ethnic tastes.

All these are the kinds of regulations one expects from a government program, and all, in the abstract, are good things, but all, in combination, make it difficult for the small meals-on-wheels programs to qualify. Of course, they can ignore government largesse and continue as they are. But even this raises difficulties: larger, better-funded government programs (and the existing, larger-scaled congregate nutrition programs are eager to expand into this new field) may take away their clientele, provide salaries to their volunteers, and altogether quite undermine the existence of the small, voluntary, inexpensive programs. In some sense, they may provide better services but, one suspects, at a much higher cost, as government workers replace volunteers.[16]

2. A second example, also suggestive rather than decisive. Robert Woodson describes the history of a voluntary program begun by a charismatic couple, Falakka and David Fattah, in Philadelphia to house black youths and rescue them from a life centered around fighting gangs and to encourage them, in an authoritarian family atmosphere, in habits of responsible work. As their work became well known, state agencies became interested in referring to them youngsters in trouble because of juvenile delinquency, or those without responsible homes in which they could live. Public funds thus became available to a small and successful enterprise, the House of Umoja, which had been dependent totally on what its young residents could earn, its founders could provide, and what local churches and merchants would offer. With resultant difficulties:

> With salaries came differential pay scales and a regular forty-hour work week. [All the residents of the house had been required to work, but now some became state employees, engaging in counseling and services, previously voluntarily performed.] Umoja residents could not understand why, if all were members of a family and therefore equally favored and equally responsible, it was necessary to pay some more than others . . . The first state evaluation claimed that David Fattah's contribution was not essential to the overall performance of the Umoja program, and recommended that his position be eliminated. David, who is the father of the house, spends most of his time in the streets helping to resolve gang disputes . . . The state also raised questions about Umoja's board of directors, which is made up of the Fattahs and their six sons. The state contended that the board of directors should be broadened to include other elements of the segments of the community.

All these were certainly reasonable state requirements, but they did not sit well with what was clearly an authoritarian atmosphere devoted to inculcating traditional values, but one which had nevertheless been successful in keeping youths out of trouble and was of interest to the state for just this reason.[17]

There was another interesting conflict between this distinctive neighborhood-based organization, with its unique culture, and state rules. The state required that a full-time social worker be employed by the House of Umoja: "His first act was to organize group therapy sessions, with himself as therapist and group leader. This proposal met with immediate resistance by the Umoja family . . . In another instance the social worker attempted to gain confidence and trust from some of the youngsters by suggesting that house rules be changed to increase allowances. He was chided by house leaders and informed that youngsters could receive additional income only if they performed an additional chore."[18]

3. The best-researched example of the potential negative effects of public funding on voluntary programs is the work of Donald A. Erickson of the graduate school of education at the University of California at Los Angeles, on the impact of a new program of provincial funding on private schools, sectarian and nonsectarian, in the province of British Columbia, Canada. He reports, to quote one summary,

> that the Canadian province's program has brought a variety of problems to participating private schools; among them:
> —Increased regulation by the province, with accompanying paperwork.
> —Less enthusiasm among students for their teachers, classes, and school, and loss of the students' sense that their schools are in some way "special."
> —Less responsiveness by the schools to parents, and more to the province, and less involvement in school affairs by parents who begin to see the schools as belonging to the government, not to them.
> —Teachers who are much more concerned about pay and fringe benefits than before; the researcher calls this a "union mentality."
> —A dependence on the new funds that could result in financial disaster for the schools if they are removed.[19]

The mechanism involved in gaining loyalty from students and parents by imperiled private schools depends in part on the necessity for all to cooperate in permitting the school to survive. A further quotation from this report:

> Mr. Erickson suspects that the social climate that distinguishes independent schools from public schools has "deteriorated" because of the inflow of public money.
> He argues that the financial jeopardy the aid alleviates often contributes positively to the climate of independent schools—conversely, the loss of that climate of jeopardy weakens the parents' sense that they "own" the schools.
> When public money is not available, he said, everyone involved in the school has an additional incentive to perform well. Because the survival of the school is directly dependent on satisfied clientele, teachers and administrators are more responsive to parents.
> "When a private school is short of money," he said, "it appears that people pull together as a result. Teachers, viewing the financial sacrifices of parents and the conscientiousness of students, redouble their efforts."[20]

The three examples are of forms of social, health, and educational services that were developed without the assistance of government and, at least in one case, because of dissatisfaction with government's ability to deal with distinctive values (mostly religious); they describe a process in which governmental assistance—admittedly desired by those conducting the service—created problems. A "substitution effect," as described by Sam Peltzman and E. G. West, came into play; volunteers provided less assistance, contributors less money, workers less commitment. A bureaucratic effect came into the picture: rules that required uniformity and better conditions for government workers, that tried to satisfy professional standards both hurt services and raised costs. So not only did nongovernmental input decline, but the new governmental bureaucratic standards increased costs—and thus there were two reasons for an increase in the costs of services.

This is undoubtedly what happened with the creation of third-party payment systems for the elderly and the poor in health: costs zoomed far beyond any projections and far beyond any parallel increase in actual services provided, or in their effectiveness. One reason is a substitution effect. For care once provided for the elderly or the poor free or at a reduced cost, providers are now reimbursed at full or close to full cost by the insurers and the government. It is interesting to work through the value of this substitution. Certainly its value to doctors is clear; their income goes up because all their time in providing medical service to the poor is now reimbursed. Hospitals are aided to increase staff and to reimburse them better. The poor now have assured access to health care, not dependent on charity, though from various accounts they are apparently treated by doctors and staff as if charity were still being provided, even though full reimbursement of their charges is made by government.

How do we draw up the balance? It may be good for the souls of doctors that they provide medical service free to the poor. But is it good for the health of the poor that they must request medical care and take it as charity?

There are two traditions at war here within the social services. One emphasizes rights independent of income. All should have the same rights to education, health, social services; and to ensure equal rights government should pay for all and put all on the same level. But can a service that involves a personal and intimate relationship work only on the basis of a market transaction guaranteed by the state? In his controversial study of blood collection services, R. M. Titmuss himself emphasized the importance of a direct human relationship, an altruistic relationship, a community-based relationship.[21] He argued for this as against a market relationship, as existed in the collection of blood in the United States. But one can make Titmuss's argument against a bureaucratic relationship as organized by government, too. We are now acquainted with the fact that it is not only the search for profits that leads to the distortion and shaving of intended objectives—it is also the search by the providers of service for a comfortable, secure, and well-paid position with government. Titmuss turned his study of blood collection services in England against the market; it can also be turned against government. The remarkable failure, both in socialism and in the early arguments for extensive governmental social services, to see that the government-paid providers of service form an interest group whose interest is not only the provision of better service but also self-interest, has in recent years been radically corrected. No one can talk about the social services without taking the interests of teachers, doctors and nurses and hospital employees, social workers into account.

We thus have, from many sources, an argument for voluntary services or for nonstate action that must be taken seriously. But if we take a larger perspective, does all this matter? In view of the enormous sums that now flow to government through the tax system for pensions, health, education, social services of all types, is it anything more than romanticism to see a role for the nonstate sector? This question cannot really be answered, but part of an answer is possible. One can see the emergence of more respect for the voluntary, nonstate, and even market sectors in social policy, and one can project a somewhat larger role for them in the future.

It is also true that one must expect very different developments in different countries. How different each is becomes evident from reading the very interesting book by Ralph M. Kramer, *Voluntary Agencies in the Welfare State.*[22] It is a major work addressed to the problems of voluntary agencies, not from the relatively narrow point of view from which voluntary services are generally discussed, but from a larger perspective which takes seriously their possibilities as major actors in the social services. Kramer concentrates on voluntary agencies dealing with the mentally and physically handicapped in four countries—the United States, England, the Netherlands, and Israel. In each the relationship of the state to the voluntary agencies is quite different. The United States has a strong tradition of voluntary agencies, and they fulfill a wide range of services. England has a similar tradition, once as fully developed, undoubtedly more seriously undermined by the greater scope of state-provided services. The Netherlands is distinctive in its social division into confessional groups which are basic providers of social and educational services, but with almost full governmental funding. In Israel a very strong voluntary tradition existed before the state itself was formed. Indeed, what became the state of Israel existed in fully developed embryo form as a group of voluntary institutions without state power. This was a unique constellation. The voluntary tradition maintained its great power, not only because of this history, but because of important religious divisions, and because religious, trade union, and party groups within the country were linked with affiliates or supporters outside the state of Israel.

I suspect one would find a similar variety of institutions in each of the major countries of the Continent. In each, traditions of nonstate action would be quite different, but I doubt that in any they are fully absent. In one country it may be local communities that have a long tradition of service (as in the case of hospitals in Sweden), in others it may be the church, in others trade unions. One must recognize that degrees of dissatisfaction with state provisions will vary from country to country; degrees of internal division which provide support for independent types of education or social or health services committed to certain values will also vary; and the notion of any uniform policy of greater dependence on nonstate social services is unrealistic. It may be that a mix of dissatisfaction with and suspicion of state services and faith in (or nostalgia for) individual and nonstate group action to deal with problems is distinctively Anglo-Saxon, characteristic of England and the United States but not found to the same degree elsewhere, and underlying both may be a stronger individualism. Some public opinion data suggest such a pattern.[23]

In the United Kingdom, as in the United States, the debate about the possible role of the nonstate sector in social service delivery is intense. Consider, as one item in the debate, an editorial in *New Society*, normally a strong supporter of the welfare state: "Lately . . . the idea of voluntary service has been making a comeback; and, as with cuts in public service, the process actually began to take real shape under the last Labour government. It was Labour . . . which expanded the housing association movement to provide an alternative to council housing in the rented market. Voluntary organizations have underpinned much of the youth opportunities and job creation activity which began in the late 1970's. But it is the advent of a Conservative government, dedicated to rolling back the frontiers of the state, which has given the voluntary movement real hope for a much larger role in the future."[24] The editorial goes on to describe a number of recent publications[25] and their arguments for the voluntary "non-statutory" sector. These arguments include such factors as the smaller size of agencies, their local and nonbureaucratic character, opportunities for participation and exchange, and cost-effectiveness. The editorial points out that an expansion of the nonstatutory sector to permit it to take up roles now performed by government would also subject it to the same bureaucratic ills that bother us in government; it urges decentralization and devolution as perhaps gaining some of the reputed advantages of the nonstatutory sectors; and it calls for cooperation between the two sectors. That President Reagan should have launched a strong initiative to expand the role of the voluntary sector is understandable; that we should find parallel rumblings in the United Kingdom is more interesting.[26]

Voluntarism evokes so many negative feelings and connotations that it is important to underscore the fact that much of the new interest in voluntarism is not in restoring a situation in which the wealthy bestowed charity on the grateful poor, but in sustaining and strengthening patterns of what might better be called self-help. Our societies are increasingly middle-class, with a broad range of rights distributed throughout the population, with destitution limited to a small minority, with the wealthy limited, because of taxation, in their opportunities to bestow charity on the princely scale of the nineteenth and the early twentieth century, and with discretionary income now available to the broad middle range of society. In such societies, the voluntary or nonstatutory sector must be, will be, very different from what it was in an earlier day. It should be noted that the three examples discussed above of voluntary action affected by the provision of state aid do not show any sharp line drawn between helper and those to be helped; in a dominantly middle-class society, this is perhaps inevitably the dominant form that volunteering, activity to provide a service independently of the state, will take.

Ralph Kramer points out that this is a new characteristic of voluntary social service: "There is a proliferation of new voluntary organizations, particularly peer self-help groups and alternative agencies, in which the line between the helper and the helped, between board member, staff member, and client, is intentionally obscured." He points out that the movements that founded organizations during the 1950s to assist persons suffering from mental handicaps, multiple sclerosis, polio, and cerebral palsy were movements of parents and family members of those suffering from these ailments. It remains the case that the best kind of help is self-help: the motivations are strongest, the controls that lead to decent behavior are most evident, the forces that undermine a commitment to the primary objective (that is, problems of money, status, permanent protection of jobs) are weakest. "In contrast to traditional agencies for the blind and the deaf, organizations to benefit these more recently 'discovered' handicaps are organizations *of* the handicapped and their guardians."

Admittedly self-help may vary in type from the direct provision of concrete assistance and sympathy to the insistence that government do more (a common role for advocacy groups), to the insistence, particularly in the United States, that the courts establish certain rights that will lead to someone—whether government, individual employers, local providers of service, or voluntary agencies—doing more under the threat of findings of discrimination. For example, in the United States, organizations composed principally of the handicapped themselves have been successful in requiring the federal government to require that all physical facilities in institutions that get some federal assistance (and it is a rare school, library, college, university, hospital, transportation facility, or local government office that does not get some assistance) be made available to those in wheelchairs.

The new forms of voluntarism and the new growth of the nonstatutory sector thus do not partake of the weaknesses that have been criticized as "Lady Bountiful" charity. It is the self-help of those who wish to escape from an overbearing government or from other large bureaucratic institutions, and who wish, too, to make their institutions more responsive.

Societies in which people are better educated, more affluent, more differentiated in tastes and needs, more self-confident of their own powers (though this last is more arguable), and less confident of their power to control large institutions and in particular large governmental institutions must explore this path to voluntary and nonstatutory approaches to satisfying their needs. And there is some evidence, apart from political or polemical urgings of the virtue of this course, that this is what they have been doing. At any rate, this is what Kramer, on the basis of his study of four countries, believes:

> Direct service volunteering [in contrast to volunteering to raise funds] can be viewed within the larger context of the great resurgence of volunteerism in the 1970's. A marked increase in the size, scope, and diversity of volunteer effort occurred in the United States and England and, to a lesser extent, in the Netherlands and Israel. In all these countries, there was greater public recognition of the value of volunteerism for society and of its contribution to pluralism, mutual aid, and individual well-being, as well as

its usefulness as an organizational resource. Aided by an increase in leisure time, a rising standard of living in the advanced industrial countries, and a wider diffusion of the norms of citizen participation and self-help, support for volunteer participation has broadened.

Kramer describes the enormous scale of voluntary action:

In England, a national survey estimated that 16 per cent of the population— 5,000,000 persons—work voluntarily for an organization each week. Almost half of the respondents were involved in fund raising, and 18 per cent reported various forms of personal service . . . In the United States, a widely publicized "guesstimate" is that one out of every four persons over the age of thirteen does some form of voluntary work weekly, of which 10 per cent is in the field of social welfare. Studies by the U.S. Department of Labor show an estimated growth in the number of volunteers from 22,000,000 to 37,000,000 between 1965 and 1974, including 4,500,000 volunteers over the age of sixty-five, representing an almost fourfold increase in this category in a decade . . . In the Netherlands, a government official estimated that there are 250,000 volunteers of all types.[27]

There are, potentially, ingenious ways of increasing the supply of volunteers. In the United States, as Kramer reports, "tangible rewards" are given, such as "high school and university course credit for students and the use of volunteer experience to qualify for admission to graduate schools." This is the sort of thing the rather free-wheeling system of higher education in the United States, with its greater diversity of institutions and its lighter controls from government and higher authority, can do—and it is true it is done less because of any desire to increase the supply of volunteers than because of the need of hard-pressed institutions of higher education to compete. This kind of "creative" approach, one suspects, would be harder to undertake on the Continent. Creative proposals can be multiplied: Roger Masters, professor of government at Dartmouth, suggests the substitution of personal labor, reimbursed at a low standard rate, for taxes. He writes: "Can the richest society on earth seriously be too poor to pay its schoolteachers and policemen?" If we take Lindbeck's analysis seriously, and if they must be paid at a high rate through taxes, the answer is clearly "yes." Masters proposes that "any individual taxpayer (or member of his family) would be allowed to pay part or all of his local taxes by working at an approved public project."[28] He goes on to develop details, which need not concern us. The point is that voluntarism and self-help can be encouraged by a variety of public measures.

*   *   *

A greater degree of voluntarism and of self-help and expansion of the nonstatutory sector can do a great deal to provide for needs and services that, if provided through the state, require a heavy burden of taxation, high deficits, and a variety of unpleasant and increasingly dangerous economic developments. High taxation reduces incentives to work and make productive investments and increases incentives to participate in the barter or underground economy or to conceal income. High deficits contribute, directly or psychologically, to inflation, again encouraging a flight from productive economic investment to various measures to escape its consequences. We should think of ways to meet needs with a lesser degree of dependence on public action. Public pensions can be supplemented by private saving; housing, whether new or rehabilitated or better maintained, can be provided through the market or voluntary organizations of various types;[29] education can also be in large measure provided outside the state;[30] and the entire range of social services for the destitute, the mentally and physically handicapped, and neglected children has always involved as a primary component family assistance and the assistance of voluntary organizations based on religion, ethnicity, locality, or charitable instincts. All this was formerly seen as a residue of the past. The growth of the welfare state, despite its enormous successes, suggests there are limits beyond which societies and states must depend on these basic and primal social ties that are created within the family or developed over time on the basis of a variety of attachments.

Certainly the role of the state is crucial. But it must more and more consider partnerships with the variety of voluntary, market, nonstatutory organizations and mechanisms that we find in each society according to its distinctive history. And states must ponder the possibility that their own actions undermine the ability of societies to respond to needs as well as or better than the state can.

8 | "Superstition" and Social Policy

The sociologist who engages himself with social policy plays many roles. In his humblest capacity, he can conduct research on what people want, what they like and don't like, their numbers and family status and the like, and certainly this is an essential base for any informed and decent social policy. Some sociologists have had greater ambitions than simply providing the data for social policy, valuable and necessary as this is. Sociology has always been more than numbers, though admittedly when it got past numbers it became, in the eyes of many, vague, diffuse, and imprecise. The large ambition of sociology in its relations with social policy has been to guide it: using its insights into what we may call the fine structure of society—family, community, informal association—sociologists have hoped to assist in creating a more humane and, by that token, more effective social policy. Sociologists have hoped that they could help create designs for housing, neighborhoods, and towns that would make the lives of communities and families and individuals more satisfying or, at the very least, would not damage them; they have hoped they could provide schemes for welfare and the support of the poor that would contribute to overcoming dependency and help develop poor children into more effective adults or, at the very least, would not contribute to family breakup and poor relations between parents and children, husbands and wives. And similarly they have hoped that they could contribute to policies for health, to policies for the treatment of delinquent and wayward children, and to other branches of social policy insights arising from their studies of communities, families, and individuals in different stages of life.

Their contribution has characteristically taken a very specific form. They have emphasized the role of informal associations and social networks based on residence in a single neighborhood in giving people a sense of security, a base of values, a location from which they emerge to do their business with the more formal institutions of society—school, workplace, government office—and to which they return to find support. They see family, nuclear and extended, playing the same role. Basically sociologists have studied the informal structure of society: not government as such, not the economy, not public administration, but social bonds. And their role has been very much one of "viewing with alarm" as they have seen these bonds weaken. Students of the family have described how its traditional functions have been taken over by school and social institutions and how the focusing of energies within the family has been weakened by work and its demands outside the family, by mass amusements and by the values spread by the mass media. Students of community have described how its bonds have been weakened as work and residence are separated, as the church and other locally based institutions decline before the competition of the mass media, and as the new values spread by school, science, and mass media make the values and satisfactions of the community appear narrow, mean, and stultifying.

If all of modern society and what underlies it—technology, economic development, rapid transportation and communication, and the new values they permit—conspired to undermine the social bonds of community and family, there would be, one might sadly conclude, little one could do about it. People would not give up the undoubted truths of science and the conveniences it makes possible; they would not give up modern economic development and its necessary separation of work from community and family; they would not give up the pleasures, specious though they may be, of rapid transportation and communication. Nothing could be done about all that—or, in any case, in modern democratic societies, very little—but something undoubtedly could be done, using the insights and research of sociologists and other social scientists, to assist social policies to enhance community and family values rather than undermine them. In particular, one would think, this task would be all the easier because the social policies in question were devised to strengthen community and family. This was the purpose of better housing for the poor, better planning of residential communities, welfare assistance for those in distress, improved health policies, and the other branches of social policy. Thus it was with a certain enthusiasm and self-confidence that sociologists in the postwar world began to get involved with the study of these policies, with high hopes that they could contribute to their design and improvement.

It is too much to say flatly that these hopes have been disappointed. There are as many sociologists—indeed more—working in areas of public policy today as ever before, and one can see the effects in public policy of various critiques that sociologists and other social-science-oriented analysts have launched against particularly egregious faults in public policy. In the United States and in Britain the massive clearance of deteriorated urban properties and the construction of tall residential blocks for low-income tenants are now in bad odor. Certainly the kind of work that Herbert Gans, Marc Fried, Michael Young, Peter Wilmott and others did in describing and appreciating the tight network of social connections that existed in what planners considered slum neighborhoods contributed to the present distaste for massive clearance and massive residential structures to replace them. Of course other things contributed too, and very likely were more influential. For example, local political resistance to mega-schemes of urban renewal and the experience of families with children in high residential towers, undoubtedly played a role, as did more sophisticated studies of relative cost, which did not give an encouraging picture of the total costs of large schemes and large structures. Undoubtedly the work of sociologists and anthropologists has led to much greater sensitivity, on the part of many social service workers and administrators, to the possible harm or ineffectiveness of policies applied across the board without sufficient regard for social networks.

Nevertheless, it remains true, in Britain as well as America, that the optimistic vision of social science guiding policy by the use of its knowledge of the fine structure of society, of how policy impinges on family, neighborhood, community, has faded considerably. One hears more and more voices raised against the impersonal administrator, the blind effects of large policies. The startling thing is that these policies were designed *precisely* to respond to human needs, to shore up families, to strengthen neighborhoods, ensure better care for damaged children, better rehabilitation for juvenile delinquents. The work of the modern state is increasingly a work for social ends: for better housing, health, education, treatment of the handicapped; for the overcoming of poverty and distress. Yet the modern state reminds one, in the descriptions of its critics, of a friendly but clumsy giant, who, in his efforts to help, tramples delicate and sensitive growths.

In the United States housing and neighborhood policies are revised, sometimes radically, every few years, and with considerable input from social scientists. And yet the cry goes up ever louder that neighborhoods are ignored, are made incapable of maintaining their distinctive values and integrity, very often just because of government policies, which make it difficult to maintain old buildings or to keep out undesirable individuals and uses. Our welfare system also undergoes continual expansion and correction, again with input from social scientists. Despite all these changes, almost everyone agrees that welfare, or some feature of it, is damaging the family, encouraging family breakup, encouraging fathers to abandon children, even though many of the changes welfare has undergone in the past twenty years were designed to overcome just these untoward efforts.

No one disputes that the welfare state is here to stay. The alarm of which I speak is by no means an alarm simply from the right, from conservative nostalgia for a time when the state stood apart from any concern for social ills and devoted itself to war and roads. In the United States, and in Britain too, the defense of the neighborhood attracts a confusing mixture of people on both the right and the left. Milton Kotler, a man of the left and a socialist, was one of its first advocates, and he has been joined by Michael Novak and Peter Berger and many others who are of a different political persuasion. The defense of the family was once reserved to Catholic bishops and conservative Republicans critical of the possible impact on the family of large-scale government programs designed to help it. But it became a leading theme of President Carter's campaign and has now lost its conservative ideological coloring. And so we have the paradox that a state increasingly concerned with social ends, with family, neighborhood, individual growth and development, and which now devotes far more of its resources to such ends than to war and traditional state functions, finds itself increasingly under attack for blindness, ineffectiveness, damage, insensitivity.

Indeed, in the present atmosphere it is not surprising to find a distinguished French social scientist, Claude Lévi-Strauss, echoing, in his suspicion of the state and enthusiastic support for small structures based on irrational custom, Edmund Burke. In a fascinating essay published in *New Society*, Lévi-Strauss came out squarely for English irrationality against French reason as a support for liberty and a defense against state despotism. He surprisingly finds a French predecessor for such a position. He informs us that the first anthropological textbook to appear in French, by Jean Nicholas Démeunier, in 1776, already made the distinction. Démeunier, after pointing out that the ancients avoided flouting popular beliefs, whatever their absurdity, went on to write:

"The same could be said of the English. The proud islanders look with pity on writers who combat religious prejudice: they laugh at their efforts; and convinced as they are that the human race is born to fall into error, they do not strive to destroy superstitions which would soon be replaced by others. But the freedom of the press and the constitution of their government allow them to attack their administrators, and they are forever sounding the alarm against despotism."

Continuing, Lévi-Strauss writes:

Almost 100 years later, in 1871, Renan in *La Réforme Intellectuelle en France* was to make similar observations: "England has attained the most liberal condition that the world has so far seen by developing her mediaeval institutions . . . Freedom in England . . . stems from the country's entire history and from the respect equally accorded to the rights of the King, the rights of the Lords and those of the Commons and corporations of every kind . . ." . . . Across the Channel, Sir Henry Sumner Maine had written ten years earlier in his famous book, *Ancient Law:* "The philosophers of France, in their eagerness to escape from what they deemed a superstition of the priests, flung themselves headlong into a superstition of the lawyers."
Of these three parallel observations, Démeunier's goes the farthest, by unhesitatingly locating superstition as the surest antidote to despotism. His opinion is relevant today, for despotism is still with us; if anyone wonders where, I would reply by borrowing another expression from Renan, even more apposite today than it was in his own time: it is to be found in the arrogant impertinence of the administration which exerts an intolerable dictatorship over every citizen.

In making these remarks, of course, Lévi-Strauss is not referring to the same contrast between France and England that Démeunier, Renan, and Maine referred to: Britain, alas, is no longer devoted to its ancient superstitions and vigorously engages in modifying daily its laws, the ancient boundaries of its communities, the rights of old corporations and bodies. Thus, in its respect for superstition, it is no longer very different from France. Rather Lévi-Strauss is pointing to the paradoxical fact that old, traditional, and unexamined institutions and customs—he does not hesitate to call them "superstitions," but we have given them milder and more acceptable names—serve as a barrier to, as he puts it, quoting Renan, "the arrogant impertinence of the administration," which is to be found in Britain today as well as in France, in our backward welfare state of the United States as well as in the most advanced welfare states, such as Sweden.

And why does he defend superstition or, as I have put, traditions and customs and institutions whose roots are obscure? Because in them we find

> that infinite number of everyday allegiances, the web of private solidarities which save the individual from being crushed by society as a whole, while preserving society from being pulverized into a mass of interchangeable and anonymous atoms; the threads that bind every individual to a certain locality, way of life and form of belief or unbelief; all of which do not merely balance each other, like Montesquieu's separated powers, but also constitute a set of counter-forces capable of resisting abuses of public power.
>
> By placing freedom on what is claimed to be a rational basis, one is condemning it to forgo this rich content and thus, to undermine its own foundations. For the attachment to freedom is all the stronger when the rights it is asked to protect are based in part on the irrational: they consist of those minute privileges, perhaps negligible inequalities which while they do not interfere with a general equality nevertheless provide the individual with some firm footholds in his immediate surroundings.[1]

I have referred before to the work of Peter Berger, who has emphasized the same theme. He speaks of family, neighborhood, church, and informal associations as mediating structures—mediating between the individual and the state—and he emphasizes, as Lévi-Strauss and those he quotes do, the significance of mediating structures in preserving liberty. Writing with Richard Neuhaus on this theme, he also summons a body of great social thinkers to the support of mediating structures:

> This understanding of mediating structures is sympathetic to Edmund Burke's claim: "To be attached to the subdivision, to love the little platoon we belong to in society, is the first principle (the germ as it were) of public affections." And it is sympathetic to Alexis de Tocqueville's conclusions drawn from his observation of Americans: "In democratic societies the science of association is the mother of science; the progress of all the rest depends on the progress it has made." Marx, too, was concerned about the destruction of community, and the glimpse he gives us of post-revolutionary society is strongly reminiscent of Burke's "little platoons."

To Berger, just as to Lévi-Strauss, an excessive rationality is suspect:

> Liberalism's blindness can be traced to its Enlightenment roots. Enlightenment thought is abstract, universalistic, addicted to what Burke called "geometry" in social policy. The concrete particularities of mediating structures find an inhospitable soil in the liberal garden. There the great concern is for the individual ("the rights of man") and for a just public order, but anything

"in between" is viewed as irrelevant, as even an obstacle, to the rational ordering of society. What lies in between is dismissed, to the extent it can be, as superstition, bigotry, or (more recently) cultural lag.[2]

And so Lévi-Strauss and Berger, from very different traditions, are willing to band together in defense of the fine structure, the mediating structure, family, community, and association, of superstition, and are willing to risk what is today lèse-majesté in criticizing an overexact attachment to equality, rationality, and the rights of the individual.

Thus they give a grand role to superstition—custom, tradition, irrational allegiances—in the defense of liberty, one to which Tocqueville and Burke also pointed, as well as Démeunier, Renan, and Maine. I would emphasize too another role: custom, tradition, irrational allegiance give people a footing, an identity, a sense of modest security, all of which are of greater importance than ever in a society in which mega-institutions, private and public, dominate and spread a sense of helplessness among ordinary people. And yet it is just this—custom, tradition, irrational allegiance, superstition—that modern social policy cannot accommodate itself to, despite all the shouting and advice from the sidelines by journalists and sociologists, anthropologists and architectural critics, socialists and free enterprisers. Despite every effort to adapt social policy to the needs of the fine structure of society, one senses, with some gloom, that it is not an easy task. It is easier to recognize these needs symbolically than to do something about them in concrete policy.

The social scientist, because he is rooted in an intellectual tradition that has emphasized mediating structures and their significance, comes to social policy with his little kit of suggestions: take into account the way the family and small informal groups use the community, note that families are linked together in self-defense and that policy should not divide them, leave space for informal associations whether devoted to religion, politics, culture, or just gossip; and to all this the administrator nods in approval. But if the voices I have quoted are correct—and I could have added many more from many political orientations—we still face, and more oppressively than ever, the "arrogant impertinence of the administration." The insights of the social scientist still seem incapable of incorporation, at least to the extent many of us would wish and many of us have believed possible, into the work of the administrator.

Why? I would like to elaborate on three contemporary sources of this inability to adapt. They are as serious, I believe, as the first consideration that generally comes to mind, the simple imperviousness of bureaucracies, their arrogance because they have power and cannot easily be disciplined, and their insistence—an insistence which in many ways we can justify—on fixed rules and regulations which they apply to all. All this is true. Bureaucracy is inevitably with us if the state tries to undertake a great deal for a great many people, as it does and as we wish it to. There are, however, some other reasons for the frustration of social scientists to which I would like to point.

The first is that we are still in large measure ignorant of how the fine structure of society works, and often we simply give the wrong advice, which if taken may only advance the sickness we are trying to arrest. A few examples will make the point.

The American poverty program, which began in 1964, and which in any recognizable form was drawing to an end in 1973, owed much to the advice of social scientists. Poverty, they pointed out, was not only a matter of money. It was also a matter of the spirit and could only be overcome, in all the senses which we consider important, by the involvement of the poor themselves in the programs that were to assist them. There was much in this insight that was correct and that we must continue to cling to. But "maximum feasible participation," the programmatic thrust that encapsulated these insights, seemed in the end to do not very much to involve the poor significantly in the programs that were to assist them. There has been much discussion of what went wrong, but it is agreed generally that one result was the creation of a new "povertocracy," a bureaucracy of the poor, drawn admittedly in part from among those who originally qualified as poor, but which was rapidly involved in the infighting for salaries, positions, and prestige that afflict all bureaucracies. Further, since local government already had a democratic base, these new poverty bureaucracies were drawn into futile conflict with more legitimately based institutions. In time one heard the same disdain for the poverty politicians from the social scientists who had assisted them in coming to their modest power as the social scientists had originally felt for the elected officials whom they had tried to circumvent with the new poverty establishment.

What went wrong? There have been a number of explanations, but the point is the advice was taken, and then the results were not those expected. I would say that our analysis was incomplete, based on ignorance and insufficient knowledge of how municipal government and local communities worked.

Another example: in 1967, the Supreme Court of the United States issued one of its most important decisions in social policy in a case titled *in re Gault,* dealing with the rights of juveniles brought before family courts. This decision laid down rules as to how these courts were to operate, which reduced their informal aspect and made them more like proceedings for criminal offenses before regularly constituted courts. These rules called for written notice, the right to counsel, and the privilege against self-incrimination. The family courts had originally been set up to deal with wayward juveniles in a way that would encourage sympathetic consideration of their problems based on wide-ranging consultation, without adherence to strict rules of procedure or evidence, with parents and teachers and others who might not, in strict legal terms, have standing to participate. But since these informal proceedings could result in serious punishment, such as confinement of juveniles in training schools, the Court decided to extend to juveniles the protection given to adults charged with offenses.

Up to now we are dealing only with the familiar extension of rights under the Constitution through interpretations of the Supreme Court, and social scientists play no role. But the Court also took notice of social scientific investigations into the operation of juvenile courts, and, as Donald Horowitz tells the story in his fascinating book *The Courts and Social Policy,* it used these findings to buttress its decision. The Court quoted a government commission report which asserted: "There is increasing evidence that the informal procedures, contrary to original expectations, may themselves constitute a further obstacle to effective treatment of the delinquent to the extent they engender in the child a sense of injustice provoked by seemingly all-powerful and challengeless exercise of authority by judges and probation officers." Underlying this quotation, as Horowitz shows, were speculations by social scientists, not evidence, for there was as yet no research on this question. In this case, evidence did accumulate later that these speculations, reasonable as they might appear, were simply unfounded: juveniles, it turns out, consider both informal and formal procedures fair.[3] This support for the new dispensation was wrong. But the replacement of the informal with the formal procedures has had serious effects: to my mind, it contributes to the undermining of confidence in and acceptance of informal social controls, which is one evil of social policy we are trying to address.

For yet a third example: in 1972, an important case was brought before a federal judge in New York, charging that a large state institution for mentally retarded children deprived them of their constitutional rights because of their poor custodial treatment and the inadequacy of efforts to rehabilitate them. The judge agreed and, on the basis of expert advice, decreed that this institution, which then contained 5,000 persons, reflecting a period in treatment when large institutions were considered efficient (and perhaps effective), treated people unconstitutionally, and that treatment must be given in institutions containing no more than 250. He set up a panel of experts to oversee the state's efforts in meeting the judgment. In the meantime New York State, apparently deciding on its own and on the basis of the best knowledge in the field that institutions for retarded children should be much smaller, commissioned a distinguished American architect, Richard Meier, to design what would be the finest institution of its type—they are now called development centers—for 384 retarded children. The institution is completed, is visited regularly by architects who consider it a wonder, but contains no children. For in the meantime experts have concluded that institutions of even 250, which they had advised the judge to consider as an upper limit, are also too large, for such children should be treated in small homelike settings. The state has been forbidden to transfer children to the new center.[4] Perhaps the experts are right, but if they are right now, they were wrong when they were advising the judge a mere five years earlier, and since any public action requires time for planning, bids, construction, and the like, one conclusion a judge may come to the next time is, don't trust the experts the first time around, for they may change their minds by the time your decree is ready to produce effects.

So, one reason why the efforts of social scientists to get social policy to take account of the fine structure of society and mediating structures fail is that they may simply be wrong and suggest something that will not have the effect they hope, even if incorporated into policy.

There is a second problem. Those of us who consider the workings of social policy in different societies have the suspicion that policy will work better in taking account of fine structure when a society is homogeneous than when it is heterogeneous. Thus things work better in Sweden, we tend to think, than in Britain; better in Britain than in the United States. Increasing heterogeneity—ethnic, racial, regional—should have something to do with it, as well as other things one can think of, such as size and political traditions. And when we consider the role of superstitions—customs and traditions and mediating institutions—we can see why. Administrators and administered are likelier to be bound by the same superstitions in a homogeneous country; what the administrator proposes or insists upon in social policy is less likely to be seen as wrong, immoral or amoral, or incomprehensible, since it is based on the common understanding of what is the proper way to raise children, or how the family should be constituted, or what is proper behavior in the community or in the search for work. In a mixed society one will run into clashes of superstitions, clashes of the unexamined grounds on which people act.

One can point to many examples. In the case of Britain, the admirable police worked wonderfully well as long as they were dealing with British people. They had more trouble with the Irish. They now have a great deal of trouble with the West Indians. Our police, who have been of Irish background, worked better when the cities were in larger measure Irish. They did not do quite as well with Italians and Jews, and have done worst of all with blacks and Puerto Ricans.

The theme can, of course, be explored through other social services too. Alvin Schorr some time ago studied French social assistants, who undertake the role of child care officer, giving advice, distributing necessary funds, and ensuring their proper use. They have a wide range of authority and act with a certain authoritativeness. My impression is that an American welfare worker would be much more inhibited in doing so. She would limit herself to the regulations. There are many reasons for the confidence and authoritativeness of the French social assistant compared to her American parallel, but one perhaps is the narrower range of cultural styles—of superstitions of child care, if you will—that the French worker meets. In the French case, there would be a less challenged national cultural norm, which the social assistant would think was perfectly proper to propose or even forcefully to insist upon.[5]

There are other examples on the Continent of close supervision of families with problems and troubles—special housing projects in the Netherlands and Germany, for example, in which problem families are concentrated for what we might call social training. We do not have anything of the sort in the United States. Once again, the question of how intrusive state authorities should dare to be with family styles would come up. The American housing administrator would be limited to either expelling or simply allowing the problem family to stay and make life increasingly unbearable for its neighbors. Of course in the case of both the welfare worker and the housing administrator, there is another and perhaps more important reason for caution and restraint in the United States, and that is the explosive development of legal rights—including rights to privacy and to services without quid pro quo requirements—that limits administrators, and that is a big story in its own right. But certainly one reason for this restraint and caution, whose other side is dependence on administrative and legal rule and bureaucratic distance, is cultural diversity.

But now what is the effect of withdrawal and distance from family and personal problems of social workers and administrators because of ignorance of customs and their meanings, and because of fear of arousing anger and distrust? (I have left out the case, probably still more common, of the unwarranted self-confidence and authoritativeness of social service providers in dealing with those of other cultures, but I do believe the trend, because of developments in professional education and law, is in the direction I have emphasized.) One effect is that teaching a common norm of behavior is radically neglected. We fail to instill the customs and habits, the superstitions, that a complex society needs to work well and smoothly. The social service provider loses authority because he is now seen as fulfilling only formal legal regulations rather than operating on the basis of a common morality, a role he has eschewed. Admittedly, there is a positive side to this development. Distinctive customs and habits can continue unconstrained; they have many virtues, like all old customs and traditions. But if our large objective is the concern of the administrator for the fine structure of society—not only what existed in the past, but what is continually being created—the results can only be negative, because the administrator and service provider withdraw from playing any role in this field, whether one of censure or approval, sanction or reward. A cold neutral eye ranging indifferently over the range of custom replaces an involved one, whether warm or authoritative, because diversity and the legal doctrines which defend it have made this appear intrusive, unwarranted, impertinent.

This diversity, most distinctive in the United States, becomes more common in countries that were once more homogeneous. England has minority races of substantial size, France and Germany have large permanent communities of North African and Asian origin, and even Sweden, until recently the most homogeneous of countries, ethnically, religiously, culturally, now has large minorities and a rising concern about them.

This new diversity is not only ethnic and racial and religious, it is also a diversity of values and customs in societies in which old superstitions have weakened gravely and new ones have not become binding. In every developed society, I imagine, the social service providers scratch their heads over the familylike commune, the homosexual couple, and other new familylike forms which their rules and regulations fit poorly.

Clearly sociologists have a role to play in the development of social policy for diverse and heterogeneous societies. But the record is not encouraging. The problems are difficult, and the social scientist is hampered first by his strong empathy for the superstitions that exist, which makes the development of a new binding norm, a new superstition, difficult, and second by his ignorance of how, without gravely interfering with human rights and dignity, a new norm is to be created and imposed.

And this brings me to the third, and to me the most important, reason why social policy finds it difficult to accept and incorporate the insights of the social sciences on the fine structure of society. It is because the doctrines of equality and human rights, the ruling doctrines of our age, make it impossible to leave superstitions, customs, and traditions in darkness, playing their role with the conscious or unconscious connivance of government. All dark places must now be illuminated by the doctrine of equality and rights. Everything must be made straight and plain and clear and equal. And this is a contradiction limiting the effectiveness of social policy that I do not see any way to overcome. Perhaps our knowledge will expand so we can give good advice; perhaps we will find ways to accommodate cultural diversity while still maintaining the authority and effectiveness of social services and social service providers. But I wonder how a doctrine that demands the most exact and severe examination of inequalities and differences in rights can be reconciled with the need to accommodate, to take into account, and, for decent social functioning, indeed to maintain social relations which have always taken for granted inequalities and differences in rights. The type case is the family, where children of different ages, mothers, and fathers, have different roles, roles which cannot be easily reconciled with our societies'—all our societies'—thrust to perfect equality.

Let me give some examples. If America is backward in social policy, it is forward in rights, and other societies, equally committed to the extension of equality and development of rights, look to the United States as a leader in this respect. If we have, as we do, lawyers and associations and movements devoted to children's rights and women's rights and minority rights, it is not because, I would argue, we are most backward in these respects, but because our constitutional and legal system makes it easier to claim and establish rights, and this is considered abroad one aspect of American practice and experience to be followed rather than avoided. Yet ľ cannot feel undisturbed satisfaction as we achieve ever more equality and protection for individual rights.

Consider the case of a girl below the age of eighteen or sixteen, who establishes in court the right to have an abortion without the permission of her parents. One wonders how, in simple practical terms, such a case is carried to court. Presumably the girl made contact with a lawyer (or perhaps vice versa) who was willing or eager to be her legal counselor and to act for her against her parents. One can argue that this is only a further step in the freeing of children from parental tyranny. Children have rights to privacy and the control of their own fate, and the state will protect these against the family. The child has been made more equal, more rights have been guaranteed to her. But one considers the other side of it. The authority of the parents has been reduced. If, as I believe, the education of children, their rearing, the establishment of moral attitudes and values in them is still primarily the role of the family, then this role has been further undermined, and it is already terribly weakened.

Another example. The Supreme Court's rulings on obscenity and pornography made it difficult, on the grounds of the right to free speech, for communities to control the rapidly growing business of pornography— pornographic movies and live displays, adult bookstores, massage parlors, and the like. Now many communities look upon these as disgusting and disgraceful, and they would like to ban such displays. They have found it very difficult. Just as a family is prevented from being the family it would like to be (and when I say this, I of course take for granted that that must be the decision of the parents), communities, through the expansion of rights, are prevented from being the communities they would like to be. (Some authoritative Supreme Court rulings do allow some rights to community attitudes in determining whether local ordinances may limit pornography, and some techniques have been developed for control.)

Another example: the Supreme Court has ruled, five to four, that a zoning ordinance which limited those who could occupy a house to a nuclear family, and which was used to prevent grandchildren from living regularly with grandparents, is unconstitutional. I personally agree with this ruling. The ordinance seems to have been applied blindly and bureaucratically, and as the majority of the Court wrote, "The tradition of uncles, aunts, cousins and grandparents sharing a household has roots equally venerable and equally deserving of constitutional recognition" as local autonomy. Different kinds of family and family structure are equally legitimate and have equal rights. But the community has been further constrained in the kind of community it creates. And when it is constrained, a cynicism and indifference develop as to the possibility of informal or formal social control, the cynicism and indifference that make large American cities harder places in which to live and raise children than suburbs.

Not all court rulings and administrative rulings move toward the establishment of equality and rights against traditional patterns and superstitions, but most do. Sometimes the right of a community as such is maintained against individuals and groups who want to change its patterns. Thus, the Supreme Court has been cautious in requiring communities to zone for poorer families or multiple dwelling units, if their plans do not call for them, though these plans have been challenged on grounds of discrimination against the poor and blacks. Some state courts have, on the other hand, required such plans. In another important case, the Supreme Court ruled that the Amish community could not be required to send its children to school until the age of sixteen, as the state of Wisconsin required, an age which the conservative Amish believed provided more education, secular and worldly, than was good for their children if they were to maintain the pattern of God-fearing living in closely knit agricultural communities that they have maintained for centuries. Here the "right" of the child to an advanced education, required by the state, was balanced by the "right" of the community to maintain its old patterns—superstitions—and the community won out.

I do not underestimate the difficulties of making such rulings, but their general direction has been to further equality, establishing the same rights for persons in different roles. It is distinctive roles that we are talking about when we consider the fine structure of society. And there is no question that rights undermine roles. And so we have Lévi-Strauss pleading for rights based on the irrational, the unequal: "They consist of those minute privileges, perhaps negligible inequalities, which, while they do not interfere with a general equality, nevertheless provide the individual with some firm footholds in his immediate surroundings."[6] The family, the community, the Amish . . . But an inequality that is negligible to one will be formidable to others, something which is infamous and must be banned by law or administrative or judicial decree.

I have suggested three reasons why the good advice of sociologists, reminding people of the fine structure of society, of mediating structures, of custom, traditions, irrational allegiance, and superstition, even when accepted, seems not to have improved social policy. Or not as much as we expected thirty years ago. Is there anything to be done? If the problem is ignorance, we can try to improve social science; although progress is not marked, I think we understand many things better today than we did ten or twenty years ago: at least we understand how much we didn't understand. If the problem is diversity of culture and ethnicity and values, the matter is more serious, but once again this is one area in which social science has not been helpless: it has been able to teach administrators and social workers the virtues of a variety of informal institutions, and it has been able to show that common functions and common roles link the institutions and customs and irrationalities of very different cultures. But when it comes to the rising passion for equality and human rights secured against all authority, whatever its sources, one sees no particular role for social science. For there we come to a real clash of values, one which will have to be fought out. And as in all serious conflicts, there is much to be said for both sides—for the insistence on a radical and egalitarian individualism, and for the defense of complex institutions and social bonds, incorporating authority and, if you will, superstition, as an unexamined but accepted element. But if the first side wins out, as it is doing, the hope that social policy will assist in creating more harmonious social relations, better-working social institutions, broadly accepted as the decent and right way to order society, cannot be realized.

9 | Why Isn't There More Equality?

Whatever justice, unqualified, may mean, it now seems established that social justice means equality. And one would think we must know much more about equality today than we did some years ago, before the publication of John Rawls's *A Theory of Justice*. That is, we must know more if the measure of knowledge is the number of books and articles that have been devoted in the years since its publication to justice as equality. Much of the discussion has been sparked by Rawls's book, which seems to have become the text and the starting point for any discussion of justice. I will also use it as such, but only as a prelude to what will be basically an empirical discussion. The question I would like to consider is: why is it, when so many philosophers agree that the measure of social justice is equality, that we do not have more of it?

There are many anomalies mixed up in this simple question. Consider that apace with this huge outpouring of discussion of justice as equality—and, for the most part, strong advocacy of justice as equality (who, after all, is for inequality?)—there seems to have been no increase in equality in this country as measured by the distribution of income. It has remained remarkably stable for some thirty years or more. This is surprising, not because of the near-universal commitment by American social philosophers to justice as equality (for, after all, philosophers do not rule the world), but because we had in the 1960s and 1970s an outpouring of measures to increase social justice—social justice *defined as* equality.

If one looks at the domestic part of the national budget, which has grown enormously in the past two decades, one finds that almost all of the growth has been occasioned by measures of social justice instituted, if not to create equality, to achieve more equality. These great measures include expansion of social security, the institution of Medicaid, Medicare, food stamps, grants and loans to college students, assistance to communities for education of poor children, an expansion of rent subsidies and of welfare, and various kinds of assistance to expand the rights (and presumably the income) of minorities, women, the handicapped, and the aged. In the face of this enormous outpouring of activity, which has greatly increased the proportion of personal income taken by the federal government for purposes of expanding equality, the distribution of income remains stable—and unequal.

Now, clearly, I am using only one kind of measure to judge the effectiveness of the expansion of social policies to increase equality, the measure of distribution of income. But that happens to be the favored measure of most proponents of more equality. By other measures, all would have to acknowledge there has been substantial movement toward more equality. By the measure of political representation, blacks are much more equal to whites than they were twenty years ago. By the measure of participation in key professions, in government, and in business, blacks, Hispanic Americans, and women are far more equal than they were two decades ago. If representation in schools of medicine, law, and business foreshadows an increase of income, then women and blacks should become more equal, so long as they follow, to the same degree as white males, the more lucrative fields of practice.

It is not only through growth of the federal budget that we can mark these enormous efforts to achieve equality. If we consider other equally important interventions, such as the expansion of regulation, they too have been motivated both by a concern for social justice and a concern for more equality. So we have created major government agencies such as the Equal Employment Opportunity Commission and the Office of Federal Contract Compliance Programs, mobilizing thousands of professionals to achieve more income equality for minorities and women, and created or expanded other major regulatory agencies designed to increase the power of consumers and ordinary people as against that of manufacturers of cars, drugs, and other products and manufacturers who pollute the air, water, and soil. But by the measure of gross income equality, despite all this thrashing and pulling, we are an unequal society—somewhat more unequal than Japan and Australia, perhaps a touch more equal than France, somewhat more unequal than other major developed countries of Europe.

Three Explanations

We do have a dilemma here. So our question: if thought, argument, and policy have been directed toward more equality, why isn't there more?

I will present three explanations for why we do not have more equality. The first is that, surprisingly perhaps, we don't want more. And by we, I do not mean the rich and powerful (that would be understandable), but most of us, including the poor who on a simple reading would be helped by more equality.

The second is an explanation of this first fact. Despite the enormous role the discussion of equality has taken in social philosophy, most people seem to hold just as strongly a number of other values, which seem to them an equal part of justice, and these compete with equality as an overriding part of justice.

The third is that because of these conflicting and competing values it is literally not possible for government, at any rate democratic government, to move to more equality in income as a *general* and overriding goal. It must move toward more equality in more piecemeal and concrete ways—for the aged, the sick, the handicapped, women, the young, students, the low-income renters, farmers, the unemployed, and on and on. It turns out, not for any reason that I can find written in the heavens, that the battle for more *different* kinds of equality, whatever satisfaction it may give one group or another, does not lead, or has not lead, to any *overall* movement toward equality.

It is the first point that is perhaps the most surprising and that receives the least attention. Yet it directly ties up with the Rawls-influenced analysis of justice as equality. Rawls argued that if we were to conduct an opinion poll under very strictly limited circumstances—under a "veil of ignorance," in which each person did not know whether he was black or white, a man or a woman, young or old, sick or able-bodied, slow-witted or quick-witted, dexterous or not—that we would then all vote (I leave aside some complexities) for strict equality. Obviously, the poll cannot be conducted. But interestingly enough, social science techniques potentially permit something like it. We *could,* in theory, conduct a public opinion survey on how much equality people wanted, and hold constant everything that might bias the results. Through statistical techniques, we could eliminate all the factors that Rawls wants us to be ignorant of, such as intelligence, skill, heredity. Nothing like this has actually been done.

Yet there is an even simpler approach to the problem. We can ask the poor what they want in the way of equality. Or, we might ask all those below the median income. This has been done, and—as we would all recognize if we ponder that this *is* a democratic society and the will of the people *does* in some rough measure prevail—*most people don't want much more equality than we have.*

Jennifer Hochschild has examined this anomaly—if anomaly it is—in an interesting book *What's Fair?* It seems to be a fact, she writes, that

> the American poor apparently do not support the downward redistribution of wealth. The United States does not have, and seldom ever has had, a political movement among the poor seeking greater economic equality. The fact that such a movement could succeed constitutionally makes its absence even more startling. Since most of the population have less than the average amount of wealth—more people would benefit than would lose from downward distribution.

Indeed, Hochschild points out:

> Redistribution has been so far from the national consciousness that even voracious pollsters and doctoral students have, for the most part, ignored it. As a result, we know very little about how most citizens actually feel about distributive changes. In the past forty years, only eight questions on national surveys have investigated some aspect of redistribution of income. Only 3 of the 8 mention wealth.[1]

These surveys do show, which is not surprising, that the poor, the unemployed, and blue-collar workers support redistribution more than do others. But even among the poor, only 55 percent (at most) strongly support redistribution. And the more radical the question, the less support. If we translate Rawlsian equality into its crudest form (it has to be crude to get into a national survey), almost no one is for it. Thus, in 1969 the question was put: "Every family in this country should receive the same income, about $10,000 or so." (To take account of inflation, if the question were asked today that figure would have to be raised to about $25,000.) The figure selected, by the way, was not unduly low—it was about 15 percent above the median income of households in 1970. It was therefore *above* what the median family was then getting, and the majority of Americans would have been agreeing to a raise of 15 percent in family income by just saying "yes." They weren't even warned about any possible undesired consequences of the redistribution. The responses, one must say, are startling, and should appear as a footnote in all further philosophical discussions of equality.

The respondents were divided into four income levels. Only 14 percent of the lowest quarter answered "yes" to the redistribution question, 17 percent of the next, 16 percent of the third quarter, and 7 percent of those in the top quarter of income. Support for a radical measure of income equality in the United States, one must say, is an eccentric minority position, not particularly affected by income earned (after all, we have millionaire socialists), and perhaps reaching significant proportions—if one may judge by the debates in philosophical journals—only among philosophers.

What is the basis for this denial of equality? Professor Hochschild has gone beyond the bare facts of public opinion survey answers—which never tell us "why"—to discuss their views of justice and equality with a few dozen citizens, rich and poor. What she discovers, I would argue, is that other conceptions of justice are at work which undermine commitment to justice as equality. Take the views of the poor: they are more interesting for us than the views of the rich, for the defense of self-interest is nothing that has to be explained, but the defense of a value that opposes crude self-interest does seem to require explanation.

So consider one of Professor Hochschild's respondents, Maria Pulaski, who cleans other people's homes. She feels her wealthy employers should pay her more—her work is worth it. But concerning their income—their $60,000 a year, as against her $7,000 (from both her efforts and her husband's; it is the 1974 recession, and he is unemployed)—she says: "They worked for it, why not? You work for it, it's fair. If I got a good education and I'm doing a different job and a harder job, I deserve more . . . I don't believe in this equal, all equal . . ." Even those who did not work for it, who "got it through their parents," deserve to keep their wealth. "Sure, if I had money, and if I gave it to my children, that's good. Good luck to them."

Or consider Sally White, now unemployed after various clerical jobs which gave her an average income of $6,000. She thinks she can make a lot of money someday, and doesn't want to give up that chance for a uniform equality. She even rejects equal pay within occupations: "Not all secretaries are the same." She even can see some point, not that she likes it, to her boss's son starting in a job that is better than he deserves and running a show he didn't start: "Somebody worked to get there in this family, and if they want to give it to him, it's their business." And when company presidents take it easy, she doesn't see why they still shouldn't enjoy their high salaries: "I know if I got my business going and I decided to be lazy and have someone else [run it], I would still expect my full share of the profits. I'm the one that got the whole thing started."

Another Kind of Justice

What we have is a strong idea of another kind of justice competing with the idea of justice as equality. It is the idea that what is legitimately acquired, and even more, legitimately handed down to one's children, is legitimately owned. People are entitled to keep what they can fairly get and to pass it on after they are gone.[2] Professor Hochschild's respondents make no sophisticated argument about inequality being necessary for economic growth or other ends. They simply believe things worked for, owned, are properly to be kept. A second belief which comes out very strongly is that one has the right to benefit one's children, regardless of their efforts. These beliefs quite overwhelm any commitment to strict equality.

But this does not mean that Professor Hochschild's respondents are rampant individualists who would let the devil take the hindmost, à la Herbert Spencer. They believe in guaranteed jobs, in minimum decency, and are quite willing to pay taxes for it. What emerges—in contrast to the philosophical discussion of social justice—is a kind of rough and ready pragmatism, combined with sympathy for those who suffer hardship, and even a willingness to provide for those who suffer hardship because of their own failures. There is also a preference for giving more, on easier terms, to those who suffer through no fault of their own—the workingman out of a job because his plant has closed—than to those who suffer because of drink, or drugs, or unwillingness to learn and work. The notion of making a distinction between the "deserving" and the "undeserving" poor may be considered old-fashioned and reactionary—it is not to be seen much any more in schools of social work, or among the majority of those who think about social problems—but it lives a hardy and determined life among ordinary people. Russell Long represented Louisiana, but the kind of values he defended in the Senate Finance Committee would find rather solid support among Hochschild's citizens of New Haven.

I would insist these are sensible views we see expressed, solidly based in deeply held values, which are in no simple sense selfish values (as we have seen, the poor hold them almost as much as the rich). They are moral rather than pragmatic positions.

Some sophisticated defenders of inequality claim we need inequality of income in order to motivate people to work and to encourage investment by those who earn more than their consumption needs, but they have argued that these objectives would not be hampered by confiscatory inheritance taxes. Indeed, they have asserted this would help implement the equality of opportunity that all favor and would have no harmful effects on the economy. The New Havenites disagree, reports Hochschild: "Respondents see taxes on inheritance or wealth as unfair, because they tax property more than once and they apparently preclude saving for the future of one's children." Or as one of the more prosperous respondents asserts: "Why should I work all my life and run the risk that three idiots who got jobs out of patronage are going to decide whether my daughter is going to get my money? No way. Before I'll do that, I'll stop working." Cutting inheritance taxes, I would guess, is one of the more popular things the Reagan administration has done. It caters to a basic and widely held sense of fairness.

Of course one question comes up about this widespread acquiescence in, and indeed favoring of, economic inequality or, more specifically, about the freedoms that lead to it and perpetuate it. Perhaps people are brainwashed—or perhaps they think that taking the egalitarian position will subject them to ridicule. In these long—very long—interviews, in which at least one respondent even felt free enough to say he was contemplating a robbery, there was simply no hint of this. This is not an issue of "false consciousness," as Marxists will have it. In any case, "false consciousness," as Guenter Lewy has pointed out in a book analyzing this peculiar idea, is a very flawed concept. It simply makes it possible for the ascriber of false consciousness to insist, quite independently of those whose interests he claims to be advancing, that anyone who disagrees with him about how to advance his own interests has been bamboozled. There is no hint of bamboozling here; there is strong enough evidence that people are using their eyes and their experience and yes, their values. They would like to restrict the role of government to limiting distress and not have it redistribute income.

Relieving Distress and Ensuring Equality

Let us leave Jennifer Hochschild's respondents and suggest a third reason why we do not have more equality. The programs that most Americans favor under the rubric of relieving distress, and that others may favor because they advance equality, have specific and discrete aims. Each may relieve a specific distress, but as a whole they seem not to basically affect the distribution of income. This is to me something of a mystery. How is it possible that the huge redistribution of income to the aged, once one of the poorest groups in the society, does not redistribute income away from the rich to the poor? This is our largest social program, and it is well known that it takes considerably less from the low-paid worker than it pays back in benefits, and, as the social security tax goes up, it takes more from the well-to-do than it returns to them in benefits.

We could make the same analysis for programs which have become quite large and didn't exist twenty years ago, such as food stamps, or for programs which did exist but have grown substantially, such as welfare. It is true that some of our major new social programs could be analyzed as not particularly assisting redistribution. For example, Medicaid and Medicare go to doctors, hospitals, and drug companies, and may well serve to redistribute more to the rich (though they have also permitted hospitals, for example, to increase the wages of low-paid hospital workers). Similarly, student grants and loans may not serve redistribution, since so much goes to the middle classes and to colleges and universities. And yet I remain mystified at the stability of the American distribution of income after all these efforts. The only explanations I have seen that make sense are two. First, as Edgar Browning and Morton Paglin have argued, if we properly value some of the elements in the redistribution that are not distributed as money (for example, health care and housing subsidies) we will find that as a matter of fact there has been considerable redistribution to the poor. There is a second explanation: the change in the composition of the bottom fifth or quarter of income earners. The bottom rung may still be getting a very modest share of income, but it is now composed of fewer families headed by working males, more families headed by nonworking females, and more people living alone.

Now this change in composition has considerable bearing on the question of why we do not have more equality after having instituted so many social programs. For the change in composition is itself in large measure the result of the expansion of social programs. This is not to say that people in the bottom fifth are not truly poor, but it is to say that the social programs have had a dynamic impact, which creates new classes of poor that take up the bottom position as those assisted by social programs rise out of poverty. Two such dynamic interactions are familiar. Social security permits more old people to live alone rather than with their children. Thus is encourages independence while also reducing the incomes of the households it makes it possible to maintain. A program giving assistance to elderly people permits them to move out of a household and set up their own. The two new households have more income than the one old household (they also have more expenses). The old couple or individual may now qualify as poor, but only because social security enabled them to maintain a poor *separate* household.

We now have much more in the way of support for young single individuals—young people who cannot work because of alcoholism or drug addiction, or the mentally ill and retarded released from institutions by the powerful movements for deinstitutionalization. This increases the number of single-person households and of poor households. Social policy has aimed at this—it is not a perverse effect—but it also thereby creates a new class of single-member households which will now join the bottom fifth, when formerly they might have lived in institutions and not been so classified. Perhaps the most important change in the composition of the bottom fifth is the increase in female-headed families, and it is clearly unnecessary to rehearse the argument that the increase in the number of such households is a result of the increase in and wider availability of welfare benefits.

Thus various social policies designed to create equality have certain effects which indeed do foster equality (the nonworking aged are now more equal to the working people; the mother on welfare is better off monetarily than she would have been before the expansion of welfare benefits), but they also *increase* certain categories which replace the groups formerly numbered in the lowest income stratum. It would clearly be wrong to say simply that efforts to increase equality are counterproductive, because what has happened to the aged who now live alone or the mentally ill and retarded released from institutions is exactly what social policy has aimed at. But in some cases, and the argument could be made for welfare, we do hit one target—the poverty of mothers without working males—but in hitting it we expand the category substantially.

The point, in a word, is that there is no final answer to social problems, including the condition of poverty. It was perhaps the great illusion of the long period of prosperity of the 1950s and 1960s that there was, or could be. We now know that that long period of prosperity, and of rising social expenditures to accommodate every major need—in some societies, such as Sweden and the Netherlands, just about every need for which public provision could be made—was based on exceptional circumstances. The rising tide of social expenditures was not yet producing massive deficits and major inflation—as was the case in the 1970s and the early 1980s. But whatever the explanation for that good period, a bad period has followed it, and poverty emerges as a problem even in societies that have gone further than we have in creating a net of services. More people are falling through the safety nets. Sometimes it seems as if poverty is an extraneous problem. In some European nations, such as France, which took in large numbers of immigrants in the years of prosperity, poverty seems to be a matter mainly of unemployed and as-yet-ill-adapted foreigners, and, perhaps more seriously, of their children now reaching working age. But then how difficult is that from the United States, where poverty is concentrated among blacks and some groups of Hispanics?

When problems are dealt with by government action, they may go away or be reduced, but they will also be replaced by new problems. The new problems may not be as bad, and they are not an argument that the old problem should not have been dealt with. The end result is that there are still a lot of people who are poor. They are different people, and the causes of their poverty are different. But the structure of inequality remains.

Government Policy and Social Justice

Can government effect social justice? Of course it can. But up to now it doesn't know how to effect social justice in a dynamic world so that poverty disappears and a substantial equality prevails. Nor has it even been successful in establishing floors of decency. We have a much more substantial floor than we did, and some countries do a better job than we do, but there are still holes and weak places, and shoring up one place often, as a side effect, increases the numbers falling through another.

This is a modest, not a revolutionary conclusion, but there is a more serious matter. Our situation is not as simple as saying, "we keep on trying, and succeed well enough here, have a modest success there, and a failure there, with an overall march toward more equality and a more satisfying society." It is also not as simple as some programs having an untoward effect. There is a greater problem, I am convinced, that is created by the mass of social programs.

Why is it that in most developed countries we now have unsettling deficits in the government accounts, deficits connected with growing difficulties in maintaining vigorous economies? These deficits have been creating huge headaches both for well-established welfare states that are not particularly increasing their defense budgets—such as Sweden and the Netherlands—and for countries, such as the United States and France, which have among their objectives building up defenses. While the increase in military expenditures contributes of course to the huge American deficit, the common element that seems to have produced a situation of permanent and rapidly increasing deficits is the social expenditures, which—on the basis of promises and commitments made, and expectations established in the mass of the population—are enormously difficult to cut. In this country, we have cut some social expenditures—those targeted to the poor. We have not been able to reduce those directed to the middle strata of the population, such as social security, which are much larger.

There is an aspect of the search for social justice as equality which has not yet been much thought about. It is that while everyone fights for equality in terms of some standard, that equality is interpreted from the perspective of a given group, comparing itself by means of benchmarks by which it shows it is unequally treated. Thus government employees claim that they are not paid as well as private employees. (Though the latter can certainly claim they are not paid as well as the public, when one takes into account pensions and vacations.) The aristocracies of American labor do not feel overpaid—by some measures they are doing worse, and they can prove it. American farmers before the current agricultural depression were the most prosperous in the world—but they could easily prove they were being compensated at less than what industrial labor got if one took into account their capital investments, the hours worked, the risks undertaken. Equality presents itself as a stable endpoint: achieve it, and no one can claim more than any other. There is a simple attractiveness to the idea, and there are enough examples in the most intimate areas of life to suggest that this is only simple justice. If you are going to divide an apple among three children, the simplest thing to do is to divide it into equal thirds. And probably the children will fight less.

It is not simple, however, to divide a wage increase or an increase in government benefits, and even harder to divide a decrease in wages or in the benefits of government. The children can divide the apple because they are in some key sense considered as equals—and indeed Jennifer Hochschild shows that when it comes to the raising of children or to political rights, Americans do believe firmly in equality. But when it comes to the *economic* sphere, Americans believe there is a rough justice to economic rewards, and thus they will fight to maintain differentials in wages. The problem is that while they believe in the rough justice of American economic distributions in general, they can also easily argue that they are slightly worse off than they should be in relation to this or that benchmark group—and particularly so if government is paying the bill. And why not? Surely it is easily possible for government to afford more? What's an extra billion or ten, when the deficit already amounts to $200 billion, and no one is too serious about reducing it? Why should the soldiers give up their pay raises, the aged their pension increases, the farmers their rise in subsidies, and so on?

Classless Resentment?

One of the problems that I suspect develops when government gets into the business of implementing social justice is that it undermines—just a bit, but in a competitive situation enough—the decent convictions that emerged among the people of New Haven that what's mine is mine, what's yours is yours, and I have a right to what I have inherited and earned, and you have the same rights. But if government is now getting into the act to correct the distribution, why then I might as well get into the game too. This is one unexpected effect of government implementing social justice. Another, I think, is that people then get resentful about whatever share government is providing to them.

When government gets into the act, we all begin to feel resentful that we are not getting our share—or are being billed in taxes for more than our share. Why is it, I wonder, that most workers (and here I am guessing) in private employment think they are getting more or less what they deserve, but that when it comes to getting something from government, everyone thinks he is not getting enough? I believe the explanation is that in private employment we see immediate connections between such things as what we earn and what others earn, between earnings and competitiveness, earnings and profits, earnings and making the company attractive for investors. We find it harder to see the connection in government. Why should we, when we can contemplate with only modest upset a $200 billion deficit?

Government benefits end up by making people greedy and resentful. That is the Tree in the Garden of social justice. Government can certainly take the road of ensuring more social justice effectively—all the governments of the democratic world have. But it does seem to get into trouble farther down the road, and just how it will get out is not yet clear.

10 | The American Welfare State: Incomplete or Different?

It is now twenty-five years since what seemed to be the final push to the completion of the American welfare state was launched. In 1964 and 1965 major action took place along three fronts. First, the largest hole in the American system of welfare provision was in some measure filled with the passage of laws setting up the system of Medicare (contributory health insurance for the aged) and Medicaid (noncontributory health care provision for the poor). Second, the United States began in some respects to move ahead of Western Europe by launching a complex group of programs designed to wipe out poverty under the auspices of the Office of Economic Opportunity (OEO). The large number of people who, so to speak, "fell through the cracks" of even the best-developed welfare systems were to be provided with activistic programs of education, work training, political organization, and community action. Third, the Civil Rights Act and the Voting Rights Act outlawed discrimination in employment and education on grounds of race, and ensured the ability of blacks and other minority groups to register and vote. The passage of effective national civil rights legislation meant that blacks and other minorities would benefit from the new social legislation without discrimination, and it opened the way to other national social legislation, such as federal aid for poor children in schools.

But in social policy, as in other forms of public action, there is no such thing as completion or finality: old problems, it turns out, have not been adequately addressed, and, even when they have been, new problems have risen almost immediately from their ashes.

Problems arose that delayed, raised doubts, and finally turned back the movement to reach a fully developed welfare state. The United States, having begun only in the 1930s to create a national system of protection against the hazards of unemployment, old age, death, and disablement (ill health remained the one great issue that the reforms of the 1930s did not settle), never did catch up with Europe and for the last few years has appeared to be in full retreat. Why is the American welfare state a somewhat abortive example, compared to the fully developed systems of other economically advanced states? What explains what remains a somewhat exceptional history?

The problem is an old one. Perhaps it is kin to another old question: why is there no socialism in America? The answer is not a simple one. The difficulties that the enthusiasms and programs of 1964 and later ran into have been chronicled by many. One favored explanation for some years was the Vietnam War, and indeed it did in some measure affect developments: apparently, intentions to have the poverty program grow were arrested by the needs of the war. However, the billion or two or three additional dollars that might have been spent on poverty programs if there had been no war shrink to insignificance compared to the expansion by tens of billions in the entitlement programs that were unchecked by the war. This is clearly a very partial and minor explanation. The Vietnam War did nothing to impede the rapid expansion of social security, of Medicaid and Medicare, of welfare, all of which expanded at a more rapid rate than anyone expected during the war in the late 1960s and 1970s. The Vietnam War had no effect in moderating the expansion of civil rights enforcement machinery, an expansion that remained unbroken until the Reagan administration. The rapid growth of entitlement programs such as social security and Medicare, and various programs for the poor, was unbroken under Presidents Johnson, Nixon, and Ford, and the rate of growth was affected only moderately, after the Vietnam War had come to an end, under President Carter.

What we have to explain is a growing disillusionment with the hope that a more fully developed welfare state would bring improvement to the conditions of life not only of poor Americans and black Americans, but indeed of all Americans. In developing the story of this disillusionment, we have to distinguish between welfare as most of the world understands it and welfare in the American context. In most countries, social welfare expenditures are overwhelmingly for education, health, unemployment insurance, and old age. The latter three are substantially insurance and contributory programs (with exceptions, such as the British National Health Service); the first is tax supported. All four major programs are seen to provide for the entire population. But the welfare state also deals with other kinds of residual distress, those that major national tax-supported or insurance-based programs cannot deal with, through the ministrations of social workers, child care specialists, and the like. In the well-designed welfare state, it is always the hope that the first type of program will take care of the vast majority of problems, and the number of people needing programs of the second type will be small and will decline, as good education and health care make almost every person someone capable of participating in the labor market and becoming self-supporting.

The two kinds of programs are sharply distinguished in the American mind—perhaps because of the nation's individualist orientation, its pioneer and immigrant origins, and the converse, the limited degree to which Americans feel part of a national community encompassing all other Americans, regardless of race, religion, or national origin.

The exceptional periods that have to be explained are those in which this mood was overcome by a national effort to deal with the problems of all Americans. Without detailing the history of the American welfare state, one can record that the first great period in its construction was the New Deal period. Even without a strong Socialist party, the United States between 1934 and 1938 had some of the elements generally associated with it, such as a growing and self-confident labor movement. The depression had cast vast sections of the population into distress, and the new national programs of the Social Security Act—old-age pensions and unemployment insurance—were seen as programs for all rather than for an unfortunate minority. It was a remarkably short time before older values and political orientations reasserted themselves, and it was not until the Great Society period—once again, a brief period from 1963 to 1968—that the next great push was effective. Part of its achievement was in welfare for all, but the most distinctive element was an effort to expand those residual programs addressed to the poor who could not take advantage of the contributory programs, and to devise new ones under the general heading of the war on poverty. By 1968, however, the moment had passed again—and the Republicans were back in power nationally.

There is a strong American bias in favor of programs for those conceived to be independent individuals, against programs for the dependent. That bias has grown. Welfare I—the contributory programs for all and for education—still expands and is almost sacrosanct. Welfare II—the residual programs for those not helped by the first type of program—is in increasing disrepute. Attacks on Welfare II by the first Reagan administration were in part beaten off, but the efforts by those committed to it are devoted to defense, rather than expansion and improvement. The same pattern for Welfare II prevailed in the second Reagan administration.

Perhaps the radical decline in the fortunes of Welfare II can be attributed to overpromising in the 1960s, when the war on poverty was launched. The promise was not only that the poor would be helped but that the poor would disappear, and that would help everybody by eliminating one of the chief environmental hazards of American life. The issue thus was not only whether the poor were affected positively by these programs. More significant politically was whether these programs were affecting the ambience of life of the great majority of Americans for the better. They hoped and expected that with the reduction in the number of the poor there would be less juvenile delinquency, less crime, lower taxes, fewer slums, and less illegitimacy.

None of these hoped-for ends has been achieved. Indeed, on most measures, things only go worse through the 1970s as expenditures for social policies ballooned. It had been promised that the poor would be raised, that the socially delinquent would be enticed away from their destructive behavior and become independent and untroublesome fellow citizens, and that crime, the ever-present accompaniment of urban life in the United States, would decline. The elimination of discrimination and the provision of political rights would guarantee that blacks would join the racial and ethnic mix of the United States on an equal footing, and would offer no more problem than the Irish, Italians, Jews, Poles, Chinese, or Greeks. When Lyndon Johnson launched the war on poverty, the enthusiastic support in almost all quarters was not based only on an altruistic commitment to raising the poorest fellow citizens and improving the lives of the worst-off among us. It was expected to have substantial benefits for the others, too—not only the psychological benefits of removing poverty in the richest nation of the world, but also the practical benefits of improving conditions in the poorest parts of our cities and reducing the incidence of crime and the costs of expensive remedial programs through a massive effort at primary prevention.

One of the most interesting and insightful evocations of the enthusiasms that accompanied the great burst of new programs in the 1960s period is from Charles R. Morris, who was a young "poverty fighter" at the time:

> When the decision was taken to eliminate poverty, Johnson's top advisors— mostly holdover Kennedy technocrats, including a number of recruits from McNamara's Pentagon—set about the task with the brisk, no-nonsense, sleeves-rolled-up, let's-get-it-over-with, grim good humor that fit the cher-

ished legend of their fallen hero. Lights burned late in brainstorming sessions all over Washington. In other times, the scale and complexity of the problem might have been daunting, but the new poverty warriors had the confidence of professional problem solvers . . .

The programs were supposed to produce results quickly. Shriver's main criterion for including proposals in the final package was that they had to promise visible progress before the 1966 midterm congressional elections. He courted conservative congressmen assiduously with detailed estimates of the cash savings that would accrue to the nation from reduced welfare, reduced crime, increased tax payments, . . . if only the programs were enacted . . . Shriver also went on a campaign to induce states to raise welfare payments out of the savings from the poverty programs, since welfare rolls would be expected to drop rapidly . . .

Such a massive conspiracy of self-delusion is altogether astonishing. There was virtually no evidence to support any of the claims that were being made . . . The slightest scraps of data and the broadest sociological associations—as that between education and income, for instance—were used to underpin huge, wobbly towers of interventionist hypothesis.[1]

Whether these programs were successful or not, and why, is now the subject of a major debate. There is hardly any doubt that from the point of view of politically effective public opinion, the expansion of American social policy in the later 1960s and 1970s was not a success: the last president who tried to expand the net of American social policy went down to defeat, and his successor, who tried determinedly to eliminate many of the programs of the preceding fifteen years, and to cut others, was returned with an overwhelming majority to a second term. The judgment of public opinion may well be wrong. There are those who argue that these programs were effective and that they would have been more effective if more money had been spent.[2] But some things that definitely failed to fulfill the hopes described by Charles Morris in the quotation above are beyond dispute: the numbers on welfare (AFDC) exploded in the later 1960s and early 1970s, until the states, which paid a substantial part of welfare costs—whether liberal Nelson Rockefeller's New York or conservative Ronald Reagan's California—imposed sharp administrative restraints. Crime increased and became more dangerous. The slums remained, and as far as simple observation could tell, became worse. The lower-class black population was more afflicted by social problems of drugs, crime, illegitimacy, education failure, and economic incapacity than ever before, despite the growth of a more prosperous black working and middle class.

These nagging problems became evident during the 1970s, even as the American welfare state was further developed under the surprising auspices of Richard Nixon. Whether this was because Daniel P. Moynihan truly convinced him that he should play the role of Disraeli, a Tory nationalist raising the conditions of the poor, or because a Democratic Congress still insisted on expansion, or because elite public opinion was not yet disillusioned with the possibilities of social engineering, the fact is that neither Nixon's nor Ford's administration indicated any retreat. Analysts of federal and other expenditure have concluded that the retreat began under Carter and accelerated under Reagan.[3]

The American welfare state came under attack long before it reached the levels of the European welfare states, whether measured by percentage of gross national product (GNP) taken in taxes for social purposes; by percentage of population in poverty; by extensiveness of protection by public programs against unemployment or ill health or loss of wages in sickness; by child care services; or by degree of subsidization for housing. Indeed, possibly in only one respect, pensions for the aged, is the American welfare state comparable to the advanced European states. Without ever having reached European levels, the American welfare state has been in retreat since 1981.

To give a simple summary of the changes that have taken place in the years since 1981 is not easy. American social policy operates through hundreds of discrete programs, but there are only a few large ones, and the course of change is clear. There have been substantial efforts to arrest and reverse the growth of programs directed primarily to the poor: AFDC, food stamps, and Medicaid. These attacks have been in modest measure successful, though not as successful as they would have been if the Congress had not resisted. (See "Low-income assistance" in Table 10.1, and Figure 10.1.) There have been less substantial efforts to arrest and reverse the growth of the largest redistributive programs: social security, unemployment insurance, and Medicare, programs that in large measure go to the middle class. Here there has been some modest reduction in the rate of previous growth. (See "Social insurance and other" in Table 10.1). President Reagan has been most successful in reducing a variety of grant programs, of which the largest were employment and training programs. (See "Other grants" in Table 10.1.)

One should neither exaggerate nor understate the changes introduced by the Reagan administration. All efforts were directed to cost cutting, and all innovations were consistent with that aim. They took a number of directions: reducing the ceilings that defined eligibility for AFDC, food stamps, and Medicare; returning programs to the states; reducing the federal directive role and allowing more diversity among the states, hoping for cost-cutting initiatives from the states (or, if they chose further program development, the states would have to pay for it); depending on, hoping for, or expecting that some of the holes opened up by the federal withdrawal would be taken up by private, voluntary, non-profit-making organizations, or even profit-making organizations.

What has been abandoned is any effort to "complete" the welfare state—for example, taking up the unfilled large gap in health cost insurance or trying to integrate, as Nixon's Family Assistance Plan and Carter's Program for Better Jobs and Income did, AFDC with other means-tested programs aimed at the poor. If the problem of the American welfare state

Figure 10.1. Basic monthly benefits for median four-person AFDC unit and single SSI (Supplemental Security Income) unit. Data points represent available information. Trend lines were drawn by interpolation. First full year of operation for the SSI program was 1974. (Reprinted from John L. Palmer and Isabel V. Sawhill, eds., *The Reagan Record* [Cambridge, Mass.: Ballinger, 1984], p. 194; based on data in Timothy M. Smeeding, "Is the Safety Net Still Intact?" in W. Lee Bawden, *The Social Contract Revisited* [Washington: Urban Institute Press, 1984].)

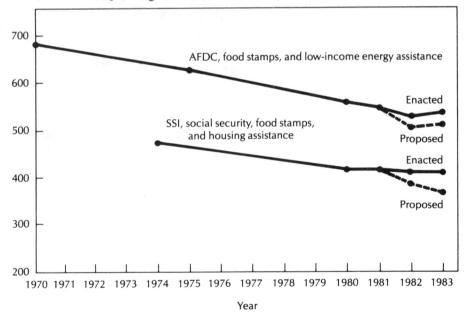

Table 10.1.
Average annual real growth rates in federal social program outlays (percentages).

Outlays	Kennedy–Johnson FY 1961–1969	Nixon–Ford FY 1969–1977	Carter FY 1977–1981	Reagan FY 1981–1985[a]
Payments to individuals				
Social insurance and other[b]	6.7	9.2	4.0	2.5
Low-income assistance[b]	8.7	12.0	4.7	0.1
Other grants[b]	37.6	9.9	0.7	−7.4
Total	7.9	9.7	3.9	1.5

Source: Palmer and Sawhill, *The Reagan Record,* p. 350.

a. Calculated on the basis of Congressional Budget Office estimates of 1984 outlays and projections of 1985 outlays based on 1984 policies.

b. See page 173 for definition.

is that it is fragmented, with too many sources of authority, too many individual programs, and that it does not reflect a national commitment and a national philosophy (as many critics assert), it is going to remain that way for a long time. Even if a new Democratic administration replaces the Reagan administration in 1988, we will probably not see as much innovation as Carter attempted.

What explains the "backwardness," if backwardness it is, of the American welfare state? "Backwardness" is placed in quotes because it seems there is now generally agreement that no one model exists for the welfare state. In the 1960s, as the Organization for Economic Cooperation and Development and other organizations wrote reports and as scholars began to analyze the comparative development of welfare states, there seemed to be an international competition; those states that collected more in taxes and distributed more in benefits seemed to be "ahead." After all, we had no philosophy, no political position, that argued that *less* should be collected in taxes and distributed in benefits. While there were always some free-market liberals who looked on these developments skeptically, these were few compared to the number in the 1980s.

That does not seem to be a sensible position any more. That Sweden or the Netherlands or Denmark collects more in taxes and spends more in benefits than some other Western European countries no longer suggests it is a beacon to be followed, a model to be duplicated. Their circumstances depend on a specific history, a specific concatenation of forces. That Switzerland and Japan bring up the rear no longer serves, except for idealogues, to indicate *their* backwardness. The mechanisms that exist in those countries are different from those in Sweden or the Netherlands or Denmark to deal with distress; and their success is indicated by the absence of a large permanent poverty population—no massive slums, no underclass threatening the life and property of ordinary citizens.

The United States, however, is different not only because it spends less on welfare and has a less complete system of protection than most welfare states, but also because, as compared to countries with well-developed welfare systems, it has a large poor and problem-making population. How one demonstrates this is not easy. International comparisons of "how many in poverty" run into the problem of not only how one defines poverty in a single nation but how one defines it across many nations. International comparisons indicate that there is indeed more poverty in the United States than in most other major developed welfare states and that there may be a somewhat more unequal distribution of income, but the facts that suggest a more severe problem in the United States are not measures of distribution. They are measures such as the amount of crime and of youth unemployment among minorities, the number of broken families and of illegitimate children, and the condition of neighborhoods in the great cities in which poor minority families live.

Few people in the United States would be worried if the only indication of American exceptionalism was that the bottom 20 percent of the income distribution had only 5 percent of the income, or that 15 percent of the population fell below an officially defined poverty standard. That would concern those committed to equality as such, but that is not the position of the great majority of the American population (see Chapter 9). The issues that concern the people of the United States are the social conditions plausibly linked to poverty, even if poverty is not the only cause. What makes the United States exceptional is the degree to which social disorder coexists with an advanced economic position.

The uniqueness of the United States consists not only in the lateness and incompleteness of its social policy system, but also in the scale of its social problems. Are the two related? It would appear so. It can be argued that if there is too great an inequality in income distribution, it is because an insufficient amount is collected in taxes and redistributed as benefits on the basis of need. If there are large numbers of poor people, it is because insufficient funds are provided them to get out of poverty. If there are slums, it is because they are not cleared by government provision. If the poor live in inadequate housing, it is because they are not provided with subsidized housing. If they are unemployed or without jobs, it is because the system of education does not have enough funds, or the system of relating education to work or of retraining workers is inadequate. And if there is family breakup, juvenile delinquency, and crime, it is because of all of the above, not to mention other inadequacies.

These not surprising assertions and conclusions are commonly made in public policy discussion. It seems reasonable that there should be such relationships. But perhaps nowhere is the challenge to the assertion of such relationships as sharp as in the United States. It is there we find arguments, whether old conservative, reactionary, or neoconservative, or even, as they are now called, neoliberal, which look skeptically at trying to deal with our social problems through expansions of government-provided social services. The socialist vision of a planned society, making rational provision on the basis of need, eliminating from society the driving force of profit, may be somewhat battered in much of the Western world, but it persists. The United States once shared in such a vision and even provided classics, such as Edward Bellamy's *Looking Backward,* that embodied it. As we know, socialism as a political force of any kind disappeared in the United States fifty years ago. While the Democratic party at one time evolved in a direction not very different from the Socialist parties of Europe, and its policies could not be sharply distinguished from theirs, there was a striking difference. In Europe these policies had been developed as part of a larger vision; they were the surviving fragments (or more than fragments) of a fallen utopia, and that utopia, perhaps to be realized someday, always existed as a support to the system of social policy. In the United States the same proposals (even though socialists or ex-socialists participated in shaping them) had to be presented on purely pragmatic grounds. They were not surviving fragments of a great utopian vision: those who proposed them had to deny they shared any part of that vision. They were simply sensible ways of dealing with problems. There must be a difference when a social policy descends from the heavens in which its complete form can be glimpsed, and when it arises from immediate needs with no necessary hint that a larger picture is to be completed. This is the ideological dimension of the problem of incompleteness in American social policy. The ideal of a planned and rational society eliminating social problems has not had the same presence or appeal in the United States.

In addition to the absence of socialist ideology, we find the weakness in the United States of the key social institution that supported this vision in Europe, a socialist-inspired labor movement. The American labor movement is not and never has been socialist, despite having socialists within it. It was characteristic that its shaping leader, Samuel Gompers, "denounced national health insurance as an unnecessary paternalistic reform that would create a system of state supervision of the people's health." In 1916, at congressional hearings on a national commission on social insurance, Gompers attacked the Socialist "belief that government had to be called in to ensure workers' welfare and gave a ringing defense of the success of trade unions in raising workers' standards of living."[4]

This position did change: the labor movement did in time become one of the strongest supporters of social security, national health insurance, and other parts of a national system of social policy, and remains so. But the unions are also a much weaker and smaller part of the working class than they are in most other developed nations, and a declining share: 30.8 percent of nonagricultural employment in 1970 and 25.2 percent in 1980.

Social policy expansion is buttressed by neither a socialist ideology nor a strong labor movement. In general, the link between a system of social policy and social problems, reasonable as it may appear, is nowhere challenged as sharply as in the United States. It is challenged on broad ideological grounds, the grounds that have put socialism to flight in the United States. It is challenged by more detailed analysis. Each of the points that might serve to support a more complete system of social policy is attacked. If there was more redistribution, it is asserted, there would be less investment, lower productivity, less competitiveness, more unemployment, and more misery. If we provided more assistance to the poor, then we would encourage the poor to reduce work effort, and if this assistance, as in AFDC, was provided because the working husband and father had left his wife and children, we would encourage more of this family breakup. If there was more generous unemployment insurance there would be more unemployment. The public housing we have provided has turned to slums in many cases, creating doubts that this expensive provision really provides better housing and environment.

The critique of American social policy has been extensive and devastating. Indeed, far from supporting the common sense that says more social policy means fewer social problems, it has argued quite the opposite: more social policy means more problems. The increase in expenditures for welfare and for activist poverty programs in the mid-1960s was accompanied by a rise in youth unemployment, withdrawal of minority men from the labor force, and the increased breakup of black families, and easier availability of welfare encouraged this.[5]

Admittedly, some of our efforts in social policy cannot be attacked on the ground of aggravating what they were meant to cure, such as Medicare and Medicaid, but these policies are attacked on the grounds that they have increased the inflation in medical costs and have not been efficient in improving health care. Only social security seems to be immune from attack: pensions do not lead to antisocial behavior in the aged. This program is alone in receiving the heartfelt support of all political tendencies.

The debate is a curious one. Much larger tax burdens for social policy and much more extensive provision for the poor and unemployed are not as problematic in Europe as they are in the United States. Of course there is controversy over social policy in Europe. But whereas we in the United States think that a tax burden of 30 percent of GNP will have devastating consequences on investment, productivity, and economic growth, tax burdens of 50 percent or higher, primarily for redistribution, seem less controversial in Europe. Wilensky has pointed out that we in the United States have tax revolts at much lower rates of taxation than is common in Europe—perhaps because a higher proportion of our taxes, such as income tax and property tax, are visible.[6]

Clearly all this points to large differences between the United States and Europe, as does the disappearance of socialism and the conservatism of the trade unions. All this helps explain why a less-developed system of social policy stalled some years ago and is being turned back.

But there are other specific features in the American political and social environment that must be brought into an account of the character of American social policy, if we are to explain why social policy initiatives are relatively stunted and incomplete in the United States. A number of characteristics of American society argue against, undermine, or prevent the universalism of social provision that has been the general ideal in welfare states. These features operated in the past to prevent the United States following in the footsteps of Bismarckian Germany or Lloyd George's England. The Great Depression reduced their effects and enabled a burst of national legislation and creation of social welfare institutions. The civil rights revolution had a similar effect in the 1960s and 1970s. But the features that hamper the development of a full-blown welfare state are resurgent today. That is why the further development of American social policy will take a course that continues to be divergent from that of European countries and from that of Japan.

The weakness of universal social provision as an ideology in the United States and the weakness of efforts to create national and uniform systems of social provision reflect five features of American society:

1. American federalism, despite the hopes of nationalists, is still strong, ideologically and institutionally. The greater role states play in social policy under Reaganism is not just a result of the effort to save money or a distaste for social programs; it is due in equally large measure to the strong hold the principle of federalism still has on the American mind, despite its obvious weakening since the depression.

2. The failure of universalism results from ethnic and religious divisions in the United States. The earliest efforts of cities and states to respond to social problems had to take into account the heterogeneity of religion and ethnic groups; universal provision was unacceptable. The development of statewide or national policies had to deal with and accept a diversity of welfare institutions that had originally been created by a heterogeneous population.

3. A separate obstacle to universalism is the problem of the blacks, originally slaves and subsequently maintained for a hundred years in a position of social and legal inferiority. This has introduced enormous complexities into efforts to establish universalism.

4. Must we also take into account a particularly strong individualistic trend in American society, to account for the resistance to national and universal systems of social policy? I believe we must, but how do we demonstrate that? It is not easy, but consider that the United States is still (or once again) a country to which 600,000 legal immigrants come every year, almost all aiming to improve themselves without state assistance, through their individual effort.

5. There is still a remarkably strong sentiment that problems should be taken care of by autonomous, independent institutions, and even by profit-making businesses, rather than by the state. That one can handle social problems, such as the problem of the poor, through profit making might seem bizarre; yet this is widely believed to be a reasonable approach, and not only by Republicans.

All these factors combine to make the American welfare state unique. Let me introduce some specifics under each of these headings.

Federalism

The unceasing effort of the Reagan administration to return a variety of programs and responsibilities to the states was a means of reducing the costs of social services. Typically, it involved a trade-off of increased power to the states and less federal funding for the programs. It was also a way of reducing the federal government's role in a host of programs in line with the administration's distaste for a strong federal role in social policy. But it also testified to the strong role that federalism retains within the American policy. Even if the states were reduced in large measure to claimants for federal funds during the 1960s, their structures existed, strongly grounded in the Constitution and in the political institutions that maintained complete constitutional governments in each state. More power to the states has been seen for many decades as a part of conservative ideology, consistent with a less activist role for government generally. But federalism is no synonym for conservatism. Today, with most of the states headed by Democratic governors, the attack on the central government's policies tends to come from the left, not the right, as it did when a liberal national government was seen as the protector of the rights of trade unions, blue-collar workers, and blacks. There are and always have been progressive states as well as conservative ones. Many states would like to go beyond what a conservative central government considers desirable— and some do, just as many in the past have resisted doing as much as a liberal government required, as in the 1950s and 1960s, when the federal government imposed liberal standards in welfare programs on resistant southern states.[7]

If the role of the states today is to serve as an alternative to the federal administration of social programs because of the ideology of a conservative government, their role in the past was to help determine the form of the American welfare state—and in doing so to prevent it from being as national, as uniform, as rational, as universal as many of the reformers of the 1930s hoped. It was taken for granted in the first few decades of the twentieth century that the states were the place for reform. One of the first major successful efforts to deal with the casualties of industrial societies were workmen's compensation laws, which spread through the states in the earlier part of this century. Progressive states such as New York, under governors Al Smith and Franklin Delano Roosevelt, and Wisconsin, with its strong progressive tradition, pioneered various forms of social policy.

When the depression struck in the 1930s, it was a president from New

York, with a secretary of labor and other major advisers from New York, combined with experts from Wisconsin, who created a cautiously drafted system of social insurance, one that took cognizance of the fact that neither Congress nor, very likely, the Supreme Court would allow for a fully national system. Old-age insurance was the only part of the proposed system of social security that was to be entirely national and uniform. Unemployment insurance was to be in the hands of the states, though an ingenious use of the taxing power of the national government forced all of them to adopt it. What was to become known as "welfare"—the noncontributory aid to the dependent aged, blind, and disabled, and aid to families with dependent children—all remained under the states, with contributions from the national government.[8] This is more or less the structure of the system today. The reforms of the 1960s and 970s added three major programs, two of which (Medicare and food stamps) were national and uniform, and one of which (Medicaid) was again diverse and administered by the states with federal aid.

Some regret the substantial role that states were given in American social welfare policy in the 1930s. But even in regretting it, they are aware of the great difficulties a fully national system would have had in getting through Congress in the 1930s. The fear of a strong government is not only a characteristic oddity of our present national mood, but also a recurrent major theme in American history. Thus, the power of the states, as represented in Congress, shaped what could and could not be done by the federal government in introducing the major programs of the Social Security Act in the 1930s.

By now there is something almost anachronistic in the complaints about the failure to establish national program standards aside from old-age insurance. It is true that national standards for unemployment insurance and for welfare might have mitigated some problems—for example, the fact that some states became more attractive to migrants because of generous welfare benefits. It may also be asked whether a substantial state role is necessary after the reduction in the difference of standards of living among regions in recent decades, and the elimination of the distinctive pattern of southern race domination that for so long was one of the principal reasons for demands for state autonomy. Yet it seems there is less demand for national uniformity today than ever before. If New York insists on paying high welfare benefits—possibly contributing to its own problems, both financial and social—no one, outside of the taxpayers of New York, is interested in telling New York that it should not. If Texas insists on paying low welfare benefits, as it does, it is recognized by now that this is a problem for Texas and does not require the interference of the federal government.

The Reagan reforms meant more power to the states and less federal money. Many states were forced to raise taxes. Paradoxically, the improvement in the national economy provided them with surpluses: they now have more programs for which they are responsible and more money to deal with these programs and to consider innovation. Their responses have been variable, reflecting their politics.[9] We see a resurgence of energy in state government. Some may consider that an unfortunate obstacle to national uniformity, but my impression is that fewer and fewer do. The state role is accepted not only out of pious respect for a 200-year-old Constitution, but because the states do reflect the inevitable diversity of a very large country, and do have the institutional and political capacity to deal with a wide variety of social problems. But even if in the mind of objective observers or analysts all this could be better managed from Washington, American political reality has never permitted it; and the Reagan changes mark a sharp shift along the spectrum from national to state power that is a permanent reality of American life.

Ethnic and Religious Diversity and Voluntarism in Social Services

Social services in the United States in their origins reflect communities. Sometimes these communities were homogeneous (as in early New England). The local community reflected the values and desires of the entire population, and thus could provide for the poor, the ill, and the orphaned without conflict. Very early in the development of the United States this homogeneity was broken. New York and Philadelphia, almost from their origins, were religiously and ethnically diverse, and social services developed for distinct groups or communities within them, a pattern that became larger and more fixed with immigration in the nineteenth century. Thus, we have the Hebrew Orphan Asylum or Catholic Charities, Mount Sinai or Lutheran or Presbyterian Hospital.

This is one key strand in the American pattern of social services. It does not affect insurance for the aged, or unemployment insurance, AFDC, or welfare. It does affect the provision of old-age homes, of children's services (for care, fostering, adoption), of work-training programs, and of the entire gamut of social services that are the pride of advanced welfare states. In the United States these functions may be carried out by public bodies, branches of local and state government; as likely, they are conducted by private, "voluntary" agencies created by ethnic and religious and neighborhood groups. Initially entirely supported by the groups that created them, in time they could lay claim to public funds for support, which were state and local in the nineteenth and the first half of the twentieth century, but which in recent decades have been increasingly federal, distributed to the states, and eventually to the host of voluntary agencies carrying out what is considered a public function. They also carry out other functions, serving for group survival, or the enhancement of group prestige, or simple institutional maintenance. The complexities of the interplay of the "private," voluntary world and the public world of social services have been studied by Neil Gilbert, and some indication of how they interact gives a sense of the scale of voluntarism in the United States:

> The distinction between financing of services through the public and private sectors of social welfare has faded close to the vanishing point. This transformation came about through the use of "purchase of service" arrangements, whereby public agencies contract with the private sector to provide social welfare services . . . Between 1962 and 1973 there was an enormous expansion in the use of public funds to purchase services delivered by private agencies . . . A study in the trend in government payments to Jewish-sponsored agencies reveals a twenty-fold increase in these payments from $27 million to $561 million. . . . In the brief span of one decade government payments as a proportion of the total income received by Jewish-sponsored agencies rose from 11% to 51%.[10]

The significance of this system of private, nonprofit agencies, in part governmentally funded, is twofold. It prevents uniformity on a nationwide (or citywide or statewide) basis, and it also provides a means of disengagement for an administration that wishes to reduce the government's role in providing social services.

Since the voluntary agencies exist, government can say that there are agencies to take care of the homeless or hungry. Indeed these agencies, which had gotten somewhat sluggish under government funding, do in fact remain vigorous, with their boards of directors, their supporters, their fund-raising mechanisms. Even while complaining, they are ready to expand the scope of their fund raising and services in response to the pressures created by government cutbacks.

The Republican administration is roundly charged with cynically making use of the voluntary sector to justify its own reductions in funding and withdrawal from public services. But just as in the case of federalism, it would be a serious mistake to see the Reagan administration's glorification of the voluntary sector as simply a conservative means of saving money. Efforts at uniform national social services have again and again come into conflict with the reality of ethnic, racial, and local diversity. Efforts have been more successful when they have tried to accommodate this diversity—as in the case of the popular preschool Headstart programs, run by local neighborhood and church groups, very often black—than when they have tried to ride roughshod over them, as in the case of efforts to create uniform standards for child care. Liberals and radicals, as well as conservative ethnics and Catholics, try to protect these local services from the imposition of standards by a central money provider that may conflict with local tastes and values.

One analysis of the impact of the Reagan administration on the voluntary sector comes to negative conclusions. Lester Salamon argues that federal cutbacks to these agencies seriously harmed them, while the concurrent tax cuts reduced the incentive of private givers to contribute to nonprofit, tax-exempt organizations. Nevertheless, there has been an increase in income of the average agency from corporations, foundations, religious funders, direct individual giving, and, most substantially, from imposition of fees and charges. A report on giving for 1983 showed an 8.3 percent increase in giving over 1982 to 300,000 nonprofit organizations of many different kinds. While the reduction in tax incentives led to a reduction in large gifts (the average gift of millionaires was 32 percent less), this seems to have been made up by the fact that there were more millionaires.[11]

The voluntary nonprofit sector does play a substantial role in American social services. It very often argues against national and uniform services, and its existence serves as an argument against public expansion of these services.

Race

The United States is not unique in having a division between the major national insurance programs (social security, unemployment insurance, Medicare) and the residual programs based on need (AFDC, food stamps, Medicaid). But the United States is unique in possessing so large a population of working age that is supported, along with their children, by residual programs, because it is not eligible for assistance by insurance programs. This population, stabilized at about 11 million since restrictions imposed on its growth by the states in the early 1970s, is about one-half black, and some other groups such as Puerto Ricans are also disproportionately represented.

While any system of social policy has difficult cases, in the United States the difficult cases form a mass cut off from the insurance programs in which benefits are provided as of right. Although noncontributory "welfare" is also a right, as courts have clearly ruled, it is a right that to the great mass of Americans is charity. The effort to surround it with the same sense of legitimacy, the same dignity, as social security or unemployment insurance or Medicare fails. The question that inevitably comes up is whether it fails because it is in large measure a program for blacks and some other minorities. The issue is not racial discrimination in administration of programs. National programs do not permit discrimination; state programs, such as welfare, also do not discriminate, and under the generally sharp supervision of the federal government arising from its substantial contribution, states that tried to treat blacks differently were disciplined. Discrimination is a matter of the past. But the fact is that there are two different systems, and one operates in large measure as a system for blacks and some other depressed minorities.

The ambitious effort to incorporate welfare into a national system in which its demeaning and isolating features would be reduced, the plans proposed by President Nixon (the Family Assistance Plan) and by President Carter (the Program for Better Jobs and Income), as I have pointed out (see Chapter 2), failed. Race came into play in this failure in a number of respects. First, the proposed reform, by reducing state control of welfare in favor of a national system, would have had a strong impact on wage rates in the South, where wage rates are lower, particularly for blacks. One reason wage rates are low is that welfare benefits in southern states are so skimpy. One reason they are so skimpy is that they go largely to blacks. Thus, the women with children who can withdraw from the labor market in the North do not find it easy to do so in the South. Domestic labor and other forms of labor are still comparatively cheap and plentiful. This was always a problem in getting southern members of Congress to accept a national system.

Second was the fear, perhaps stronger in the North than in the South, that reducing the stigma of welfare by incorporating it into a national system would not reduce the behavior that makes welfare necessary (that is, withdrawal from the labor force, male irresponsibility toward their children, creation of broken families, and the increase in illegitimacy) but would simply make it more acceptable. This seemed to be the finding of the income maintenance experiments. These behaviors—withdrawal from the labor force, female-headed families, illegitimacy—are far more marked among the black population. If a national and uniform system would only accentuate these effects, as the experiments showed, there seemed to be no reason left for the reform.

National systems, treating everyone alike, based on insurance and dignity, do not work in the United States as they do in Europe or in Japan because America has large differences, related to race and ethnicity, in how people behave. Group differences in behavior exist presumably because of the enormous impact of a heritage of severe discrimination. Group differences are barriers to universalism. In one respect the United States bears comparison to developing countries, where the protection of labor tends to involve only a small elite of government workers and workers in large firms, whereas the great mass of the population, without access to regular jobs, is outside the system of social policy. In the United States the numbers are reversed. A large majority of the working population has protection through insurance against unemployment, old age, disability, and illness, and only a small minority is dependent on public charity, but the two categories exist. Undoubtedly, one reason they exist is that our largest minority was held as slaves, and held down by discrimination for a hundred years after emancipation.

When there are large differences in a population, differences of race and ethnicity related to differences of income, productivity, culture, and values, the introduction of a national, uniform system is difficult. Differential behavior leads to greatly disproportionate claims on the system; it is then seen as a system for "them," not "us."

It is easier to create a nationally uniform system where there is an expectation that behavior throughout the society will be similar, values will be similar, responses will be similar. Once such a uniform system is in place, it will not be abandoned if strains are introduced into it by differential behavior related to differences of race and ethnicity. Thus, European countries now accommodate large numbers of foreign workers and their families, who may make larger claims on the system of social provision than natives. But a commitment once having been made to the uniform system, it will not change. When a nation is ethnically homogeneous, it is easier to see social benefits as designed for "us"—all of us—rather than for "them," a minority.

Individualism

Yet it may not be the sheer objective fact of ethnic and racial diversity that determines whether people see social benefits as designed for all, and therefore desirable, or designed for others, and therefore to be restricted. There may be another factor that the word individualism suggests. There are substantial differences among nations in the degree to which they *desire* egalitarianism or blame the poor for their troubles (see Table 10.2). Why do so many more of the British attribute the causes of poverty to "laziness and lack of willpower" of the poor? Why do so many fewer feel it is important to reduce inequalities? Rudolf Klein describes Britain as "a relatively inegalitarian society, with little support for egalitarian policies— and unique in that the British people tend to blame the poor for their own poverty." That sounds like the United States. His tentative explanation is that "support for 'altruistic' policies is a function of economic prosperity."[12]

Table 10.2
"Egalitarianism" in four countries.

Country	Income maintenance expenditure (% GDP)[a]	"Egalitarian" (% of population)[b]	Blaming the poor (% of population)[c]
Germany	12.4	30	23
France	12.4	49	16
Netherlands	14.1	36	12
United Kingdom	7.7	18	43

Source: Rudolf Klein, "Values, Power and Policies," in *The Welfare State in Crisis* (Paris: Organization for Economic Cooperation and Development, 1981), pp. 169–170.

a. Table 1, *Public Expenditure on Income Maintenance Programmes* (OECD, July 1976). The figures refer to the early 1970s. GDP: gross domestic product.

b. Appendix Table 1, *Euro-Barometre*, no. 5 (July 1976). The figures refer to the proportion of people who consider it "very important to try to reduce the number of both very rich and very poor people."

c. Table 29, *The Perception of Poverty in Europe* (Commission of the European Community, 1977). The figures refer to the proportion of people who attribute the causes of poverty to the "laziness and lack of willpower" of the poor.

I suspect that comparable public opinion evidence would show the United States is in the same position, but it could not be explained here by lack of economic prosperity. Is there an element of Anglo-American "individualism" here? This term is unsettlingly vague, and yet I think it can be argued that Americans are more likely to expect to make in on their own, and are scornful of those who do not. This is, after all, a society of free immigrants and their descendants (except for Indians and blacks), who came expecting to work hard and get ahead—and until recently expected no or very little assistance from government in doing so. It is a country of markedly greater and easier mobility than other comparably highly developed states. One might think that home ownership, characterizing a majority of Americans, might anchor people to geographical locations as housing subsidies do in Britain, but this does not seem to be the case. In the United States it is easier to open a business and to close it when it fails, easier to sell a house, more common to move in search of jobs. One of the chief and most successful charges of Reagan against the federal government was that it regulated business too much, and he has made a determined effort to reduce regulation. As in the case of so many Reagan proposals, one can see this as simply class interest; businessmen do vote Republican. But there are not enough businessmen in the electorate to make it as attractive as all that. Rather, Americans generally appear to be hostile to the idea of regulation, even when regulation is designed to reduce monopoly profits or protect consumers and workers.

American blue-collar workers are considered among the most conservative in the world. They own their own homes, go hunting or fishing on their vacations, have small hunting camps in the woods—at least that is the image. Those who know the unionized workers of the great mass-production industries of the heartland of the United States, now in decline, insist it is so. Blue-collar workers are likely to be suspicious of a socially enlightened leadership pressing for extensions of social benefits, because they are also homeowners and taxpayers and make a close calculation of whether it will result in a net benefit or cost. They are likely to vote Republican in disconcertingly high percentages, albeit this conservatism may be due to Catholicism and European peasant background, rather than to "individualism."

Americans will take government benefits as readily as the next person does. But they like to see government benefits assisting their own hard efforts, rather than simply maintaining others in failure. So they see social security and other popular programs as "insurance," which is true only in part, and deductions for home mortgage payments and local taxes as assisting the individualistic, upwardly mobile homeowner.

There is no operational test for individualism: I speak of a mood, a feeling, a tendency, which many observers suggest characterizes the United States, and there are enough facts to support the possibility that it is really so. I believe individualism plays a role in making the ideal of a uniform and universal welfare state less attractive in the United States than it is in many other countries.

Voluntarism and Profit-Making Agencies in Social Policy

It would be normal for voluntary agencies to resist public agencies taking over their roles. On the whole, public agencies also are happy not to have to undertake what are often delicate tasks affecting religious and racial and ethnic sensitivities (for example, foster care for children and child adoption), preferring simply to provide money so the voluntary agencies can carry on.

The United States, like other capitalist countries, has major enterprises that make profits from doing the kind of thing government does, for example, insurance companies selling pensions, insuring life, and insuring against ill health. The private sector has always been a major obstacle to national, uniform social policies because it saw these as competition. Can one say that American insurance companies were more potent in their resistance to health insurance than those in other countries? Very likely, simply because political movements for public health insurance started later, and American insurance companies were already on the scene ready to fight national programs, and perhaps they were more aggressive and expansive.

In almost every area the American social system seems to throw up more resistance from profit-making enterprise than other countries do. It may perhaps be explained by the fact that government was always more sharply limited here (no supreme executive, no supreme parliament, and only recently a supreme judiciary), surrounded by suspicion, such that our greatest work of political philosophy, *The Federalist,* had to be penned as a cautious defense of central government. The private sector, voluntary or profit-making, always has had more prestige in the United States. Whether or not it has prestige, it certainly has strength, and plays a much larger role in social policy than in any other country. Examples are rife:

Proprietary [that is, profit-making] agencies are prominently represented in many social service programs including homemaker/chore, day care, transportation, meals-on-wheels, and employment training. The most conspicuous area is that of nursing home care. Between 1960 and 1970 the number of nursing home facilities increased by 140% and the number of beds trebled. Close to 80% of these facilities are operated for profit; public funds, mainly from the Medicaid Act f 1965, account for $2 out of every $3 in nursing home revenue. This area of service is typically referred to as the nursing home "industry"; the childcare "industry" looms just over the horizon . . .

Tender Loving Greed, the title of a study of abuses in the nursing home industry, is an evocative expression of the antipathy toward having the functions of family care assumed by agencies committed to economic gain. However, it must be said that this study found the quality of care at nonprofit homes was not necessarily better than that offered by proprietary homes.[13]

Recently, we have had an astonishing rise in the number of proprietary (for-profit) hospitals, which many look upon as a means of relief from the rapidly growing costs of health care. Paul Starr concludes his fascinating account of the distinctive structure of American medicine with the prediction that this sector, which organizes chains of hospitals, will become dominant in American medicine, and that the powerful, independent American physicians, who have made the principle of the exchange of medical services for fees their Ten Commandments, will be increasingly forced to submit to the control of medical corporations. The most surprising branches of social policy, it turns out, can be made to turn a profit, as when major corporations entered the field of training poorly educated and unskilled youth for jobs under the poverty program. Even profit-making jails have developed. Of course, the income for all these forms of profit making in the fields of custody of prisoners, health, nursing care, child care, work training, comes almost entirely from government.

Why, then, doesn't government do the work itself? In the United States, we seem to be convinced that when government does it, it becomes more expensive and less effective. Even Richard Titmuss's impressive attack on commercialism in American blood services has stimulated a counterattack in the United States.[14] Profit making may have a bad name in much of the world and may be surrounded with restrictions. Despite the strong suspicion of business in the United States, it still retains a surprisingly strong hold and is expected to provide solutions to a host of problems that in other countries government undertakes to solve directly.

American social policy is different. The United States is far more dependent on a great variety of private, voluntary, ethnically and religiously sponsored, nonprofit and profit agencies to maintain the public welfare—even if in a somewhat private and individualistic way. Nonpublic resources in American welfare are greater than in any other major nation. American health, welfare, and education statistics regularly indicate the role that private expenditures play, and it is considerable. Thus in 1982, private expenditures for health exceeded public ($186 billion to $137 billion). In elementary and secondary education, $14.5 billion of a total $124 billion was private, and in higher education, $40 billion of $77 billion was private. In 1978 even in income maintenance there was a private total of $31 billion against a public expenditure of $178 billion.[15]

The present mood of the United States does not favor a fully developed national system of social policy; that mood seems to be based on more than economic exigency. It reflects rather a considered judgment by many Americans that despite the cost in social disorder that prevails in their society, they prefer it that way.

Notes

1. The Limits of Social Policy

1. See, for these issues, David M. Gordon, "Income and Welfare in New York City," *The Public Interest* 16 (Summer 1969): 64–68; Edward Banfield, "Welfare: A Crisis without 'Solutions,'" ibid., pp. 89–101; for a counterview that welfare was not a major issue, see Martin Rein and Hugh Heclo, "What Welfare Crisis?—A Comparison among the United States, Britain, and Sweden," *The Public Interest* 33 (Fall 1973): 61–83.
2. Nathan Glazer, "Beyond Income Maintenance—A Note on Welfare in New York City," *The Public Interest* 16 (Summer 1969): 102–122.
3. Nathan Glazer, "Reform Work, Not Welfare," *The Public Interest* 40 (Summer 1975): 3–10.
4. Charles Murray, "Have the Poor Been 'Losing Ground,'" *Political Science Quarterly* (Fall 1985): 427–446, an answer to the critics of his *Losing Ground: American Social Policy, 1950–1960* (New York: Basic Books, 1984). The chief of these were Sheldon Danziger and Peter Gottschalk, "The Poverty of *Losing Ground*," *Challenge* (May–June 1985): 32–38. See, too, David T. Ellwood and Lawrence H. Summers, "Is Welfare Really the Problem," *The Public Interest* 83 (Spring 1986): 57–78, and an answer from Murray, "No, Welfare Really Isn't the Problem," *The Public Interest* 84 (Summer 1986): 3–11. And for the controversy generally, see Nathan Glazer, "The Murray Phenomenon," *The Tocqueville Review* 7 (1985–86): 331–336.

2. Reforming the American Welfare Family, 1969–1981

1. For the story of welfare reform, see Daniel P. Moynihan, *The Politics of a Guaranteed Income* (New York: Random House, 1973); Vincent J. Burke and Vee Burke, *Nixon's Good Deed* (New York: Columbia University Press, 1976); Leslie Lenkowsky, *Politics, Economics, and Welfare Reform: The Failure of the Negative Income Tax in Britain and the United States* (Washington, D.C.: American Enterprise Institute, 1986); Gilbert Steiner, *Social Insecurity* (Chicago: Rand McNally, 1966); Gilbert Steiner, *The State of Welfare* (Washington, D.C.: Brookings Insti-

tution, 1971); Gilbert Steiner, *The Futility of Family Policy* (Washington, D.C.: Brookings Institution, 1981).

2. Steiner, *Social Insecurity* and *Futility of Family Policy.*

3. Steiner, *Futility of Family Policy,* p. 97.

4. Daniel P. Moynihan, "The Negro Family: The Case for National Action," in *The Moynihan Report and the Politics of Controversy,* ed. Lee Rainwater and William Yancey (Cambridge, Mass.: MIT Press, 1967).

5. Sheldon K. Danziger, "Budget Cuts as Welfare Reform," *American Economic Review* 73, no. 2 (May 1983): 65–70.

6. Steiner, *Futility of Family Policy;* and Joseph A. Califano, Jr., *Governing America* (New York: Simon and Schuster, 1981).

7. *Welfare Research and Experimentation,* Hearings before the Subcommittee on Public Assistance of the Committee on Finance, United States Senate, Nov. 15, 16, and 17, 1978, p. 90.

8. The theory is presented by Robert Spiegelman in *Welfare Research and Experimentation,* p. 77, and more formally in Michael T. Hannan, Nancy Brandon Tuma, and Lyle P. Groenevald, "Income and Marital Events: Evidence from an Income Maintenance Experiment," *American Journal of Sociology* 82, no. 6 (May 1977): 1186–1211.

9. *Welfare Research and Experimentation,* p. 79.

10. Gordon Green and Edmund Welniak, "Changing Families, Shifting Income," *American Demographics* (February 1983): 40–42.

11. Susan Sheehan, *A Welfare Mother* (Boston: Houghton Mifflin, 1976); Ken Auletta, *The Underclass* (New York: Random House, 1982).

12. F. Ivan Nye and Louise Wladis Hoffman, *The Employed Mother in America* (Chicago: Rand McNally, 1963), p. 8.

13. *Statistical Abstract of the United States, 1981,* Table 653.

14. Nathan Glazer, "Beyond Income Maintenance—A Note on Welfare in New York City," *The Public Interest* 16 (Summer 1969): 180–87; and "Reform Work, Not Welfare," *The Public Interest* 40 (Summer 1975): 4–10.

15. Blanche Bernstein, *The Politics of Welfare: The New York City Experience* (Cambridge, Mass.: Abt Books, 1982); and David K. Chambers, *Making Fathers Pay* (Chicago: University of Chicago Press, 1979).

3. The Social Policy of the Reagan Administration

1. In this chapter I lean on the following studies of the impact of the early Reagan administration on social policy: John L. Palmer and Isabel V. Sawhill, eds., *The Reagan Experiment* (Washington, D.C.: Urban Institute Press, 1982); John William Ellwood, ed., *Reductions in U.S. Domestic Spending* (New Brunswick, N.J.: Transaction Books, 1982); Joseph A. Pechman, ed., *Setting National Priorities: The 1983 Budget,* and *Setting National Priorities: The 1984 Budget* (Washington, D.C.: Brookings Institution, 1982, 1983).

Other studies of social policy of the early Reagan administration are: Fred I. Greenstein, ed., *The Reagan Presidency: An Early Assessment* (Baltimore: Johns Hopkins University Press, 1983). My conclusions in this chapter are similar to those in chapter 5 of that book: Richard P. Nathan, "The Reagan Presidency in Domestic Affairs," and in chapter 3: Hugh Heclo and Rudolph G. Penner, "Fiscal and Political Strategy in the Reagan Administration." Richard P. Nathan, Fred C. Doolittle, and associates, *The Consequences of Cuts: The Effects of the Reagan Domestic Program on State and Local Governments* (Princeton: Urban and Regional Research Center, Princeton University, 1983); Richard P. Nathan, "Retrenchment Comes to Washington," *Society* 20, no. 2 (January/February 1983): 45–48.

2. A news article reviewing the findings of the Princeton University Urban and Regional Research Center suggested that the study, which covered fiscal year 1982, dealt with most of the change we were likely to see: "Congress has since been unwilling to give Mr. Reagan new cuts he has asked for and the change from 1981 to 1982 is expected to remain as the domestic high-water mark of his current term" (John Herbers, "Study Tells How 14 States Countered U.S. Aid Cuts," *New York Times,* May 8, 1983.

3. Pechman, *Setting National Priorities, 1983,* p. 25.

4. Ellwood, *Reductions in U.S. Domestic Spending,* pp. 24, 320.

5. John Palmer and Gregory B. Mills, "Budget Policy," in Palmer and Sawhill, *Reagan Experiment,* p. 78.

6. See Table 2, "Growth Rates of Federal Outlays during the Carter Years," in Nathan, "Reagan Presidency in Domestic Affairs," in Greenstein, *Reagan Presidency,* p. 59; and Table 2, "Federal Expenditures for Transfers to Individuals and Families . . . ," in Benjamin A. Okner and D. Lee Bawden, "Recent Changes in Federal Income Redistribution Policy," *National Tax Journal* 36, no. 3 (September 1983): 349.

7. Palmer and Sawhill, *Reagan Experiment,* pp. 17–19.

8. Ibid., p. 67.

9. Pechman, *Setting National Priorities, 1983,* p. 31; *Setting National Priorities, 1984,* p. 204.

10. For a fuller account of this attempt at reform, its underlying rationale, and ultimate rejection, see Chapter 2.

11. These and other changes in AFDC are from Ellwood, *Reductions in U.S. Domestic Spending,* pp. 300–302.

12. Nathan, "Reagan Presidency in Domestic Affairs," in Greenstein, *Reagan Presidency,* p. 62. I am indebted to Wendell E. Primus, of the staff of the Committee of Ways and Means of the House of Representatives, for a summary and analysis of the Research Triangle study. For press coverage of the study, see Robert Pear, "Most of Those Taken Off Welfare Are Said Not to Leave Their Jobs," *New York Times,* April 29, 1983; Burt Schorr, "Study of Welfare Indicates Success of New U.S. Rules," *Wall Street Journal,* May 2, 1983.

13. I learned at a conference at the Urban Institute that this interesting proposal had been "on the shelf" for a while and owed nothing to the personnel or philosophy of the Reagan administration. This might be the case, more or less, with many of the proposals I discuss in this article, but I leave aside the question of specific provenance of any proposal. Many had been around for some time. The point is that the administration adopted them.

14. Ellwood, *Reductions in U.S. Domestic Spending,* pp. 196–198.
15. For an initial survey of the issues, see Lester M. Salomon and Alan J. Abramson, "The Nonprofit Sector," in Palmer and Sawhill, *Reagan Experiment,* chap. 7.
16. Richard P. Nathan, in Ellwood, *Reductions in U.S. Domestic Spending,* p. 318; Palmer and Sawhill, *Reagan Experiment,* p. 21.
17. James R. Storey, in Palmer and Sawhill, *Reagan Experiment,* pp. 373, 374–375.
18. On the question of suffering, there are some oddities. Many have noted that despite ominous predictions of riots in the summer of 1982 because of program cuts, it was a relatively quiet summer. See Nathan Glazer, "The Reagan Administration and Social Policy—Is a Counterrevolution Under Way?" *The Tocqueville Review* 4, no. 1 (Spring–Summer 1982): 118–126. Nor were there major disturbances in subsequent summers. An interesting study of Stamford, Connecticut, conducted in the early summer of 1983 showed remarkably little perception of program cuts, very little perception of actual loss of services. Nor did the poor particularly report a greater loss of services than the rich. Oddly enough, the greatest perception of an "area in which you think there has been or will be a real loss of services" was in social security and services for the elderly. G. Donald Ferree, Jr., W. Wayne Shannon, and Everett Carl Ladd, "Stamford, Connecticut Weathers Reagonomics," *Public Opinion* (February/March 1983). The one area of increased distress that has aroused the most attention is homelessness. Part of that is owing to deinstitutionalization of the mentally ill and the mentally retarded. But family homelessness has also increased. The causes are obscure. Few, however, believe the answer is a resumption of massive housing projects for the poor at a time when thousands of apartments in such projects lie abandoned and when huge structures are dynamited in the poverty-stricken city of Newark. There may be answers in government policy to the problem of family homelessness, but it is not yet evident what they are.

4. Education, Training, and Poverty

1. Henry Levin, in *A Decade of Federal Antipoverty Programs: Achievements, Failures, and Lessons,* ed. Robert H. Haveman (New York: Academic Press, 1977), pp. 160, 170, 179.
2. Burton Weisbrod and Wilbur J. Cohen in Haveman, *Decade of Federal Antipoverty Programs,* pp. 188–196.
3. Raymond Boudon, *Education, Opportunity, and Social Inequality* (New York: Wiley, 1974); Lester Thurow, "Education and Economic Equality," *The Public Interest* 28 (Summer 1972): 66–81.
4. Charles Murray, *Losing Ground: American Social Policy, 1950–1980* (New York: Basic Books, 1984).
5. Andrew Hahn and Robert Lerman, *What Works in Youth Employment Policy? How to Help Young Workers from Poor Families* (Washington, D.C.: National Planning Association, 1985), p. 7.
6. Christopher S. Jencks et al., *Who Gets Ahead? The Determinants of Economic Success in America* (New York: Basic Books, 1979), pp. 223, 226, 230.
7. Ibid., p. 311.

8. Stephen P. Mullin and Anita A. Summers, "Is More Better? The Effectiveness of Spending on Compensatory Education," *Phi Delta Kappan* 64, no. 5 (January 1983): 339.

9. Richard B. Darlington et al., "Preschool Programs and Later School Competence of Children From Low-Income Families," *Science* 208 (1980): 202–204. See, too, correspondence titled "Duration of Preschool Education on Later School Competence," *Science* 213 (1981): 1145–1146. *Lasting Effects after Preschool,* Report of the Consortium for Longitudinal Studies under the Supervision of Irving Lazar and Richard B. Darlington, DHEW Publication no. (OHDS) 79-30178 (Washington, D.C.: U.S. Department of Health, Education and Welfare, October 1978). Irving Lazar, "Early Intervention Is Effective," *Educational Leadership* 38, no. 4 (January 1981): 303–305.

10. Richard B. Darlington and Irving Lazar, letter to the editor, *Phi Delta Kappan* 66, no. 3 (November 1984): 231–232.

11. Peter Skerry, "The Charmed Life of Head Start," *The Public Interest* 73 (Fall 1983): 18–39.

12. *The Condition of Education: A Statistical Report, 1982* (Washington, D.C.: National Center for Education Statistics, U.S. Department of Education, 1982), p. 12.

13. Launor F. Carter, "The Sustaining Effects Study of Compensatory and Elementary Education," *Educational Researcher* 3, no. 7 (1984): 4–13.

14. *Condition of Education, 1982,* pp. 184, 188.

15. Nancy W. Burton and Lyle V. Jones, "Recent Trends in Achievement Levels of Black and White Youth," *Educational Researcher* 11, no. 4 (April 1982): 10–17.

16. *Condition of Education, 1984,* Table 5.1.

17. *Condition of Education, 1983,* pp. 54, 194, 196.

18. Ralph Hoepfner, Henry Zagorski, and Jean Wellisch, *Report No. 1: The Sample for the Sustaining Effects Study and Projections of Its Characteristics to the National Population* (Santa Monica, Calif.: System Development Corporation, 1977), pp. 97–104.

19. *Compensatory Education Services* (Washington, D.C.: National Institute of Education, 1977), pp. 1–3.

20. Rexford Brown, "Public Policy and Pupil Achievement," *State Legislatures* (October 1983): 40.

21. Jeanne S. Chall, "Literacy: Trends and Explanations," *Educational Researcher* (November 1983): 6.

22. David Savage, "Scrutinize Students' Test Scores, and They Might Not Look So Rosy," *American School Board Journal* 171, no. 8 (August 1984): 21–24.

23. Thomas Cook et al., *Black Achievement and School Desegregation* (Washington, D.C.: National Institute of Education, 1984), pp. 9, 85.

24. John C. Pittenger and Peter Kuriloff, "Educating the Handicapped: Reforming a Radical Law," *The Public Interest* 66 (Winter 1982): 92.

25. "Disabled Students Classes Are Called Failure by Koch," *New York Times,* November 22, 1983, p. Y13.

26. "State Education Statistics," *Education Week,* January 18, 1984, pp. 12–13.

27. Russell W. Rumberger, "Dropping Out of High School: The Influence of Race,

Sex, and Family Background," *American Educational Research Journal* 20, no. 2 (Summer 1983): 202.

28. *Digest of Education Statistics* (Washington, D.C.: National Center for Education Statistics, U.S. Department of Education, 1984), p. 13.

29. Richard B. Freeman and Harry J. Holzer, "Young Blacks and Jobs: What We Now Know," *The Public Interest* 78 (Winter 1985): 18–31.

30. Robert I. Lerman, "Do Welfare Programs Affect the Schooling and Work Patterns of Young Black Men?" in *The Black Youth Employment Crisis,* ed. Richard B. Freeman and Harry J. Holzer (Chicago: University of Chicago Press, 1986), pp. 403–438.

31. Rumberger, "Dropping Out of High School," p. 201.

32. Robert Taggart, *A Fisherman's Guide: An Assessment of Training and Remediation Strategies* (Kalamazoo, Mich.: W. E. Upjohn Institute for Employment Research, 1981), p. xi.

33. Ibid., p. 28.

34. Ibid., p. 128, based on MDRC reports.

35. Ibid., pp. 311–312.

36. Judith M. Gueron, "Lessons from a Job Guarantee: The Youth Incentive Entitlement Pilot Projects," Manpower Demonstration Research Corporation (1984), p. 1.

37. Ibid., p. 5.

38. Nathan Glazer, "The Problem with Competence," *American Journal of Education* 92, no. 3 (1984): 306–313.

5. Universal and Income-Tested Social Programs

1. Dick Martz, "Rx for Lower Doctors' Bills," *Newsweek,* March 19, 1979, p. 17.

2. The Credit Income Tax is a type of demogrant. Its effects are analyzed through econometric methods in three chapters in *Income-Tested Transfer Programs: The Case For and Against,* ed. Irwin Garfinkel (Academic Press, 1982): David Betson, David Greenberg, and Richard Kasten, "A Simulation Analysis of Alternative Program Structures: The Negative Income Tax versus the Credit Income Tax"; Jonathan R. Kesselman, "Taxpayer Behavior and the Design of a Credit Income Tax"; and Efraim Sadka, Irwin Garfinkel, and Kemper Moreland, "Income Testing and Social Welfare: An Optimal Tax-Transfer Model."

3. Jonathan R. Kesselman and Irwin Garfinkel, "Professor Friedman, Meet Lady Rhys-Williams: NIT vs. CIT," *Journal of Public Economics* 10, no. 2 (October 1978): 181, 183.

4. James Coleman, "Income-Testing and Social Cohesion," in Garfinkel, *Income-Tested Transfer Programs.*

5. Arnold Heidenheimer and John Layson, "Social Policy Development in Europe and America: A Longer View on Selectivity and Income-Testing," in Garfinkel, *Income-Tested Transfer Programs.*

6. Harold W. Watts, George Jakubson, and Felicity Skidmore, "Single-Parent Households under Alternative Transfer and Tax Systems," in Garfinkel, *Income-Tested Transfer Programs.*

7. See Nathan Glazer, "Reform Work, Not Welfare," *The Public Interest* 40 (Summer 1975): 4–10.

6. Crisis and Redirection in Social Policy

1. John Rawls, *A Theory of Justice* (Cambridge, Mass.: Belknap Press, Harvard University Press, 1971), p. 63.
2. Harold Wilensky, "Taxing, Spending, and Backlash: An American Peculiarity?" *Taxing and Spending*, July 1979, pp. 6–11; Frank Levy, "On Understanding Proposition 13," *The Public Interest* 56 (Summer 1979): 66–89.
3. For two particularly valuable compilations of material and analyses of this problem, see *Welfare Research and Experimentation*, Hearings before the Subcommittee on Public Assistance of the Committee on Finance, United States Senate, 95th Cong., 2nd Sess., 1978; and *How to Think about Welfare Reform for the 1980s*, Hearings before the Subcommittee on Public Assistance of the Committee on Finance, United States Senate, 96th Cong., 2nd Sess., 1980. On youth unemployment, see Eli Ginzberg, "Youth Unemployment," *Scientific American* (May 1980). And for both, see Chapters 2 and 4 in this book.
4. See Robert Schrank, "First, Get Good Job Data on Youth Joblessness," *New York Times*, July 6, 1980.
5. Ginzberg, "Youth Unemployment," p. 48.
6. Sidney Webb, *The Necessary Basis of Society,* Fabian Society Tract 159 (1911), quoted in Norman Dennis, *People and Planning* (London: Faber and Faber, 1970), p. 290.
7. Peter L. Berger and Richard J. Neuhaus, *To Empower People: The Role of Mediating Structures in Public Policy* (Washington, D.C.: American Enterprise Institute, 1977).
8. Hans Zetterberg, "Maturing of the Swedish Welfare State," *Public Opinion* (October–November 1979): 45–46.
9. Rosemary Taylor, "The Free Clinic: Case Study in the Survival and Adaptation of Organizational and Social Innovation," doctoral thesis, University of California at Santa Barbara, 1975.
10. Michael Walzer, "The Pastoral Retreat of the New Left," *Dissent* (Fall 1979): 407–408.
11. See David Rogers and Norman H. Chung, *110 Livingston Street Revisited* (New York: New York University Press, 1983).
12. John E. Coons and Stephen D. Sugarman, *Education by Choice: The Case for Family Control* (Berkeley: University of California Press, 1978).
13. Bernard Frieden, "Housing Allowances: An Experiment That Worked," *The Public Interest* 59 (Spring 1980): 15–35.
14. Hans Zetterberg, "Maturing of the Swedish Welfare State."
15. See Nathan Glazer, "Should Judges Administer Social Services," *The Public Interest* 50 (Winter 1978): 64–80.
16. Bradley Graham, "W. Germany, No Melting Pot, Faces Migrant 'Time Bomb,'" *Washington Post*, April 13, 1980.

7. Toward a Self-Service Society

1. Richard Eder, "Mitterand's Modest Revolution," *New York Times Magazine*, February 7, 1982, 66–67.
2. Ibid.
3. See Lowell S. Levin and Ellen L. Idler, *The Hidden Health Care System: Mediating Structures and Medicine* (Cambridge, Mass.: Ballinger, 1981). This is part of the American Enterprise Institute series on mediating structures initiated by Peter Berger and Richard Neuhaus.
4. See Chapters 2 and 3.
5. See, for example, John E. Coons and Stephen D. Sugarman, *Education by Choice: The Case for Family Control* (Berkeley: University of California Press, 1978); E.M. Gaffney, ed., *Private Schools and the Public Good* (Notre Dame, Ind.: University of Notre Dame, 1981).
6. It is interesting that in the United Kingdom one finds many parallels to American developments, undoubtedly arising from similar causes. Note, on the issue of accountability, the discussion of police in *The Brixton Disorders, 10–12 April 1981*, Report of an Inquiry by the Rt. Hon. the Lord Scarman, O.B.E., Cmnd. 8427, pp. 92–97; on teachers, Tessa Blackstone and Robert Wood, "Making Schools More Accountable," *New Society*, December 24/31, 1981, pp. 531–532; and a flurry of recent works critical of social workers: Colin Brewer and June Lait, *Can Social Work Survive?* (London: Temple Smith, 1980); Digby C. Anderson, ed., *The Ignorance of Social Intervention* (London: Croom Helm, 1980).
7. The inadequacy of the private sector in providing such services has been widely analyzed as well as assumed; but see, as a counterexample of cogent analysis of the ability of the public sector to manage social services well, Charles Wolf, Jr., "A Theory of Non-Market Failure," *The Public Interest* 55 (Spring 1979): 117–133.
8. See, for example, Nathan Keyfitz, "Why Social Security Is in Trouble," *The Public Interest* 58 (Winter 1980): 102–119.
9. A letter to the *New York Times*, January 27, 1982, makes a surprisingly persuasive case for private prisons; some are already in operation.
10. Arthur Seldon, *Wither the Welfare State* (London: Institute for Economic Affairs, 1981), p. 11.
11. David Donnison, "The Empty Council Houses," *New Society*, June 14, 1979, pp. 635–637; and "Difficult to Live In," *New Society*, October 16, 1980, p. 122: "We are currently facing a new phenomenon in the British public scene—public housing only a decade or two old being vacated and demolished."
12. Seldon, *Wither the Welfare State*, pp. 20–24.
13. E. G. West's case is presented in *Education and the Industrial Revolution* (London: Batsford, 1975); and *Education and the State* (London: Institute for Economic Affairs, 1965, 1970). West leans on the argument of Sam Peltzman that government intervention may *lower* total levels of expenditure ("The Effect of Government Subsidies in Kind on Private Expenditures: The Case of Higher Education," *Journal of Political Economy* [February 1974]). As in the cause of health, the high expenditures (and in particular the high costs to individuals) in American

higher education are seen not as an example of the waste caused by competition and lack of an overall system, but as an example of the efficiency of the market in permitting people to allocate expenditures so as to maximize their welfare. For additional argument on the willingness of Britons to spend more on education and health if they could spend it freely and in a free market, see Ralph Harris and Arthur Seldon, *Over-ruled on Welfare* (London: Institute for Economic Affairs, 1979).

14. "Sweden: The Limits to the Welfare State," *Wall Street Journal,* September 9, 1981.
15. See *After Industrial Society? The Emerging Self Service Economy* (London: Macmillan, 1978).
16. Michael P. Balzano, *Federalizing Meals on Wheels; Private Sector Loss or Gain?* (Washington, D.C.: American Enterprise Institute, 1979). This analysis, on which I have leaned heavily, was written too early in the history of the federal meals-on-wheels program to permit a follow-up on whether the fears expressed were well founded. But a later news item gives a revealing glimpse of the character of federally funded meals for the poor. President Reagan, in a speech urging a greater role for the voluntary sector, referred to a program in which volunteers had replaced paid employees at a considerable saving. Not so, asserted the director of the program: it is true that the staff had acted as volunteers for a while, between the ending of one federal grant and the beginning of another, but it was a paid staff. She reported that the program cost more than $50,000 a year, of which $7,000 or $8,000 was spent on food. Without making any study, one doubts that any voluntary program would spend seven or eight dollars for each dollar spent on food ("Meal Chief Says Reagan Had Figures Wrong," *New York Times,* January 22, 1982).
17. Robert L. Woodson, *A Summons to Life: Mediating Structures and the Prevention of Youth Crime* (Cambridge, Mass.: Ballinger, 1981), pp. 59–60.
18. Ibid., pp. 84–85.
19. "Public Aid Hurts Canadian Private Schools, Report Suggests," *Education Week,* December 21, 1981; see, too, Donald A. Erickson, "The School as a Mediating Structure: Some Concerns about Subversion and Co-optation," in *Church, State, and Public Policy: The New Shape of the Church-State Debate,* ed. Jay Mechling (Washington, D.C.: American Enterprise Institute, 1978).
20. Ibid., p. 14.
21. R. M. Titmuss, *The Gift Relationship: From Human Blood to Social Policy* (New York: Pantheon, 1971).
22. Ralph M. Kramer, *Voluntary Agencies in the Welfare State* (Berkeley: University of California Press, 1981).
23. See Table 10.1 in Chapter 10.
24. "1945 and All That," *New Society,* July 9, 1981; p. 47, and references there.
25. Adrian Webb, *Collective Action and Welfare Pluralism* (Association of Researchers in Voluntary Action and Community Involvement); Francis Gladstone, *Voluntary Action in a Changing World* (London: Bedford Square Press, 1979); *Beyond the Welfare State* (London: National Council for Voluntary Organizations, 1980).

26. See "President Pleads with Civic Groups to Help the Poor," including sections from a speech by President Reagan, *New York Times,* January 15, 1982. The president also established a task force to explore the possibilities of voluntary action.
27. Kramer, *Voluntary Agencies,* pp. 195–196.
28. Roger D. Masters, "Inventing Your Very Own Tax Cut," *Washington Post,* January 10, 1982, p. D-1.
29. See John J. Egan, John Carr, Andrew Nott, and John Roos, *Housing and Public Policy: A Role for Mediating Structures* (Cambridge, Mass.: Ballinger, 1981), another in the series of volumes of the American Enterprise Institute's mediating structures project, directed by Peter Berger and Richard Neuhaus.
30. See David S. Seeley, *Education through Partnership: Mediating Structures and Education* (Cambridge, Mass.: Ballinger, 1981).

8. *"Superstition" and Social Policy*

1. Claude Lévi-Strauss, "Reflections on Liberty," *New Society,* May 26, 1977, pp. 387–388.
2. Peter L. Berger and Richard John Neuhaus, *To Empower People: The Role of Mediating Structures in Public Policy* (Washington, D.C.: American Enterprise Institute, 1977), pp. 4–5.
3. For this story and analysis, see Donald L. Horowitz, *The Courts and Social Policy* (Washington, D.C.: Brookings Institution, 1977), pp. 171–193.
4. There are other reasons why the panel of experts appointed by the judge to advise him consider the new center inadequate, but this was one. See "New Center for Retarded Opposed as 'Obsolete,'" *New York Times,* May 3, 1977, p. 39.
5. Alvin Schorr, *Explorations in Social Policy* (New York: Basic Books, 1968), pp. 232–237.
6. Lévi-Strauss, "Reflections on Liberty," p. 388.

9. *Why Isn't There More Equality?*

1. Jennifer L. Hochschild, *What's Fair? American Beliefs about Distributive Justice* (Cambridge, Mass.: Harvard University Press, 1981).
2. This is just about the position argued in Robert Nozick's *Anarchy, State and Utopia* (New York: Basic Books, 1974). The fact that a lot of people—and a lot of poor people—agree, is no argument among philosophers. Yet, though Nozick has made his argument not on the basis of what ordinary people believe, but on the basis of the kind of reasoning that passes muster among philosophers, there is a surprising similarity between his position and the popular one.

10. *The American Welfare State*

1. Charles R. Morris, *A Time of Passion: America, 1960–1980* (New York: Harper & Row, 1984), pp. 90–92.
2. Michael Harrington, *The New American Poverty* (New York: Holt, Rinehart &

Winston, 1984); Harrell R. Rodgers, Jr., *The Cost of Human Neglect: America's Welfare Failure* (Armonk, N.Y.: M. E. Sharpe, 1982); John E. Schwartz, *America's Hidden Success: A Reassessment of Twenty Years of Public Policy* (New York: W. W. Norton, 1983).

3. Richard Nathan, "Retrenchment Comes to Washington," *Society* 20, no. 2 (1983); John L. Palmer and Isabel V. Sawhill, eds., *The Reagan Experiment* (Washington, D.C.: Urban Institute Press, 1982); Palmer and Sawhill, eds., *The Reagan Record* (Cambridge, Mass.: Ballinger, 1984).

4. Paul Starr, *The Social Transformation of American Medicine* (New York: Basic Books, 1982), p. 249.

5. George Gilder, *Visible Man* (New York: Basic Books, 1978); Gilder, *Wealth and Poverty* (New York: Basic Books, 1981); Charles Murray, *Losing Ground: American Social Policy, 1950–1981* (New York: Basic Books, 1984).

6. Harold Wilensky, "Taxing, Spending, and Backlash: An American Peculiarity?" *Taxing and Spending* (July 1979): 6–11.

7. Gilbert Steiner, *Social Insecurity* (Chicago: Rand McNally, 1966).

8. C. John Ikenberry and Theda Skocpol, "Expanding Social Benefits: The Role of Social Security," *Political Science Quarterly* 102, no. 3 (Fall 1987): 389–416; Theda Skocpol and C. John Ikenberry, "The Political Formation of the American Welfare State in Comparative and Historical Perspective," *Comparative Social Research* 6 (1983): 87–148.

9. Richard P. Nathan and Fred C. Doolittle, "Overview: Effects of the Reagan Domestic Program on States and Localities," manuscript, Urban and Regional Research Center, Woodrow Wilson School, Princeton University, June 7, 1984; George E. Petersen, "Federalism and the States: An Experiment in Decentralization," in Palmer and Sawhill *Reagan Record.*

10. Neil Gilbert, *Capitalism and the Welfare State: Dilemmas of Social Benevolence* (New Haven: Yale University Press, 1983), p. 7.

11. "'83 Charity Gifts Put at a Peak $65 Billion" *New York Times,* May 2, 1984; Lester M. Salamon, "Nonprofit Organizations: The Lost Opportunity," in Palmer and Sawhill *Reagan Experiment,* pp. 261–285.

12. Rudolf Klein, "Values, Power and Policies," in *The Welfare State in Crisis* (Paris: Organization for Economic Cooperation and Development, 1981), pp. 169–170.

13. Gilbert, *Capitalism and the Welfare State,* pp. 10–11.

14. Richard Titmuss, *The Gift Relationship: From Human Blood to Social Policy* (New York: Pantheon, 1971); Harvey M. Sapolsky and Stan N. Finkelstein, "Blood Policy Revisited—A New Look at 'The Gift Relationship,'" *The Public Interest* 46 (Winter 1977): 15–27.

15. *Statistical Abstract of the United States, 1981* (Washington, D.C.: U.S. Department of Commerce, Bureau of the Census), p. 319; *Statistical Abstract of the United States, 1984,* p. 103, 138.

Credits

Chapter 1 is based on a lecture delivered as the first of a series of Saposnekow lectures at City College of New York in 1970 and published in *Commentary,* September 1971. The title of this chapter is the same as that of the lecture and article, but the chapter has been extensively revised. Chapter 2 was published in *The Tocqueville Review,* Spring–Summer 1984. Chapter 3 appeared, in somewhat abbreviated form, in *The Public Interest,* Spring 1984, and in D. Lee Bawden, ed., *The Social Contract Revisited: Aims and Outcomes of President Reagan's Social Welfare Policy* (Washington, D.C.: Urban Institute, 1984). Chapter 4 appeared in shortened form in Sheldon H. Danziger and Daniel H. Weinberg, eds., *Fighting Poverty: What Works and What Doesn't* (Cambridge, Mass.: Harvard University Press, 1986). Chapter 5 was given as a paper at a conference in Madison, Wisconsin, in 1979 and has not previously been published. Chapter 6 appeared in the volume *The Welfare State in Crisis* (Paris: OECD, 1981) under the title "Roles and Responsibilities in Social Policy." A shorter version of Chapter 7 appeared in *The Public Interest,* Winter 1983. Chapter 8 was delivered as the first John Madge Memorial Lecture to the Regional Studies Association in London, September 1977, and was published in *Regional Studies* 12, no. 5 (1978). Chapter 9 was delivered as a Stokes Lecture for the Department of Politics, New York University, February 1983, and was published in *This World,* Fall 1983. Chapter 10 appeared in Richard Rose and Rei Shiratori, *The Welfare State East and West* (New York: Oxford University Press, 1986). Chapters 6 and 7 reflect the influence of Peter Berger and Richard Neuhaus's Mediating Structures Project, funded by the American Enterprise Institute, in which I participated.

Index